D0975875

The Art of

SPIRITUAL
PEACEMAKING

Secret Teachings from
Jeshua ben Joseph

Also by James F. Twyman

Emissary of Light: A Vision of Peace

The Secret of the Beloved Disciple

Portrait of the Master / The Prayer of St. Francis

Praying Peace
(James F. Twyman in conversation with Gregg Braden and Doreen Virtue)

The Praying Peace Cards

Ten Spiritual Lessons I Learned at the Mall

Emissary of Love: The Psychic Children Speak to the World

Messages from Thomas: Raising Psychic Children

The Proposing Tree

The Art of

SPIRITUAL
PEACEMAKING

Secret Teachings from
Jeshua ben Joseph

James F. Twyman

FINDHORN
Press

© James F. Twyman 2003, 2006

First published in book form by Findhorn Press in 2006

ISBN 1-84409-079-5

British Library Cataloguing-in-Publication Data.
A catalogue record for this book is available
from the British Library

Cover design by Damian Keenan
Illustration of Emissary Wheel on page 22 by Mikael de Fauw
Interior design by Thierry Bogliolo
Proofread by Jean Semrau

Printed and bound in the USA

Published by
Findhorn Press
305a The Park, Findhorn
Forres IV36 3TE
Scotland, UK
tel 01309 690582/fax 690036
info@findhornpress.com
www.findhornpress.com

Contents

Introduction

Three events led to the composition of this book, or should I say the translation of this material. On one hand, I'm not quick to claim that this is channeled material, primarily because I tend to disagree with the common understanding of the phenomenon. More about that later. Yet, I am also fully aware that most of the information in these two collections, the original 33 Spiritual Peacemaking lessons as well as the Daily Lessons, did not come from my own conscious mind. Even today I read them and am amazed at their insightfulness, their depth, and their profundity. In fact, if I were to choose two or three books that I would take with me to a desert island, this would be one of them. This doesn't mean that I like reading my own words; rather, there is something I find within these words that I have only discovered a handful of other times in my life. What I discovered is Truth, pure and simple, and that is something to acknowledge and honor, whatever the source. The lessons in this volume came "from" me and they came "through" me. Both seem to be true and, as I have recently learned, in the end they are the same.

Let me begin by describing the second of the three events that led to my writing, or perhaps scribing, this text. In 2003 I had the privilege of leading a group of about 65 pilgrims to the Holy Land, a journey I had made three other times on my own. In both Israel and Palestine I discovered a phenomenon that probably doesn't exist anywhere else in the world.

On one hand, the ground seems to vibrate with the spiritual energy which the great prophets, from Abraham to Jesus to Muhammad, left in their wake. Jerusalem itself is the most sacred city in the world to both Jews and Christians, and the second most sacred city to Muslims. It is like Disney World to devout seekers, whether they be "religious" or simply "spiritual." On the other hand, the Holy Land is one of the most troubled areas in the world, as it has been for over two thousand years. It is a wonder, then, that Jerusalem, a city whose name translates to "City of Peace," is viewed by many as ground zero for the New World where cooperation and inclusion finally prevail. Perhaps the thinking is, "If they can get it right there, the rest will be easy." These are the main reasons I believe modern Spiritual Peacemakers need to come here, because in many ways it is a profound contradiction, but one that is essential for anyone focused on peace and reconciliation.

After ten days of visiting many holy sites around the Holy Land and sitting with spiritual leaders from many traditions, most of the group returned to their homes. Five others, including myself, stayed behind for three days to relax and visit several of our favorite spots without the constraints of a large group. One of those sites was the Dead Sea, particularly a resort and hot spring where the saline-rich water flows directly from the earth's core. The spring had been filled with tourists when we visited a few days earlier, but upon our return I was happy to find it nearly deserted. Of the five people in my group, only two of us decided to enter the pool, and I was excited to have it so clear.

To back up a bit, a month earlier I had announced to my international e-mail list that I would soon be offering a web-based class called "The Art of Spiritual Peacemaking." The fact that I had absolutely no idea what this class would include did not dissuade me from sending the announcement to over fifty thousand people. Weeks went by and excitement for the lessons began to build. Hundreds of people sent letters asking when the class would begin, a question I was still asking myself since I still had not received the inspiration required to write word one. I was beginning to wonder if I would ever receive clear direction, and worry was starting to build.

I believe I was thinking about this when I was soaking in the spring. Whether I was or not is of little consequence, though. I do know for sure what happened next.

The water and the minerals seemed to inspire a deep contemplation, and I was unaware of anything other than the waves of deep relaxation washing through my whole being. Nothing else existed, and my spirit seemed to shake free from my body, my friends and the motionless sea. I was at peace, vast and unfathomable peace, and I felt as if nothing would penetrate the stillness I felt.

Then I felt a presence, as if someone was standing next to me. I instantly realized, however, that it was not a body I felt beside me, but the spirit of a person I felt I recognized. In my mind I saw this spirit as a man who seemed to have walked straight out of the desert, his hair matted and his dark skin covered with sweat. But there was something else that caught my attention: his eyes. I had never seen eyes like this before, radiant and dazzling like the sun. He looked at me as if he saw more than the person floating there in the spring. He saw *me,* the me I rarely if ever saw myself. The love that shot from his eyes wrapped around me and filled me with Divine radiance. I knew, without his saying a word, that this was *he*: Jeshua, the real man who walked these same paths and roads two thousand years earlier.

I use the Aramaic name rather than the more common "Jesus" for a good reason. This was not the character from a book I met, nor was it the man that had been painted by the great masters or whose image had been immortalized in statues on altars around the world. This was the real guy, the authentic man who walked and talked and ate with his friends two thousand years ago. The man I sensed next to me wasn't the cookie-cutter Jesus but, rather, the mystical and passionate master who inspired or inflamed the land we now call holy. In an instant I knew why he inspired them so, for my own heart began to race.

All of this occurred without anyone around me even knowing. In other words, what I saw was within me, not without, and yet it was more real than anything I had ever known before. Jeshua was there, and a conversation began that has shaped my life ever since.

"Would you like me to help you?" Those were the words I felt extending from him, and they startled me. What did he mean? What could he help me with? It was as if he immediately knew what I was thinking. As he smiled I realized that he meant The Art of Spiritual Peacemaking course. "Would you like me to help you with it?" he asked again.

The way I was raised, you don't question such an extraordinary offer of support, especially when it comes from *him*. Still, I felt myself hesitate, as if I wasn't sure what it meant, or what I would be agreeing to. Luckily, the hesitation passed and I was convinced. "Yes, I do need you to help me."

Instantly, I felt something happen, as if information was being downloaded into my heart and my mind, information that I would have to access at a later date, regardless of how anxious I was to know what it was. He smiled when it was complete, then said to me, "When I was with my friends, I told them secrets that I couldn't reveal to the masses. They weren't ready...but now they are. I told them stories, but now is the time for everything to be revealed. That will be the course we will write together. I say together because it would be impossible for me to do it alone. We need each other in this. And so, the lessons will be 33 in number, and each one of them will have exactly 999 words. Within them will be a code, and it is this more than anything else that will teach them."

"What do you mean by code?" I asked.

"It is simple," Jeshua continued. "The information we will write will have great significance, but there will be hidden information that the conscious mind cannot comprehend. This information will be encoded in the words. The soul will then hear what the mind cannot. In this way the secrets of the Kingdom will be revealed. They will be revealed in a way that each person may know and live them, for that is what is so needed today."

He smiled and I felt the vision begin to disappear, and whatever had been placed inside me seemed to glow and radiate. I immediately jumped from the spring and ran to find my friends. I needed a pen and paper so I could write down everything I had just learned. When they saw me running toward them, they could see by the look in my eyes that I wasn't the same. They asked what had happened to me, and I told them I couldn't talk then. I found what I needed and disappeared to a secluded table where I wrote everything I had heard from Jeshua.

Over 30,000 people signed up for the Art of Spiritual Peacemaking course, and I wasn't at all surprised by the response. I wasn't surprised because I shared their enthusiasm. I, as much as anyone, couldn't believe the power and insight of every lesson. Each day I would soak in hot water, just as I had done at the Dead Sea, and wait for something to happen. As I relaxed and felt myself expand, it was as if a door opened, and the next lesson would appear in my mind. I would then rush to the computer and write down what I felt, following the inspiration as long as it would last. And then, as suddenly as it had begun, it would end, and each time I would look down at the word count on the computer: nine hundred ninety-nine words, each and every time. Jeshua had been true to his word.

The second event that impacts the information in this book took place eight years earlier when I was traveling through war-torn Croatia and Bosnia. In the book *Emissary of Light* I described meeting a community of masters who claimed to have been fulfilling an ancient pact for the evolution of humanity. Each night these thirteen men and women would enter a small meditation hut and would sit around a twelve-spoke wheel I later came to call "the Emissary Wheel." During the time I was with them I would sit in the domed hut as they conducted their rite, and I reveled at the power and energy that seemed to emanate from the geometric form drawn on the floor. Though I never understood the effects intellectually, something within me understood how important this wheel was. It was more than a symbol; it seemed to be a portal of some kind, with the power to transform and heal.

As the lessons with Jeshua proceeded, the Emissary Wheel became a focus of the instruction. Whether this was because it was something I had already embraced or was a tool Jeshua himself used 2000 years ago is still a mystery. I do, however, believe that he knew the sacred formula that is contained in the wheel. Jesus chose twelve apostles to stand around him and learn the mysteries he came to reveal. There was no coincidence here, for the entire technology of the Emissary Wheel is based on the "twelve around the one" energy, something that had been practiced in many esoteric fields of study. The Emissary Wheel, in all its forms, is one of the most magical and mysterious tools since the beginning of time. It is no wonder, then, that Jeshua places so much importance on its power throughout these lessons.

The third event was actually a realization that shaped my understanding and appreciation of this text. It would be easy to say that the material presented here was channeled: information from a being possessing the great wisdom and integrity it would require. There have even been times when it felt I was nothing more than a willing instrument to this power and that I was being used, albeit in a Divine manner, to bring this ancient wisdom to a modern era. And yet, as I said earlier, I believe that this explanation is too convenient and ultimately ineffectual. The purpose of this wisdom is to empower and reveal the inherent wisdom hidden within each one of us. So, beginning with a concept that there is another Master-Being outside of me, or outside any of us for that matter, communicating what we would not otherwise understand, would be the opposite of the real purpose and goal.

When I was in the hot spring at the Dead Sea, Jeshua asked me if I would be willing to write this "with" him. From the very beginning a pact seemed to exist making us equal partners, and though this was difficult to reconcile when I began to perceive the depth of this wisdom, it was nonetheless real. The information was not just coming "through" me, but also "from" me. If the basic premise of the lessons is true, that we are one with God and with each other, then the undeniable conclusion is that Jeshua and I are the same. In fact, it means that we are all the same, shining in the holiness in which we were created. It was not for me to "take" credit for this, but rather, to "accept" credit. In doing so I was accepting that Christ lives within me, and that there is nothing I can do to change that. This was the most empowering discovery of my life, and it is the real heart of this course.

Therefore, channeling in the traditional sense is impossible, since there is no one outside of me possessing any quality or innate wisdom that is not also mine. Perhaps this is the only message that has ever been received by such instruments or channels—namely, that we are still and will always be exactly as God created us. Once we realize that, as I did through this course, the rest happens on its own.

And so I present this as it was given. There is nothing here that you do not already know; perhaps it offers a window into what you already know. The secrets that Jeshua taught his friends 2000 years ago are not secrets at all, though we have not been able to understand them till now. I know that this wisdom is real, and that it presents a key to remembering who we are and who we have always been. I pray that this key will unlock for you the very same door that I discovered within, and that once you enter you will realize that you never truly left your home.

James Twyman
November, 2005

The 33 Lessons

Lesson One

Are you ready?

What other question need I ask of you? And what answer will you give, now that it has been asked? Will you step forward, or back? There is no other choice. You have tried to hold still, but the days of waiting are now behind you. Are you ready to accept your mission, the one that was given to you before you were born? Are you ready to bring peace to all beings by BEING peace? Say YES! Say it loud enough that you may hear it. No one else need know. Only you. Only your soul.

You have been called to be a bearer of peace in this world of dreams. There is a reason for this. You want to wake up from this world, and it is the only way. Do you understand this? The only way for you to awaken is to awaken others. And yet, no one needs to wake up but you. Think about this for a moment. No one needs to awaken but you. Why, then, do I say that you must give this to receive it? It is so simple. Because you are only giving to yourself. There is no one there but you to give or receive.

Are you ready to see this, to know it, and to love it? If so, then you are ready to heal the whole world by being a Spiritual Peacemaker.

This whole course can be described in one sentence: "Give everything as if it is the only thing that matters, while knowing that God's will is perfect every moment." Meditate on this sentence for a moment. Give everything! It is already perfect! Nothing is required but your willingness to give everything to everything, and yet nothing you ever do will change the will of God that is fulfilled in every situation, no matter how it appears. Does this seem impossible to you? Why would you be asked to work for something if its outcome doesn't matter? That is what you are going to grapple with for the next 99 days, and when it is done you will understand, not with your mind, but with your soul.

Let me explain what I am leading you to. There will be 33 lessons in this course that will flow through 99 days. Can you guess why this number is so important? Thirty-three is not an ordinary number. It is the number of your Christ consciousness. It is the number of your awakening. And why are these lessons being presented every three days? I laid motionless in the tomb for three days so that life would take me into itself. I died that I might live forever, and you are being asked to do the same thing. The only way you can be a Spiritual Peacemaker is if you become the fulfillment of peace, or, in other words, if you become the Christ yourself. Do not be afraid of this, for I have gone before you to make straight the way. But make no mistake: now you must walk the path yourself. No one can do it for you. No one can accept life but you, and once done, it is accepted for all. This is the moment you chose, and it is fulfilled.

I am speaking to you on more levels that you know, for you exist on more planes of existence than you could ever realize with your mind. That is why these sacred numbers are so important, and these symbols I use will awaken this information in ways words never can. You will read the words and your mind will understand the concepts. Your life will benefit and you will touch the lives of countless others through the peace you offer. But there is so much more that the mind will never understand, and this is the critical place I am leading you. These are the secrets that will transform your existence, just as they transformed me. Yes, I too underwent this transformation, and now I am a way-shower. You too will open the heart of this truth to those whom the Beloved gives you, just as you were given to me. There is no other reason you were born. Nothing else will mean anything to you, and yet you will not understand that until you offer it.

So now we will begin, for the journey has been laid out before us. Walk with me these 99 days, and let your mind be opened.

Two thousand years ago I shared mysteries with my friends that they held very sacred. They were only shared with others once they were prepared for the powerful impact of the truth upon their hearts and souls. Many of these secrets were encoded in a geometric symbol that was being passed down from one community to another, and yet only a few of the people who were exposed to this symbol were able to unlock the secrets found within. Their souls knew and understood, but their minds were not yet ready to enter the sacred chamber.

But now it is critically important that all of you access this information. The secrets of the Kingdom of God are reflected there, for they are within you now. In the next 99 days I will open each lock and reveal for you the mysteries of life and death. Then you will understand the immortal nature of this quest, and you will know that you are one with the goal you seek.

So I will ask you once again: Are you ready to enter upon this path? There will be moments when it will seem very dark, and others where the Light will almost blind you. Know that every step will be guided by me, for I have walked before you and I know every dangerous place. But you must know that your whole life has led to this moment. Then it will fall upon you like rain, refreshing your very soul.

—Brother

Lesson Two

Beloved. I call you by your name, for only then will you know the truth about your Self. Only then will you adopt the Holy Sight with which I see you and all beings. Then you will do as I do, extend that vision. The world is already healed, Beloved. That is what you have come to realize and learn. The world of dreams is now passing away, and you are left only with the Light of Peace. Welcome, Beloved, to your home.

It is important at this early stage for you to realize why you are here. First of all, why are you here on this Earth? Was it an accident of fate that brought you here, the aligning of circumstances beyond your decision? Or have you come far enough to realize that there is nothing beyond your decision? Nothing! Your birth at this time was predestined. It was predestined by you!

You are here because you chose it before time began. It was only an instant ago when you decided this, and now you are here. What will you do with this knowledge?

I will tell you. You will use time wisely to heal your split mind, then see the world as healed. Then it will be so, for you have the power of God within you. This is the moment when you are choosing to see your Christ-Mind reflected everywhere, including where war seems to rage. Your decision alone will shed Light upon all these shadowy places, for the Light that proceeds from you is Holy Light. It is the Light that proceeds from my mind, and you are included there. You have come to KNOW this, and to heal through this knowledge. Blessed is the moment of this decision. And Blessed too is the world you will now heal.

Throughout the course of these 33 lessons I will offer suggestions to speed this process along. You are needed NOW. It is not because this time is any darker or more in need of your Light than any other time. It is simply because there is no other time but this. You are the one who chose this time. And you will fulfill everything you have set your heart upon. That is why it was important for you to open your heart before you could begin this stage. That is why you underwent the lessons that preceded this course, and now you are ready. You will bring it all with you, and you will see clearer than you have ever seen before. You are needed NOW, Beloved, and we will move forward with great speed.

It is not important that you understand or even accept the mind that is sharing this information with you. It is your mind as well. But the reference may be different, just as your view is different depending upon where you stand at a given moment. My reference is whole,

✳ *heart* ✳

while yours is still a bit splintered. That is about to change. It must change if you are to adopt the vision I would offer you. We will understand what we need to understand, and then we will set the intellect aside. It will not take us to where we need to go. But your heart, yes, this is where we will focus our attention. It is there already.

I want you to focus for a moment on the name I was given when I was born. Jeshua. If you can understand what this name means, and that it is yours as much as mine, then you will understand where we are headed together. You have been taught to chant the word YES to open the channels of your soul, preparing your heart for the Great Work that lies before us. It doesn't matter what language you use. It is the feeling you generate that creates the opening. There is a sound in Hebrew that essentially means "It is so." This is a more powerful interpretation of the word YES. The sound is "Yesh." Say it a few times out loud. Make the sound long and draw it out for at least a few seconds. "Y-E-S-H." The sound generates a powerful response within your heart. See if you can sense the feeling. As one who has awakened his heart and mind to the experience of Christ consciousness, I can tell you that your dedication to this one word will lead you to where I am standing now. "It is so." Your Christ-Mind is so, this very moment. It is happening NOW, not in the future, not in the past. As you chant this sound over and over, let your heart awaken to this knowledge. "Y-E-S-H." It is so within you now. Your awakened mind is present, waiting for you to claim its power.

Now add the final sound "U-A." "Y-E-S-H-U-A." I am not the one you are chanting to. Do you realize this? I do not need this recognition, BUT YOU DO. My mind is your mind, and my name is yours. It is time for you to claim who you are. Chant it over and over, as often as you can. Call to the Christ in You, and it will awaken.

Will you believe me when I tell you that the rest will happen on its own? What do you wish to see in the world? Peace? Harmony? Adopt the vision that was given before time began and these things will appear before you. Why haven't they before now? Because you needed the world to reflect what you believed to be true. It is that simple. But now you are ready to allow a new Truth to dawn upon your mind, one that is eternal and beyond all change. It has always been there, but your eyes have been closed to its brilliance. Open now! This is the essence of being a Spiritual Peacemaker. It is an art. It is your path to freedom. Choose peace now. You are ready.

—Brother

Lesson Three

Today I would speak to you about your passion and desire.

What do you hold dear in this world? Are you willing to offer everything you love to the One from whom all Love flows, knowing that only Love will return to you? Or do you believe that you must sacrifice what you love in order to have everything you desire? Be honest with yourself. What do you hold dear in this world?

Perhaps you will say your children, or your special relationship. What would happen to them if you completely accepted your role as an Emissary of Love, leaving behind all the things that do not serve that end? Would you still be able to provide for their needs? Would your relationship end, unable to compete with the great tide of energy that flows toward you even now?

Whether you are aware of it or not, these are some of the questions in your mind. You believe that a sacrifice is required of you, and that God would ask you to surrender all the things of time in order to embrace the eternal within. It is the natural state of the ego, which you still cling to. And yet, our goal is not to erase these conditions, for that would only amplify them. We desire only to focus on what is true, and to let that truth grow in our hearts and minds till all the symbols of fear are replaced.

You are afraid of love! Take a deep breath now. You will not be able to heal that wound until you embrace it. You will not be able to move to the next level of your Self unless you first accept your fear of love. Then your passion will be released on its own, without effort on your part. Then you will open like a flower, and your Holy Task will enfold you. Your fear of love will ultimately catapult you into a life you can only imagine now, for then you will have compassion for yourself and all the world. This is what an Emissary of Love, or a savior, must learn. That is why you are here now, reading these words and accepting these Blessed thoughts. You are ready to move forward now.

Your passion has been sleeping within you and must now be awakened. This will happen the moment you desire one thing. Your challenge has been that you desire more than one thing, and so you are not able to see that all desires are the same. If you choose in darkness, then shadows will enfold everything you perceive. But if you choose in the Light, then they will shine as you shine, and be blessed by your Holy Desire. Passion and desire stand together in your mind and cannot be separated. We will now open to the One Desire that will lead you to the goal you seek – the Peace of God. Nothing else in this world can satisfy you now. You have come too far.

Desire only the gifts God would offer.

· If I told you that you must desire only love, it would only confuse your mind. (Though this is, in fact, the final path we will walk together.) You have been given so many concepts of what love is and isn't, and they have only clouded your thoughts. Therefore, what we seek is the Peace that your mind can never comprehend, the Light that extends beyond all thoughts of time and space.

Your passion and desire are the keys that unlock this door. You must desire this over all things. All things! You must be willing to give up everything you perceive in this world in order to enjoy the Light that extends past this world. YOU MUST WANT IT ABOVE ALL THINGS. Only then will it be yours.

Pay attention for a moment to any emotions you are feeling right now. Did the thought of lack, in any degree, enter your mind? "What will I lose?" "Whom will I lose?" This is the basic dilemma of the ego: it has linked gain and loss, thinking that to accept everything you must sacrifice something else. Pay attention to this! WHEN YOU ACCEPT EVERYTHING, NOTHING IS LOST! I once said that if you seek only the Kingdom of God, then everything else will be given to you automatically. When you seek only love, then love will return, and this is where your truest desire lies hidden. Love will flow to you from every direction, not just the ones you ordain. Life will find you; you won't have to find it. Therefore, let your passion be released and desire only the Gifts God would offer. Then your hunger will be satisfied, and your thirst will be forever quenched.

Then you will enter the Wheel of life. Then you will know yourself to be an Emissary of Love.

You are not here to bring worldly peace, but the Peace of God. You cannot understand this yet. Your mind will never be able to understand it. But the wider you open your heart the simpler it will become, until it is like a game children play. Then you will laugh where before you cried. Then you will know that love cannot be replaced by anything this world holds dear, for only love truly exists, now and forever.

Your desire is mine, and mine is yours. Are you willing to link your mind, and your passion, with mine? It is not the personality you are linking with, but the force behind the personality. This is what animates your Spirit and mine, the Life that ignites all Life. This is the time you chose to undergo this transformation. Time can be your ally or a thief. Choose to use it wisely, and it will reveal the gifts that exist beyond your concept of time. There is nothing left for you to do now but embrace your passion for peace. Your desire is the path that will lead you to your chosen goal.

—Brother

Lesson Four

There was a time when you saw yourself as very distant from me. That time has now passed, for I have called you my friends, not my disciples. Now we can sit together by the fire, and I can tell you all the things that are so clear to me now. And then they will appear the same to you, not clouded and indistinct as they once were. Now is the time for us to relax and be as a family, for only then will you see that we are the same. My mind is yours, and the moment of my awakening was yours as well. Knowing this, I would like to share a story with you. Let the details sink into your mind, and the lesson into your heart, that you may understand where this path is leading us.

Imagine a house that is filled with Light. There is nothing in this house save a small, unimaginably brilliant crystal in the very center that reflects and magnifies the Light that streams in from every window. The room needs nothing, though there is nothing there. The Light vibrates with an essence that in unseen, indescribable, and you are content to exist there in Perfect Joy.

Then one day a new thought arises. It will not do to have such an empty house. It is so calm and comfortable there that there should be a place for "You" to sit. Many chairs are brought in and couches that fill every room. Then the thought arises that there must be a place for "You" to dine, for eating in the comfortable chairs will not do. And so you buy tables and place them in the appropriate places, and more chairs to place around the tables. Then you look around and see that there is no bed for "You" to sleep in. And so you go out and purchase a bed for yourself that is soft and luxurious, and others beds in case you have guests. Day after day you fill the house with all the furnishings you desire, until the moment comes when you see that there is enough.

But something else has changed as well. You look around the house and realize that the Light that once radiated from every corner has been dimmed. You find lamps to add more light, but no matter how many lamps you buy it never equals the brilliance you once knew. You go and sit in your favourite chair, the one in the very center of the house. As you sit, you remember the crystal. It was almost forgotten in the rush of filling the house with everything "You" needed to be comfortable. You look at the crystal and you can see a faint glow you once knew, the Light that once filled your days. Then a new thought enters your mind. You look around for the "You" that was so important, the one you bought so much furniture and decorations for. Where is this elusive being that required so much? No matter how hard you look you cannot find the "You" that was so important a short time ago. Maybe there is too much furniture to find "You." One by one the chairs are removed, then the couches, and even the tables. You go upstairs and remove the beds, and the lamps, and everything else that you bought. Finally, you look around and notice something amazing.

8/12/06 8/13/06 8/18/06

The Light has returned.

And you are standing right where you started. All the furniture that blocked the Light from the crystal is gone, and the whole house vibrates with Life. And you vibrate as well, for you know that you are that crystal, and that Light, and that house, and that "You."

The time we are spending together, all these lessons, are meant to help the Light return to your mind. We will not accomplish this task by adding anything, but by subtracting all the things that have blocked the Light from your conscious experience. The crystal, or your awakened soul, will be enough. Nothing else is required.

Where is the "You" you are seeking? Does it exist at all, or was it simply a concept used to distract your pure awareness? Who is it that is seeking? Your thoughts have created this being, and your thoughts can uncreate it as well, revealing the Truth that you can neither create nor uncreate. This is what we are seeking today.

Simply put, the "You" that is being sought does not exist. Rejoice in this, for the realization of this fact is the beginning and the end of your journey.

Who are you, then? You are the crystal that reflects the Light. The Light is full within this crystal, fully contained and fully realized. You cannot change, and whatever there is in you that seems to change is not who you are. Play with it if you choose, but do not cling to it. Cling only to the eternal essence beyond your influence, and then you will see that there is nothing beyond your influence. Do you understand the subtle difference here?

The Art of Spiritual Peacemaking is the art of removing the blocks to your Light. Then the Light shines on its own. You do not need to "do" anything. You just need to "BE" who you are. You are the Light of Eternal Grace. You are the Pure Essence of the Being of God. Stop trying to understand this with your mind. It is the surest way to never KNOW it. Simply understand that it is true NOW, this very instant, fully revealed, WHETHER YOU ARE AWARE OF IT OR NOT!

The Art of Spiritual Peacemaking has nothing to do with changing anyone, including yourself. It is the deep comprehension that there is no one to change, including yourself. Then your eternal Self is revealed, and everything falls into its natural place. If you decide to enter this portal now, you can.

You are ready!

—Brother

Lesson Five

I have called you to remember the reason you chose to be born. You have chosen to answer that call, for the song that was planted in your soul is now ringing in your ears. This is the time YOU chose to awaken and BE. The time of dreams has now passed, for your help is required to initiate a world that has never been threatened, except in your imagination. You will now release those imaginings for the world Peace will show. This is the only thing you desire now, and thus is your release assured.

I will not call you to BECOME anything, but to BE all things. How can I ask you to COME to me when I do not see any distance between us at all? I ask you to BE me. Are you beginning to understand? There is nowhere for you to go. You need only open your eyes and see where you have always been. Will you answer this call and assume your rightful place at my side? Does it help to say that I need you here, for the All is not known in my mind unless it is known in all? Stand now and be seen with the family you have chosen to awaken, and be awakened by. Know that the time is NOW. There is no other path for you to walk now but the path of Peace. All is answered there.

I will begin speaking to you now about the wheel of wisdom and life. You have called this the Emissary Wheel because it was the sacred focus of many ancient communities and groups for thousands of years. It contains information, profound information, and we will now begin using this information consciously that we may comprehend the proper way to accept our role of being Spiritual Peacemakers in this world. These ancient groups have closely guarded this information, but there is no more time to waste. The wheel itself will speak to your heart and mind, but only if you possess the foundation that will allow this knowledge to take root in your soul.

(For a reference point, you can see the Emissary wheel on page 22. I suggest making a copy of it to have at your side when you read these lessons.)

Look at the wheel for a few moments and let it speak to you. Don't worry about focusing at one particular point. Let your eyes move where they will and trust that they are being guided by the energy emanating from this sacred geometry. The mysteries of peace and life itself are encoded here, and you have the key that will unlock the door that leads to all the answers you desire. Let your soul absorb this code, knowing that it will be revealed when the time is right. You may feel powerful pulsations moving through you as you look. Do not resist any of it, but allow yourself to flow into and through this portal. It will be your teacher, and you will grasp its secrets. That is all you need to know for now, only that the ending is sure. That should be enough to inspire your continued movement toward the Center that does not move.

Now, pay attention to the twelve points that touch the outer circle of the wheel. This is where we will begin our lessons, for it is here that you will touch where you are and who you are this and every moment. Each of these twelve points represents a quality of energy associated with a Spiritual Peacemaker. These are the qualities you must amplify during the next several months as you progress through this training. You may want to have a separate copy of the wheel where you will write these qualities at each point. Always begin at the twelve o'clock point and move clockwise around the wheel. Here are the twelve qualities:

Courage, Patience, Wisdom, Certainty, Compassion, Joy, Clarity, Understanding, Depth, Generosity, Abundance, Agape.

Over the next four lessons we will discuss these qualities in groups of three, since the qualities themselves are grouped energetically. In three days we will begin with Courage, Patience and Wisdom. I will ask you to join me in experiments that will enlighten these qualities and help them dissolve into your soul. Once you have integrated each of the twelve, then we will begin moving in through the spokes and explore the deeper lessons the wheel can teach us. For now it is enough to know that all your questions will be answered here, not with words, but with the Light that transcends all words. It is this Light we are seeking together.

Over the next three days meditate with the Emissary Wheel as much as you can. You may feel powerful releases taking place in you as you conduct this practice. If this happens, simply breathe deeply and let them flow in whichever direction needed. Even if your experience is profound and rapturous, know that the energy itself is clearing a path for you to walk toward your Self. All is well. There is nothing that can happen to you here. You need only surrender to the current of grace that is flowing through this symbol and realize that the current is your very life.

Which brings me to the final and most important thing I can tell you at this time. This wheel, this symbol, is who you are. It is nothing more, and nothing less, than a geometric representation of your Highest Self. It is Perfect Balance which you can know and enjoy this moment. Do not think that these mysteries will lead anywhere but back to where you are now and always. There is nowhere else for you to go. The wheel is meant to awaken the part of you that is still sleeping, the larger part of you that has hidden from your Divinity. There is no reason to hide now. You have come too far to turn back. There is only one direction: Forward. Focus now on the wheel, and in doing so, on your Self. This is the moment you have been waiting for.

—Brother

Lesson Six

Today we enter a sacred wheel that is the symbol of your enlightened mind. Know that you are being called to see yourself as you are, and as you have always been. Let me try to express that thought more clearly. You are here for one reason and one reason only: to know that you are enlightened NOW. No other goal will do. You can step into this experience right now if you choose. Do you? Let me tell you the first thing you must do if you are to accept and embrace this Holy Mind:

Let go of every thought you have ever had about what it means to be enlightened.

I mean this literally. Do not hold onto a single concept of what you think it means to walk the earth as an enlightened being. Why? There is only one thing I can guarantee at this point—that every thought you have about this is wrong. How do I know this? Because the goal we seek has nothing to do with the concepts and thoughts you hold. They are all blocks to your Holy Awareness, no matter how sacred they seem. If you want to KNOW who you are, then KNOW who you are. No thought can take you there, only your recognition of what has always been true and can never change.

Today we will enter the sacred wheel that has been a symbol of this awakening for thousands of years. You will be asked to embrace each of the twelve qualities of an Emissary of Light, which are the portals into the experience we are seeking. As you read this information, look at the wheel itself.

Let your eyes wander through the geometric patterns that are meant to awaken your soul at a super-conscious level. You do not need to understand it intellectually. In fact, you cannot understand it intellectually. Strive to embody the qualities I will offer your mind, and let your soul seek its own path through the spokes of the wheel. These are the qualities we will explore for the next three days. If possible, read one of these sections each day, or refer back to them every day. Breathe them into your life, and they will exhale you into a New Life.

Courage, Patience, Wisdom

Courage:

It is not the courage of this world we are seeking, but of the Real World from which you came and where you have always belonged. You have forgotten this Sacred Home, and yet you have never really left. Courage is the first path that will lead to your Remembering. Everything in the world of form forces you into a place of weakness. Separation itself is weakness, and so you must deny its effect before you can adopt true courage. You aren't alone. The "you" that you think you are doesn't exist in truth. Only the "You" God perceives exists, and this is where we will gain our courage. It cannot be threatened. Such a thing is impossible. Death cannot touch the "You" God perceives, so there is nothing to be afraid of in this world. To the ego, death is victory, for it proves its version of the world true. But the death the ego perceives is an illusion. It is not a real end. Why, then, would you choose to be afraid of this impossible conclusion? Be courageous and know that you are an eternal being. The body's decay is not yours, for you are not your body. Are you afraid of the clothes you wear falling to ruin on some future date? Why would you be afraid of the body's natural end? Release this fear and everything else will fall into its natural place, and you will be afraid of nothing. To be an Emissary of Light means that you focus on what is, not what isn't, and you find your courage there. Let go of the concept of death, and you will discover a wealth of strength you didn't know you possessed. Today I ask that you imagine yourself to be the enlightened being I perceive, filled with courage. Imagine how you would walk through this world if this courage were yours. Your meditation will be to spend some time imagining this new life today.

Patience:

There is no time in which you will be judged. There is only NOW, and you have already accepted the finality of your soul's TRUTH. Understand this and Divine Patience will be yours. Then time will have no meaning to you, for you will know the ultimate conclusion of your life: Full knowledge of your True Self. How can you be anything but patient if you know the path you walk? Even if you do not see the castle in the distance, still you are certain of your eventual arrival. And the more certain you are of this, the sooner you will perceive this reality. Only Divine Patience offers immediate results. There is no hurry, then, for the ending is sure. Enjoy the path you walk and admire the beauty of the landscape. Turn one more corner and you are there. Today I ask that you imagine yourself to be the enlightened being I perceive, filled with patience. Imagine how you would act toward others if this patience were yours. Imagine this new life, and embrace it now.

Wisdom:

Is it the wisdom of the world you seek, or of God? Which will you choose, for I tell you, they are not the same. The wisdom of the world tells you to understand the multitude of differences that lie before you, while the wisdom of God tells you there is no difference. There is no real difference between you and anyone else, and there is no time in which the holiness you share is compromised. How can this lead to anything but Perfect Joy? Imagine that you are an enlightened being, filled with wisdom. You are. I see it so clearly. Can you?

—Brother

Lesson Seven

We have embarked on a Sacred Journey together. It is a journey without distance that leads to where YOU have always been. The mind has been laid aside, as has the body that you made with your mind. Your thoughts have brought you to this place, but they cannot lead you to where you really belong. We travel from here together, wrapped within one another, one heart and one mind ascending to the Higher Kingdoms. You have tried to come alone, but have seen that such a journey was impossible. Everything you created comes with you now to the Home you never left.

You may wonder about the value of the geometric form we have chosen to employ on this journey, the Emissary Wheel. It is true that no symbol can cross this barrier, and yet it can aid you in your journey to the gate of that Holy Experience. Ultimately the only symbol you are being asked to lay aside is your own "self concept." You have forgotten who you are and have adopted an image you cling to till your body's death, and you continue on with a new image that seems to change. And yet, who you really are does not change, for it exists beyond the world of transient reality. This is what you are here to discover, and the symbol of the Wheel will serve as a tool to initiate that awakening. Then we will lay it aside, just as we will lay all symbols aside, and rest together in the Kingdom beyond your dreams.

The twelve spokes of the Emissary Wheel represent the twelve aspects of your ego's dream. Their points exist on the outer fringe of the wheel, and therefore seem most separate. But now we have given them new meaning, and have adopted the tools of transformation that lead to the inner dimensions of your Life. These are the experiences we are looking at now, and as we continue walking this path we find ourselves moving closer to the center of the wheel. Then we exist in the place that does not move, the place where your dreams of separation have no meaning. That is the goal of this course, and it is how you will know yourself to be a Spiritual Peacemaker and an Emissary of Light.

Today we will open our hearts to the next three spokes and the experiences they inspire. You will find that they are grouped together in threes, resulting in four triangles, or twelve spokes. Each experience leads to the next and is meant to deepen your comprehension of the Truth within. We will deal with the concepts for now since we cannot describe Reality itself. Open your heart to them and gaze at the wheel, and the lessons I cannot describe with words will be revealed on their own.

The fourth spoke:

Certainty:

You are not asked to believe anything, but to KNOW. In the past I spoke of the importance of your belief, but that was when you were a child. Now you are mature, and so I treat you in a new way. Lay your belief aside, and KNOW that you are One with me and all Reality. Your belief has led you to the door of Awakening, but only your Certainty will allow you to enter. Otherwise you will stand there and never comprehend. I will lead you forward, for I am Certain of who you are. But it is time for you to be Certain as well. Only then will you be able to See the Beauty that I perceive within you. You will not be able to See it anywhere until you KNOW it is yours. Your Certainty is required now.

The fifth spoke:

Compassion:

Perfect Certainty leads to Perfect Compassion. When you are Certain of who you are then you will Know that it extends beyond the shallow definitions you once held of yourself and the world. How can you experience Compassion for what lies beyond you? But what lies within, yes, this you can have Perfect Compassion for, and everything lies within. I will say that again so there is no possibility of confusion: Everything lies within. When you know who you are then your Wisdom is Perfect, and your Compassion is perfect as well, for you will realize that every gift you give is given to yourself. Open your heart in Love, and know that love returns to you. Where else would it lead but to the source you never left?

The sixth spoke:

Joy:

Perfect Compassion leads to Perfect Joy. Are you beginning to see how each one of these Holy Experiences leads to the same place and cannot exist without the others? Your Joy has never been complete because your awareness was splintered. You have chosen to look upon what is not real and deny what is. There have been moments when you have laughed and moments when you have felt the sudden movement of your heart. But the joy we seek now does not depend upon the movements of this world but of the Real World that cannot change. Then you will live where you choose to live, and do what you choose to do, and yet never leave the Sacred Ground of your Perfect Joy. Your heart will be fixed on what is Real within you, not that which has never existed. Simply put, you will finally be able to understand the difference. Do you understand how valuable this will be? You will walk upon the Earth as I walked, untouched by the changing tides of unreality, blessing everything you touch because you see the truth that exists within YOU. You will be a Savior, and the example of your life will be enough to enlighten any darkened mind that comes to you.

You have been called to save the world by Seeing as God Sees and Knowing What God Knows. Will you accept this commission? Will you finally choose Peace?

—Brother

I gaze upon the Light in you, regardless of what you perceive.

Lesson Eight

You have chosen to be an instrument of peace, or a Spiritual Peacemaker. I have not chosen you, you have chosen yourself. I want you to understand this subtle but important difference. I cannot ask you to do anything that you have not already chosen. Even if I could I would not try, for it would place you below me, and such a position is not appropriate. We stand together, and so I have called you my friends. The work we have chosen must be completed by us all, since it is "for" us all. Are you beginning to understand how important your role is?

I would like to speak to you now about the attributes you are learning to embody that will allow you to step fully into your role of being a Spiritual Peacemaker.

You now realize how each of these attributes, all of which an Emissary of Light must fully contain, all of which you do fully contain this moment, deepen as they progress. Each one prepares the way for the next, until the each spoke of the whole wheel has been gathered together as one radiant form, representing the radiant YOU that is emerging from the place you have hidden.

As I said, you contain each of these this very moment, whether you are conscious of it or not. It does not matter if you are conscious of it at this point, and the moment you realize that your conscious recognition of this does not matter will be the same moment they break through. All that is important at this stage is that you recognize each of these traits as yours NOW — not becoming, not gradually integrating, but fully present this very moment. Then you will be given a marvellous gift from the Spirit of Truth that waits for you now. You will be able to see it everywhere else, and then you will stand at my side as a miracle worker, a Spiritual Peacemaker, and an Emissary of Light.

Do you think that it matters to me what you think of yourself? It doesn't. Do you think that it has ever occurred to me to enter into your self-concept and validate it in any way? It hasn't. My joy is to see you as you really are, not as you imagine yourself to be. It does not occur to me to ask you if you see it as well, for such a thought would give reality to what isn't real. I gaze upon the Light in you, regardless of what you perceive. You are now ready to see that this is what you are being asked to do, as well, for it is the highest calling. And this is the time you have chosen to do this, for your brothers and sisters need you now. Look upon them with gentle eyes and do not acknowledge the visions of separation they perceive. Acknowledge only the Truth, the Grace that flows through them this moment and the next. That is how you will ground the same vision of yourself, for you cannot give this gift without receiving it.

The seventh spoke:

Clarity:

You have been looking at the world with unfocused eyes and have made all your decisions based upon subtle misunderstandings of the Universe you thought you saw. And yet you have not realized your misperception and believe that you see clearly. Now a friend, a Brother, comes to you and gently points at the things you thought you saw, and helps you understand that they are not the demons and monsters you thought they were. It is like putting glasses on for the first time. My Clarity becomes yours, and you are finally able to See. How will you do this? First of all, by accepting that you have not seen clearly until now. Without Guilt. Then you will trust that I understand what you have confused. Finally, your gratitude for your meaningless error will bring the Clarity you have lacked till now, and everything will make sense again.

The eighth spoke:

Understanding:

Until now your goal has been to be understood by others, and so you have lacked the understanding that you really desire. You cannot understand something until you See it clearly, comprehending what it really is. And you cannot know who you are until you are willing to offer that same gift to another. Try to understand the Holiness of whoever is standing in front of you now, not with your mind, for you will surely fail. Try to feel the Grace, and then KNOW that it is yours. I ask only that you understand who you are. You will not be able to accept your role of power until then. You will know this by giving it, for understanding is a gift that is given and received at the same moment. Do you long to See who you are, then understand that it is the same SELF God perceives? Then SEE as God SEES, and Understand what is real. Your Seeing is the key to everything.

The ninth spoke:

Depth:

It is not the depth of this world we are seeking together, but of the world beyond your imagination. And yet, when you finally begin to perceive this Real World as it truly is, then it impacts the world you created with your mind. In truth they are the same, though one is only a splinter of the beauty you could know, if only you would open your heart. It is the choice you must make, and this is the moment you will decide. It may be better to say that it is the moment you "did" decide, since the choice was already made. This is the thought that inspires your depth, the understanding that your decision has already been made, and so has the result of that decision. And what is the result? Simply this – perfect acknowledgment of who you are. What else is there to seek?

—Brother

Lesson Nine

Today we will begin with a thought that is the foundation of your work as a Spiritual Warrior. It is the experience you seek and the reward you will enjoy. When it is full within you, when you can say this phrase with complete confidence, then you will know that you have arrived at the place where your gifts can be offered to the Spirit of Truth. The Spirit will then use you, as you, and you will KNOW why you arrived on this planet.

"My cup runs over."

Say this phrase over and over and try to feel the energy that enfolds your soul. What does this mean to you, and how can you become the cup that flows with Divine Grace? Isn't this what you are really seeking? How can you give something to another unless you have fully realized it yourself? Do not think that in your humanness you are able to purge the urge toward self-promotion: it may not reflect the Truth in you, but the ego has always been a welcomed guest in your home. You soon forget that it was invited to remain, though you did not have to extend its stay. You cannot purge it, but through Grace it can be removed from you. This will occur only if you fully accept it and offer it the opening it desires: Integration rather than extinction. Then it leaves on its own, and you are able to See who you really are, the Self you have remained even while you dreamed of impossible worlds.

"My cup runs over."

Be filled with the Peace you desire to share. Don't ask for anything, for it is the admission that it is not already yours. How can you desire something that you do not know, and ultimately, do not have. What is needed is an expansion of what it means to possess something. Your role is simply to realize that there is nothing in this universe that is not full within you. There is nothing you can conceive that is not already yours. This realization, then the experience, is what it means to "Spill God's Grace Everywhere." You are a living vessel, a holy tabernacle, and yet, God cannot use you until you step toward your Self, the "You" that cannot be threatened by your illusions. Until now you have stepped away into the dream you created, and so you have understood what it means to be weak and alone. But every dream must end, and so do you now step away toward the reality we share. KNOW this, then give it to all. Only then will your cup continue to overflow. Only then will you enjoy the riches that have always been yours.

"My cup runs over."

This will be your prayer for the next few days. Meditate with it, but most of all "feel" the prayer in your heart. It is true, but you will directly experience this truth only as you extend it to others. This brings us to the final three spokes of our Emissary Wheel.

Tenth Spoke:

Generosity:

Why would you hold back when you realize you are only denying yourself? This is the single barrier that needs to be removed, for there is still a place in you that believes that if you give something to another, then you have lost it yourself. Loss can only occur in your mind, but is then translated into your physical life. Were you to remove the concept altogether then you would not think to look at the outward appearance of things to determine anything. You would feel abundance because you would offer it to everyone. Your cup would run over and would be continually refilled. The universe itself is conspiring to bring you this, but you have resisted it and have therefore created an experience that seems to set you at odds with reality. Stop trying to determine what is yours and what belongs to another. There is no other! There is only You waking from the dream of separation. You have been called to be a Spiritual Peacemaker, and the world cannot possibly understand what this means. That is because everything in the world you created reflects the laws of a world that does not exist except in your imagination. Give everything to everything! If you hold back your gift then you are the one who will suffer, and suffering is no longer necessary.

Eleventh Spoke:

Abundance:

Do you want the world of form to reflect your inner KNOWING? You already realize that each spoke in this wheel leads to the next, and so your generosity automatically leads to your abundance. It is almost redundant to speak of this for if you have been following the direction of this Divine Thought then you would know this already. You are here to have everything you desire. There is no sacrifice for you to make, though I guarantee that your priorities will change when you accept this new role. You may begin to define abundance in new ways when you don't expect the outside world to reflect your inner reality. There are those among you who have next to nothing by the standards of the world, and yet they are the most abundant. There are also those who have everything, and yet they are the poorest among you. Make your choice about what you desire to fully receive. Once again, GIVE EVERYTHING TO EVERYTHING and you will remember who you are and why you are here.

Twelfth Spoke:

Agape:

You are here to adopt the vision of God that automatically leads to the Love of God. We call this agape, for it indicates an experience wholly unlike your concepts of love. God's love depends on nothing, and so it is unconditional. You have been called to Love as God Loves. Quite simply, it is the only thing that can give you everything you desire. Are you ready to lay everything else on the altar now?

—Brother

Lesson Ten

The Three Enlightenments

Now that we have finished examining the twelve qualities of the Spiritual Peacemaker we are ready to consider the real function of the Emissary Wheel. To some it is a simple geometric symbol that communicates information on psychic and spiritual levels. I have also said that it is an outer symbol of an inner journey, or in other words, the journey of your personal transformation. Now we will open our minds and hearts to its true function, that of being an energy portal able to shift the intention of your human experience into a Divine context. When you realize and experience this Divine Context, then you will be able to fulfill your role on this planet.

You may have already noticed certain powerful or subtle shifts that occur within even when gazing at the Emissary Wheel. We will discuss this at great length as we progress through this course, but it is important for you to realize that what you are feeling is very real. Certain geometric shapes have the ability to produce physical and spiritual reactions just by focusing on them. Most of you have already realized this and have had your own experiences that help you understand. The particular form that we have employed has been used for thousands of years by the ancient mystery schools in Egypt, then later adopted by certain esoteric Christian traditions, most particularly the "Community of the Beloved Disciples" founded by the man you refer to as St. John, and whom I call my friend. He was able to crystallize the truths and teachings I offered, then activate them through the wheel. It has since been used by the extensions of that original community to project a powerful energy, or focused communal prayer, that has kept humanity moving forward on its spiritual evolutionary track. The Emissaries of Light were the most recent group to conduct this powerful meditation and use the wheel, but they were far from the first. Now it falls to you, for the fact that you are reading this now means that you have been called. The form you choose to extend this is up to you. It does not matter at all. But the transformation the wheel will cause is important indeed, and that is why much of this course will be focused on it.

For the next three weeks we will focus our attention on the fruit of this transformation, what we will call the "Three Enlightenments." They are

> Illumined Mind
>
> Awakened Heart
>
> Realized Soul.

The twelve qualities we have examined for the last several lessons make up the first Enlightenment, the second is found in the inner triangle, and the circle in the middle of the wheel represents the third. Ultimately, here is what you have come to learn through all of this: The quality of God's Love is the same as the quality of your Love of God. That is what we are here to achieve, this recognition. Your first inclination will be to try to understand this statement intellectually. Hopefully you will realize the impossibility of this rather quickly. The mind cannot understand what it has no relationship to. And yet there is an experience that exists beyond the mind that can translate these concepts into tangible truths. The mind will be empty and serene, yet will you understand. It has been set aside for a moment in favor of a deeper ocean, one that will withstand the crashing waves of thought. Once you have touched this place, nothing else will suffice. Then the Peace of God, that which surpasses all thought, will be yours, and you will stand at my side to save the world.

Today we begin by considering the quality of God's love, that which you must understand even at the most basic level, then compare it to your love of God. There is a mystery here, and if you are able to see the correlation between these two, then experience it in your heart, your progress will be swift. We will begin in the mind but, as always, seek the deeper pulse from which all real learning occurs. One of these extends from God while the other returns. The mind believes that these are two actions; you have already come far enough to realize that it is really one. What extends from God stays with God. What extends from you stays with you. If there really are two of you in this equation, you and God, then it would mean that no movement has occurred at all. God has not moved toward you and you have not moved toward God. Therefore, one of two things is false, either the premise itself, or the concept of "two." You can decide for yourself. What extends from God is perfectly received by God. God gives but to Itself, and you are not separate from that giving. YOU ARE THAT GIVING. It is who you are, yet you have tried to deny who you are. Thankfully, you have failed miserably at this attempt, and nothing has changed at all. You seem to have changed since the perceived Split, but there is a rather large difference between something "seeming" to happen, and actually happening. Your failure is your salvation. It should be embraced, not decried. Then you can look at yourself again and see that you are the Gift of God and the Giving of God at the same moment. Another more simple way of saying this, which you already know, is that you are One with God. Now we come full circle, back to the place we began. I could have said this at the beginning and you would have understood, but this winding path has a purpose, though you are not able to perceive it quite yet. That moment, however, is fast approaching.

So what is the experience that exists beyond the mind that can translate this into tangible truths? Your Unconditional Surrender! Embrace it now.

—Brother

Lesson Eleven

We are on a journey of awakening. In reality this is a journey that leads back to where you have always been. No distance has been crossed, for you have never truly left your Home. The Thought of God has never left its source, and that thought has been identified as You. And now a new Light dawns upon your open mind, for you have begun to embrace an ancient experience that leads to your full Illumination. Your enlightenment is at hand, and the Grace of your birthright suddenly fills your soul.

The awareness of your enlightenment will occur in three stages. This is what we are calling the "Three Enlightenments."

Illumined Mind

Awakened Heart

Realized Soul

Notice that I referred to this as the "awareness of your enlightenment." This is the critical distinction that must be observed then accepted before any real shift occurs. YOU ARE ALREADY ENLIGHTENED! In fact, there is nothing but this seemingly elusive state in the whole Universe, perfectly revealed every moment as You. You cannot choose whether this is true or false, but you can choose whether you are conscious of it. Until now you have chosen to live within the ego's tight constraints, completely misidentified by its version of who you are and what the world is for. But now a Light has opened in your mind, and you are at least able to consider the possibility that you are so loved of God that Grace wrapped itself around you the instant you were conceived by Eternity, and enfolds you still. As you surrender to this Love you will feel yourself waking up to the vision of the Real World, a place where time does not exist and your Holiness shines forever. First your mind will open, then your heart, and finally your whole soul. Over the next several lessons we will examine these stages and how you can use the Emissary Wheel to excite the process.

The First Enlightenment:
Illumined Mind

This is the Light that shatters your perception of everything you thought was real and everything you value in the world. Its effect is stronger than anything you can consider with you mind. Imagine that you have been sitting in a dark closet for many years when suddenly the door opens to a cloudless sky. The sun is directly above and you are blinded by its effect. Now multiply this by one hundred, then one thousand, and you are then close to the powerful opening you will experience when the First Enlightenment dawns. You will see the world through new eyes and believe that you have finally arrived at the end of your journey. But you have not. It is but the first stage of your awakening, and it is essential that you do not accept this. The contrast alone is enough to convince you that you must have achieved full illumination, but the ego still clings to the walls of your mind and is afraid to move forward. (We will define the ego as the part of YOU hat believes it is separate from everything that exists. It is not real, just as YOU, or the concept of YOU, is not real. This is your salvation.) You now look out upon the world you created and realize that you created it. Do you understand? You are no longer the effect, but the cause, and thus do you realize your power. But power without an awakened heart is nothing, and so we move on to the second stage.

The Second Enlightenment: Awakened Heart

You will recognize a master who has achieved the second stage by their willingness to give everything to everything. How can you hold back when the whole universe is giving to you every moment? Your heart explodes and becomes a river of refreshment to all beings. They come to you with parched tongues and drink from the Grace that flows from deep within. When you look upon them you see only the Beloved, for you know that only the Beloved exists, and your praise is unmatched. Words cannot speak of this state, for they are but the concepts of a world that no longer exists for you. And yet there is a new language you have learned, the language of the heart, of Love itself. You are that Love NOW. The instant the Second Enlightenment occurs the first thing you will say to your Self is "How could I have not seen this before? It is the most obvious thing in the Universe." And so it is with you and all beings, for the Awakened Heart reveals that which cannot change within you. But you are still not finished. There is still one final opening, the third stage.

The Third Enlightenment: Realized Soul

Of this we cannot speak. The moment you try to conceptualize this state is the instant you return to the world of form, the world the Realized Soul views but through half-opened eyes. It would not be true to say that they are in the world at all, just as you are not in the world even now. But the true master sees both within them, and thus becomes the bridge that leads others into the vast Light of Realization. Stand beside them and you are but a step away. Enter yourself and you realize that there is no step at all. It was all in your mind, then your heart, and it is now but a memory that fades as does the darkened sky come dawn. The shadows that frightened you so appear as harmless friends, and you find yourself wrapped in a deep incomprehensible peace. You are home, the home you never left except in your imagination. There is nowhere for you to go now, for the Light has come to you at last.

And yet, through these three stages of your enlightenment, nothing has changed at all. You are the same as you have ever been.

—Brother

Lesson Twelve

I have called you my Beloved Friends, my family, because I have looked upon your Love and recognized you as my own. Now you must do the same, for to fully enjoy this Sacred Union we must see with the same eyes, perceive the world through the same heart, and know the Beloved every moment we live. The Three Enlightenments are not real, for they do not indicate any real change in you. But they seem real because your heart has been closed for so long, and it is finally returning to its most natural state. That is the only thing that is important right now.

I have said that you are already enlightened, and that is why I know myself, because I have seen this in you. How else would I understand the ways of my Father/Mother if not by giving what I have received? Are you willing to step into this same Light now? You have come here only for this, and this is the moment you decided to awaken long before you were born into this body. Look upon the world with new eyes now, and you will understand everything I have said, not with your mind, but your whole Self.

Look upon the Emissary Wheel for a moment and notice the outer circle where all the points meet. Let your gaze soften and you will notice that the Wheel seems to move on its own. Your focus will shift from one place to another, and you will see triangles upon triangles, all leading to the very center where no movement occurs at all. This is your goal, perfect stillness. We begin on the outer reach where the circle encloses the wheel, then begin to move inward through the spokes until we arrive at the center triangle. You are now a step away from Heaven, for there is nothing left but to release everything you thought was real. Then all your questions fade and melt before this altar of Grace, and you at last perceive your Blessed Holiness. Scales fall from your eyes and you see the world as if for the first time. Nothing can invade this calm, for you have broken free from the restraints of what never happened at all. This is the only moment that exists, for you remember who you are, and all is well.

I have called you to stand at my side as Spiritual Peacemakers. This is what is meant by the phrase: "Be in the world but not of the world." You must become the bridge that leads others into the Light we share, away from the world you thought was real, into the World where reality is never threatened. A simple loving glance in the direction of another can bring more peace than all the governments in the world. A hand extended to another frees more energy than all the sources of power on this planet. We lay aside our former judgments and view the world through spiritual eyes. We are not interested in results, but in the peace that surpasses all understanding. The Emissary Wheel is valuable only because it is patterned after your Awakened Self. On its own it has no value at all, but when applied to this holy moment it releases you from the prison you placed yourself within.

Is this what you choose now? You must have realized that you are in prison; otherwise you would have never answered the call I sent forth. And how do you feel when I tell you that the door to your cell was never locked? You could have left at any moment, and yet your fear of what lay outside kept you from experiencing the freedom you deserve. Reach out and turn the handle and you will see for yourself. It turns easily, almost too easily. You may feel the temptation to criticize yourself for not having left before. But how could you be of service to others if you never experienced all these things? I too felt this prison, and now I look back upon you and call you forward into the Light I enjoy. As soon as you leave you will do the same, then you will know what a peacemaker really is. Until now you have imagined that a peacemaker is one who brings peace to the world. All I am here to show you is that there is no world to bring peace to. Don't try to understand these words with your mind for you will surely fail. You have come far enough to comprehend these things with your heart, for that is where the release occurs. Open now and let me reveal the Truth. You are ready!

I will continue leading you on the path of the Three Enlightenments. Now that you have begun feeling the effects of the Emissary Wheel that awakens at a cellular level, you are ready to understand the path you have entered. The Wheel naturally contains everything I will share, so continue to meditate with it as often as you can. Do not direct the course of this meditation, but let it direct you. Simply gaze upon the geometry and let it pull you in. The rest, however glorious, will happen by itself. Over the next three days I will share more information regarding the Three Enlightenments. At this point it is still important to move between the soul and the mind with gentle ease, until the point comes when we will lay aside the mind for what will serve you more. There is nothing for you to fear in this. I am at your side and have walked this path before you. I will never lead you astray.

You have nearly made the final turn on the path that leads to your home, the place where the Beloved waits for you. I can feel the joy of my Father/Mother coming from that palace, for you have been away for a very long time.

—Brother

Lesson Thirteen

Are you ready to SEE the Door that opens before you, allowing you to step into "Your Truest Self"? This is the door you must pass through if you are to join me as a Spiritual Peacemaker. It has always been open, but your eyes have not. They have been closed, and you therefore thought the door was closed as well. But now you have progressed far enough to realize that there is nothing for you to fear, and no reason to remain blind. Open your eyes and step forward. I am waiting for you on the other side.

Your forgiveness is all that is required of you and is the path that leads to the First Enlightenment. But you must first release every idea you have ever had about what forgiveness is, otherwise it will not have the power to liberate you from the world you created in favor of the Real World. Liberation is required, for a master does not base his or her power in a world that does not exist. They seem to live in the world, just as you, but they are not of this world. Make no mistake about it – you have been called to do the same. You chose this path before you were born, the path of mastery, and now is the moment you must embrace it. A new definition of forgiveness must replace the old; then you are ready. Then the door will pull you, rather than you having to exert any effort at all.

The First Enlightenment: Illumined Mind

The Door that leads to the First Enlightenment is simply your willingness to forgive yourself. Until now forgiveness has been a concept in your mind, not a real experience. That is because you have perceived another person outside yourself that seems to need your forgiveness, and so you have ignored the real lesson, that which leads directly to the Illumination of your Mind. The possibility of "Perfect Unity" must first be accepted by your mind because you have given your mind so much power. The mind's power is extremely limited, but you have forgotten where your real source of power lies and have unknowingly bolstered the weakest part of you. And because the Holy Spirit would never deny you anything, it begins the process where you are, not where you are not. It uses the concepts you have accepted into your mind to ultimately release the concepts you have accepted into your mind. Did you understand that statement? We are using thought to release thought because you have given your thoughts so much value. Their value ultimately has no meaning outside of time, and therefore chains you here, blocking your awareness of what is true, your timelessness. And yet, there is nothing we cannot use to initiate the transformation that is required, even that which has no purpose at all.

There is only one statement you must learn and fully embrace to welcome the First Enlightenment. Repeat it over and over throughout the day, and at every time you feel yourself entering into judgement.

"My perfect release comes from forgiving myself for what never occurred."

An Illumined Mind has directly experienced "Perfect Unity," not as a concept but as a real, tangible thing, and therefore has realized the futility of forgiving anything or anyone outside itself. There is nothing to forgive because there is no one outside you to forgive. (You will ultimately discover that this statement applies to you as well, for the concept of "you" is the only true hurdle to your awakening. But we must begin by drawing your attention inward, away from the world of form, the world where you seem to be vulnerable to attack.) You are experiencing the projections of your own split mind because it keeps you from taking full responsibility for everything that happens to you. Forgiveness is the only path you must walk now, for it reveals everything you really desire. You are ready to lay down your sword and stop hurting yourself. Then the door swings wide and you enter with ease.

Perhaps it would be best for me to lay this step out as clearly as words will allow. If this seems to threaten you in any way, or shakes the foundation of the world you cling to now, then bless that experience and do not resist it at all. Your resistance will only lead to greater pain. Simply take a deep breath and allow everything, but open your heart to these truths. I am telling you these things because I care for you so deeply, and because of the agreement we made before time began. We agreed that we would work together to end all things of time in favor of the reality that cannot be threatened by any illusions. I intend to keep that agreement.

Jesus

Do not try to understand these thoughts with your mind, but let your heart absorb them all:

The world you think you live in is not real.

There is no one for you to forgive, including yourself, since your concepts of yourself are as unreal as the world you created to hide in.

You cannot hide forever.

God does not even know you are here. You are like a child that fell asleep and dreams. The child's parent sits beside him/her and will not move until the fever breaks. And yet there is no time in which the parent gives reality to what it knows doesn't exists.

Your fever is breaking now.

When you wake up from the dream the first question you will ask is: "Why did I keep my eyes closed for so long?"

This is the moment you chose to remember who you are. Nothing is important but this. Your forgiveness is the path that leads you to this moment.

Finally,

These thoughts, if you are willing to fully accept them into your mind, lead to the First Enlightenment. Breathe them in, and you will realize peace at last.

—Brother

Lesson Fourteen

Your Mind is now Illumined and you have opened the first door that leads to the Truth within. You have done this by forgiving yourself for an offense that never occurred in reality, and have therefore seen past all the walls that seemed to separate you from the Real World. And though you will now be tempted to believe that you have finally achieved the goal established for you before time began, you must not stop. Though the new world you perceive with your Illumined Mind will appear in a light you could have never before imagined, your journey has only begun. Move forward and prepare your Heart for the next movement, for your Spirit dwells in this Sacred Chamber and needs to be released now. It is the next step, the second door, and you are ready to enter.

It is important that we define forgiveness so you will not be confused. I have said that you must forgive yourself, and others, for the offenses you perceived with your mind but which in reality never occurred at all. What does this mean? I have also said that your salvation comes naturally when you realize the difference between the world you made for yourself and the world made for you by God. The ego sees everything as separate and alone, waiting for death as if it was the natural ending to all things that live, and it created a world that reflects this decision. God knows that anything that lives at all lives forever, and that separation and isolation are impossible. Therefore, the world you presently perceive is directly opposed to the Real World, and must therefore be released before you can enter. Both cannot be real, and you are choosing which one you will see every moment. You can choose again whenever you want. Let this be the moment of your release, for delay is unjustified. If you knew the sacrifice you were making by denying the world God has made, then you wouldn't wait another second. Take my hand now, for I have seen both worlds and can show you the one where Love alone is real. It is not here, the place of separate bodies and broken dreams. And yet it is but a step away, a simple shift in your mind, then in your heart. That is the journey I am leading you on, and you can trust me not to lead you astray.

You are not bound by the laws of two worlds, but by the world you choose to SEE.

Ultimately only one is real, but both will "seem" real to a confused mind. Are you willing to accept that until now you have been confused? This acceptance is not meant to increase your guilt, but to end it. You are ready to release the world that never gave you what you really wanted, and accept a New World where all those things are already yours. Your willingness to lay aside one leads to your acceptance of the other, and the limitations that bound you in the first are then set aside. The world of bodies will not fade, but its effects will. Do you understand the difference? Until now you have been afraid that to accept the world God has prepared for you means you must leave behind all the things you love in this world. Nothing you love can ever be lost, for loss directly opposes love. The nature of love is gain, not loss. You will bring it all with you, and time cannot leave its deadly mark upon your soul. And yet, you will know that you are the Love you seek. It has always been yours and cannot change. You are that love, and it will never fade away.

The Second Enlightenment: Awakened Heart

I would like to share a thought that has the power to undo all the illusions you have ever held about yourself and the world. If you accept it into your heart, and follow its inner promptings, then it will open the second door.

The Thought:

Your willingness to forgive others as you have forgiven yourself is the Door that leads to the Second Enlightenment.

Are you able to see how these two things exist together as a single Holy Action? Your mind opens when you realize that the sins you thought you committed have been forgiven already, and then your heart is awakened the moment you extend this gift to others. The love of God is a circle and must flow in every direction. Until now it has encompassed a narrow field, usually the one you inhabit moment to moment. Open your heart and give this gift freely, and then you will have it freely. There is only one way for you to keep this vital flow alive, and that is to share it. Forgiveness is the path, but seen in a new light, wholly free from the restraints of the ego's world. There is nothing for you to forgive now, and within this truth does your freedom lie, and the freedom of everyone you touch.

There are two things I would ask you to focus on for the next three days. The first is a simple formula that will help you understand how the Three Enlightenments work:

First the Mind surrenders, then SEES; next the Heart surrenders, then SEES; finally the Soul awakens, then KNOWS.

Meditate on this formula and you may begin to discover its simple design. All I can tell you now is that it is related to the code that has been inserted into each lesson in this course. I told you that these lessons are meant to activate your soul at different levels, both gross and subtle. This formula will bring these two closer than you can imagine.

And as often as you can these next few days, chant this single word:

YES!

You already know what it means and where it leads. Open to it now.

—Brother

Lesson Fifteen

The formula that was offered last week is a key that will help you understand, first intellectually, then in your soul, the process of enlightenment. We will leave our discussion on the Three Enlightenments for a moment while we enter into this more fully.

The Formula:

First the Mind surrenders, then SEES; next the Heart surrenders, then SEES; finally the Soul awakens, then KNOWS.

This formula applies both to the order in which you are experiencing enlightenment, as well as the method. Notice the way I expressed those words. I did not say, "the order in which you WILL experience enlightenment," for that would mean that it is not yours now, or that I am somehow different than you. There is nothing that is full in my mind that is not also complete in yours. I know this, and now it is time for you to know it as well. I have said that you are already awake, and the only difference between your mind and mine is that I believe these words fully. You have considered them, but it is not the same as realizing that any other thought would be impossible, especially now. It is who you are, and I constantly look upon this reality. Open your eyes and you will do the same.

The first experience you must embrace over all others if you are to fully integrate these lessons is "Surrender."

Why is surrendering so important before your mind and heart can fully open? The reason you seem lost is because you have been fooled into believing that you can find the Light on your own, or that your mind alone is capable of establishing the path that will lead you home. If this were true then you would have done it a long time ago. The fact that you are experiencing time at all indicates that you are incapable of doing anything on your own. You need help. Eternity is still nothing more than a concept in your mind, not an experience. A concept is a belief and can never be substituted for the truth. The first step is to release the concept completely and to realize that you DO NOT KNOW THE PATH TO WALK. You cannot be shown where to go or how to proceed until you admit that you do not know. Then the path is illumined at your feet, and the memory of your home returns.

To the ego the statement, "I don't know," is a sign of weakness or failure. In reality it is the first step toward wisdom, and sets you firm upon the path of realizing your enlightenment. There is so much help that you can receive, but not until you surrender and admit that on your own you have failed. This is not because God wishes to ridicule you, but because

Present Moment

you will not be able to fully embrace the truth until you realize that you are helpless on your own. Embracing the fact that you DO NOT KNOW THE PATH TO ENLIGHTEN-MENT is the only thing that the Holy Spirit needs to show you everything. It is like crack-ing a door open and letting the light stream in. The objects in the room that a moment before seemed dark and ominous, now appear as they really are – harmless projections of your sleeping mind. Let them go and they are gone, but you must surrender what you thought they were in order to be shown the truth.

The Mind cannot KNOW anything. This is reserved for the Soul. The Mind assumes and judges and all its judgments are based upon its past experiences. And because it places so much importance on the past, it seeks to make the future like it. It therefore drags its lim-ited knowledge of everything like a weight into every experience, never once considering that the very premise of its thought system is insane. The present moment is never seen at all, for it is nothing more than a bridge that exists between the past and the future, hardly worth considering. The mind never realizes that resting for a moment in this Holy Instant could solve all its troubles. This is the most threatening thing in the whole universe to the ego, for it means that you have to admit that you never knew where to go, what to do, or anything at all. You are admitting that you are like a child, completely helpless. To the ego it means you failed and deserve nothing at all. In reality, it means that you are very near your greatest success.

Let the past go and do not consider the future at all; then the present moment will appear before you as a great beacon of light leading you to the place you never left except in your imagination.

Rest for a moment in the "I don't know" experience. Let it wrap around you like a warm blanket, keeping you free from all the empty snares of this world. It could be your salvation, if only you would allow it. There is nothing for you to fear when letting go could give you everything you desire. Nothing temporary will suffice now. The complete abandonment of the ego is the only thing that will lead you to where you really want to go.

The second word for you to consider in this formula is "SEE."

Your eyes were made not to see, or to see what isn't really there. The SEEING you are being led to is not a function of this world, but of the world reserved for you in eternity. When you open your spiritual eyes, which is what enlightenment really means, reality appears before you as it really is. You SEE what is there, instead of what never existed at all. Are you willing to consider that it is this simple? Are you willing to surrender everything you thought you saw a moment ago and SEE what has never changed?

—Brother

Lesson Sixteen

Today's lesson begins a gentle shift in focus. You are here because your soul is choosing to be a Spiritual Peacemaker. It may seem like you made this choice with your mind, or even with your heart. In reality it was made in both your mind and your heart, which then activated the place within your soul that IS this. We will now begin to explore this movement, the manner in which your soul chooses the experience it lives, and how you will integrate these three into one perfect extension of your Holiness and Grace.

You will also be offered ways to ground this awakening into your conscious Self, moving enlightenment from a concept in your mind to a reality you can know and live. Until now I have shared the concepts of the Illumined Mind, but they will not take us where we need to go. The Awakened Heart is the real first step, as it unites with the Mind. These two together present the final possibility, the full remembrance of your Divinity. We will not stop until we cross that final bridge and set your feet upon solid ground. Then you will not need these lessons, or anything this world can offer. Then you will KNOW that you are Home, and that all things are contained within that Perfect Light. You will not judge anything as right or wrong, good or bad, but will look upon it all with forgiving eyes. And your forgiveness will be whole, for there will be nothing left to block the radiant flow of the Beloved's Love as it washes you clean from all the broken promises you made yourself. You are that Love, and you are ready to embrace your Self and BE as God perceives you.

The Second Enlightenment:

You will not be close to fulfilling your role as a Spiritual Peacemaker until you have achieved the Second Enlightenment, Awakened Heart. Countless people have achieved the first level, and yet the energy of their Illumined Mind was not strong enough to catapult them past their illusions. The Illumination of your mind involves seeing what is in front of you every moment. It is a vast achievement because you have been spending all your time seeing what is NOT in front of you. Do you understand this now? Everything you thought was real was merely a shadow of the reality you are about to perceive. Seeing what is real and acting with Spiritual Integrity are not always compatible, however. The ego's grasp upon a person who has only achieved the First Enlightenment is still very strong, and without the empowered heart the temptation to use the new awareness for the ego's glorification will persist. That is why it is so important that you resist the urge to believe you have done anything at all. If you look around you and SEE what is real, that you are one with all beings and possess the power of that wholeness, do not consider it an accomplishment. Keep moving forward, into the heart, for only it is able to untie the knots that bind you to the ego's desire.

The Illumined Mind is achieved so simply. You have convinced yourself that it may take years of study and sacrifice, but it is not true. It is as easy as opening your eyes and admitting you were fooled before. I have already shared how important it is for you to joyfully accept the failure of your entire system of thought. Do not bemoan what has had no effect at all, but release it with eagerness and delight. Your goal isn't to be right, but to be happy once and for all. Being right in this world is such a limited frame, while happiness is a true gift from God. But it will not come to you until you admit that you were looking at shadows while the world of your dreams was lived just beyond your reach. This admission is the simple first step to the Illumination you have asked to receive. Once you admit you were wrong, then you can choose to see everything in a new way, the only way that reflects the truth you feel deep within your heart. Open your eyes and see what has always been real. There is no need to recreate the world, for your vain imaginings have never changed it at all. Your full and open gaze is all that is required now; then your Mind will spring into a new life.

You are now a single step away from bringing Peace to the world. You have learned to SEE what is true, now you must FEEL it as well.

I want to share a simple exercise that will help you prepare yourself for the initiation that lies ahead. You will likely immediately feel power in these words and actions. Practice them as often as you can, not only for the next three days but for the rest of this course. It is like a key that will open powerful energy centers within. The more you dedicate yourself to this exercise the more value it will hold.

If possible, do this at a time when you are very relaxed and at peace. You may choose to do it in the shower, or after you have prayed or meditated. When you have centered your mind, turn to your heart and let it open wide. The purpose of this exercise is to begin the process of FEELING who you are, and then knowing you are awake. Here is the exercise:

Wrap your arms around yourself and say these words over and over, meaning them with your whole heart:

"You are the awakened Heart."

Do not think about what this means with your mind, but with your heart. Think with your heart. There is a secret I could share with you about this chant, but I will wait until the next lesson. For now, only FEEL. And then, KNOW.

—Brother

Lesson Seventeen

Welcome again, Beloved Friends, to this dialogue on awakening. The words we speak are but the symbols of the Light we share, and it is this Light that leads you to the true goal, the Home you never left.

The dream of separation ends when you ask it to. What can this mean but that you have not yet asked it to end? Why? Because you were afraid of what might be waiting for you, what reward or punishment you may enjoy or despise. Your Brother's job is simply to report back to you what he has seen, and to remind you how safe it is to remember who you really are. I have seen the path that lies before you, for I have walked it just as you are walking it now. I too felt the pain of forgetfulness, but then the dawn of a new world flooded my heart, and I was able to see again. And now are you waking up, and your Brother takes you by the hand while the sleep still fills your eyes. I am here, and I will not leave you until our job together is done.

You have asked to become a Spiritual Peacemaker, and you are beginning to realize what that means. It does not require a sacrifice at all, unless you still believe that giving up what was never true is a sacrifice. You have come far enough to realize that the only thing that is real is Love itself, and all the loving extensions of your Healed Mind will come with you into the world God has prepared. You will bring peace by BEING Peace. That is why peace is not a function of this world, for true peace is impossible here. It is a function of the Real World, and that is where I am leading you to now. Open your eyes, Beloved Friend, and SEE what you have hidden from. There is no reason to be afraid now, for Love has come to greet you.

Last week's exercise was very important, for it was meant to give you a tangible experience of your Healed Mind. I asked you to wrap your arms around yourself and say these words with profound conviction: "You are the Awakened Heart." If you did this then you will have felt a movement that is impossible to describe. If you really meant these words, not with your mind but with your whole heart, then your life has changed.

Some of you may have wondered why I asked you to say, "You are the Awakened Heart," as opposed to, "I am the Awakened Heart." There is a very good reason. The real purpose of this exercise is to train you to become a Bridge to others, for that is the true function of a Spiritual Peacemaker. You are being led to imitate one of the most vital aspects of the Beingness of God. It is the Holy Spirit, and you are being led to this now. You are being called to be the physical counterpart of the Holy Spirit's function on earth. Do you feel how important this job is? Let's look for a moment at what this function is so you may understand the Holy Benefits of this exercise.

The Holy Spirit's only job is to act as a bridge between the Real World and the world you are perceiving now. It speaks both languages, though it has not forgotten which is real and which isn't. Therefore, it is a gift to all who would remember the truth within them, for it reminds you that you are not at home here. It reinterprets the function of the world and reestablishes your role as Healer and Guide. Why? Because you will integrate this gift only by sharing it. Therefore, you are being asked to imitate the Holy Spirit's function, or in other words, to be the body, the mind, and the heart through which it expresses its only thought: "Only God's Will is True." This is why you were born, and it is the truest purpose of your life.

There is no difference between the "You" that you embraced through the last exercise, and the "You" you will embrace this week. They are the same, and you will be asked to FEEL them as the same from this moment on. Only then will you touch the heart of this gift, and begin to experience the Second Enlightenment – Awakened Heart.

At least three times in the next three days, find another person that you can serve. Here's all I ask of you – wrap your arms around them and say, either in your mind or out loud, "You are the Awakened Heart." Try to feel this energy in the same way you felt it before, when you were wrapping your arms around yourself. You may want to do that a few times before you extend this exercise so you can remember the feeling. You are saying the same words, and you are giving the same gift. There is no difference at all, and this is what you are trying to have a tangible experience of. Practice this as often as you can. This will test the level of serious-ness you bring to this course. I cannot overemphasize the importance of this, because without the experience I am leading you to here, all these things will only be concepts in your mind. As I said before, concepts in your mind, even if they are illumined, will not help you now. Your heart must now FEEL what you know in your mind. Then you are ready to move into the Third Enlightenment – Realized Soul.

These were the lessons I offered my friends two thousand years ago, and only a few were able to integrate them. But now there is enough energy present, and enough people have walked this path at my side, to allow you to enter.

This is the moment you have been waiting for.

—Brother

11/5/06
11/7/06
11/9/06

Lesson Eighteen

You are undergoing an intense training, though you may not realize where it is leading you. You have asked to become a Spiritual Peacemaker, but it is still impossible for you to understand what this means. It is very different than the world's idea of peace or how that can be accomplished. This is already clear to you. Your eyes are beginning to open to the reality we are seeking, but they are still only half open. You are seeing two worlds at once, one of imagined dreams where you created a world built upon an impossible foundation, and the world where you can clearly SEE the truth that never changes. You may find yourself moving between these two worlds without even knowing it, for the differences are often subtle and hard to perceive. But they will soon become more obvious, and you will not be able to deny the truth any longer. Soon your eyes will open wide, and the world of dreams will disappear completely. Then you will KNOW what it means to bring peace, not with your mind but your whole Self. Then you will be a true servant of humanity, of reality, and everything will make perfect sense to you.

We are going to stay with the Second Enlightenment for one more lesson before we move forward. There is a step we must take together before we can consider the Third; otherwise it will be nothing more than a concept, not a real experience. The Awakened Heart is where we must devote most of our attention because it is where the real foundation lies. Achieving the First Enlightenment is significant but nowhere near the goal, and the Third Enlightenment occurs on its own, without any effort at all, once you have fully opened to the Second. You have come a long way, but there is a step you must take now that you cannot take on your own. That is why I am here, for this is function of an Enlightened Guide.

In the last two lessons you were asked to first embrace yourself as the Awakened Heart, and then embrace another in the same way, knowing that it is the same. The "You" you embraced does not change simply because the frame of reference is different. In other words, the ego believes that because you are more intimately aware of your own self, symbolized by the body, it must surely be different than the self of the other. It sees through your eyes, not theirs, and therefore builds a solid case for its theology of separation. What it does not remember is that it made the body for this very purpose, and claims it still. It has forgotten that the Vision of God extends past all bodies and form and claims them as one. Therefore, when you claim the Awakened Heart within anyone, whether it be yourself or a person who seems to be separate from you, you are the one claiming it. Is this beginning to make sense? This is what we mean when we say, "It is in giving that we receive." What I give to thee is received by me.

And though you have begun to understand and even experience this truth, it is still like a fog in your mind. It is for this reason that you have been given a Master Teacher, one who has cleared the mist that claims you now, and can hold your hand while you do the same. Your Teacher is not here to stand above or beyond where you claim to be, but to simply create a bridge between your mind and heart, much as you are becoming a bridge to others. When seen in this Light then the function begins to make perfect sense. Your Teacher has not come to take anything away from you, but to help you claim everything you thought you lost.

I am within you now, alive and open, ready to show you the heart that loves the world. It does not matter whether you claim my personality as your guide, or the personality of another. It is all the same and makes no difference at all. But you must at this point reach out your hand and ask for help. There is a subtle shift that needs to take place in your heart now, and it will not occur if you convince yourself that you have come further than you actually have. The Teacher appears to lead you home, so that you may in turn offer the same to those that will be given to you.

The Teacher asks you to SEE through his or her heart, not your own. Your heart is not open enough to contain the Light that would flood your being the moment you fully surrender. That is why the first role of one who has achieved the Third Enlightenment is to be a bridge to those who walk behind them. I can offer you the only bridge you need, and yet it is not about any particular identity. The nature of the final stage in your awakening is that you will no longer identify yourself as different from any other being— in particular, other beings that are also awake. Turning toward the Buddha nature within is the same as turning toward your Christ Consciousness. Each is a reference, nothing more, which will link your mind to the eternal movement of Spirit that flows through us all. We are the same in this, and this is the purpose of the bridge I offer.

For the next three days, look through my heart often. Consciously see the world and everything you experience as if I am the one experiencing all of it, not you. When you cross this bridge and reach the other side, then you will see that we are the same, that we share the same heart. Then you will KNOW and you will SEE. The next step will then be yours.

—Brother

11/10/06 11/12/06 11/13/06 11/14/06 11/25/04

Lesson Nineteen

We stand together on a bridge so sacred that words can never describe the grace we feel. We will stop and consider this final step for a moment, the journey from one holy thought to another, from the place you never left to the home where you have always lived. Your mind wandered away for a moment, but your Spirit has always remained, and we will rejoin it now with the awareness of your Illumined Mind and Awakened Heart. This is the only thing that has been lacking, your awareness of who you have always been, but now even that fades into the ocean of timelessness. Nothing has been lost, and all thoughts of separation dissolve into the Holy Vision you now perceive. One final step and you are there. Take my hand, and I will lead you into the safety of your Sacred Self.

I want to describe the single action of this final step, what we are calling "Realized Soul." It is the Third Enlightenment, and you already possess the fruits of this gift, though until now you have closed your eyes to them all. As we stand together on this Bridge of Awakening, I will share the single lesson that will mean more than all the rest, and yet it is the one your mind will be most unwilling to grasp. That is because this Holy Action is so foreign to its current system of thought, that which separates everything from itself. If you can lay aside this resistance, even for a moment, and enter into this current like a child, then your Realized Soul will dawn, and you will remember all the things you once tried to forget.

Open now and try to understand what I will now describe.

A fully Realized Being moves through all worlds with one word, one thought and one feeling surrounding their heart. This word is the bridge we have been discussing. Though a thousand words move through their space, there is only one that is heard. Though a million thoughts enter their mind then leave, only one remains. And though their feelings may change as all emotions change, there is one that remains full and real. I will describe this as a single word, though even this word does not approach the Holy Altar I am offering to you now. If you can access the Light that lies behind the word, and then KNOW that you are that Light, then you will realize with your soul what may have seemed hidden for a time, but which has always been right in front of you.

YES! ★ ★ ★

Are you surprised? Did you expect a word you have never heard before, one with mystical powers you can never understand with your mind? I am telling you now that this word does have mystical powers you cannot understand with your mind. What I am asking is that you allow it to rest alone, isolated from all other words and thoughts for a moment, and see what magic it holds. If you do, then you will see that it is the only word you will ever need, though your mouth will continue to speak so many more, and your mind will race with other thoughts. Still, at the very center of it all, this one reality will exist, and it will pull you into an experience no word or thought can ever propel. Though you may speak a hundred million other words, they will all spring from the experience of YES! Though you will think an unthinkable number of thoughts, still will your YES be at the center of them all. And though your actions will vary from one moment to the next, they will not escape the YES that motivates them all.

When an enlightened being speaks, every word is YES. When they think, every thought is YES. When they act, every action is YES. And now as we stand together on this bridge preparing for this final step, I see this YES moving through you, acting as you, motivating every movement of your soul. This is the only thing you need to know, not with your conscious mind, for it will never be able to grasp what I am saying to you now. But there is a place that has been prepared, and you have been breathing life into this place from all the other lessons and thoughts we have shared. From this place will your YES awaken, and then you will fully grasp what I am saying to you.

In the next lesson I will offer several ways for you to access the Gift of this experience. In this lesson I have offered it as a concept, but as we have said so many times before, a concept will not help you now. It is like swimming at the surface of the ocean when all the treasures you seek lie far below. We are preparing to dive to that sacred chamber where the pearl of highest wisdom is sleeping. As it awakens, so will you. But you must be ready to leave the surface, and I believe you are ready. All the words you have spoken till now, all the thoughts and actions that have defined your life, have not given you what you really want. But this word, YES, radiating through them all, will show you that you have always had what you always wanted. Do you understand that this is the real goal we have set for ourselves, to KNOW that you have possessed this Holy Gift from the beginning of time? Nothing else matters now. Nothing will satisfy you but the Realized Soul you are about to enter.

Lay aside all your idle dreams and let them pass away from you. I have told you that nothing real will be threatened in this transition from illusions into reality. You will bring all your loving thought with you, for love itself is the only reward you will receive.

—Brother

Lesson Twenty

I have said that a master who has attained the Third Enlightenment, Realized Soul, lives within the Eternal Yes. What better advice could I give to you? If there were only one gift I could give, a single reward you would value over all others, it would be this word, this experience, this Holy Offering that has the power to transform the whole world. Live within the YES! I cannot tell you how to do this, for this gift is revealed to each one of us in its own unique way. All I can tell you is that the gift is before you now, and you have the power within to activate it. Choose it above everything else and it is yours. Do not wait another moment.

The first step in living within the Eternal Yes is realizing all the ways you have lived within the experience of "no." This is demonstrated by the ego's insistence that it is "not" everything. The whole universe conspires to reveal the truth to you, and yet you cling to the walls of your sleeping mind and say, "I am not That." The ego refuses to clearly identify what "That" is, for it knows in its heart that all questions would be answered within this Holy Light. The Spirit of Truth says, "You are That," and then proceeds in showing you what that means. The Spirit begs you to look around at the gifts of the universe and then tells you, "You are not separate from any of them." It looks upon the Highest of the High, and the Lowest of the Low, and it says to you, "You are all of That." Thus was YES born, and thus does it live within you now, if only YOU would live within IT now.

This is the beginning and the end of this course on Spiritual Peacemaking. I have saved this simple lesson for a time when all the other concepts and thoughts would be already before you, and after your heart and mind were opened sufficiently enough to accept the most essential teaching I can offer. Let your whole being claim the YES that is at the very core of your being. You are not here to reject anything, but to claim it all. This is what God does, and it is time for you to begin imitating God. You are ready for this, whether you realize it consciously or not. I would not have called you here if you were not ready, and if we had not made an ancient agreement to stand together in this Light. The YES of your soul has been ignited, and it sings to the whole world the Song of Remembrance.

I would like to offer two images to help you understand, and even practice, claiming the YES of your being.

Imagine yourself standing straight with your arms open. (For better effect, do this physically after you have read the descriptions.) Begin chanting the word YES over and over, and as you do, feel the energy of this word filling you. Now move your hands in an outward motion, as if you are giving this energy to others. Every time you say the word YES, push the Light away from your heart. Let it extend from you completely.

Now we will change the meditation to reflect how you have lived your life till now. (I do not mean to discredit you in any way by saying this, but it is important for you to know and embrace the guidance that has come from your ego, guidance which until now you have chosen to heed.) Begin chanting the word NO, and as you do, pull the energy toward your body. Every time you say the word NO, sweep the energy in toward you as if you are not willing to share it.

Now we will examine the meaning of this meditation. It was not a metaphor as much as a clear illustration of what you do in spirit whenever you make any decision at all. Ultimately, every decision or choice is a choice between YES, and NO. Do you see this clearly? When you live within the YES, the natural movement is to give away the same gift you have chosen to receive. The natural action of YES is expansion, whereas the natural action of NO is retraction. NO seeks to hide within its projections while YES chooses to give so that it may receive more. God is constantly giving, and so must you give everything if you are to "Be as God." The Divine does not hold back; therefore, it does not understand the experience of NO. Give all to have all. This is the true path to enlightenment.

If you changed the order, it would also provide a powerful lesson. Imagine that when you chant the word YES you are pulling the energy in toward yourself, and when you chant the word NO you push it away. In this example, the energy of YES seeks to contain all reality within itself, while the energy of NO seeks to project it onto others. YES takes full responsibility for everything it perceives, while NO takes no responsibility. The second experience chooses to reject itself by rejecting others. Thus does it find itself isolated and alone, while the whole world rotates around its center.

Find as many ways as you can in the next three days to live within the YES. This is one of the most valuable tools I can offer, for it is in living this that it becomes real to you. Be aware of the ways you are currently saying NO to the universe. Allow a new vision to take hold, one where YES is the only reality you embrace. Chant the word over and over. Clap your hands together, or pat all over your body in order to ground the experience. I am asking you to join me in the Eternal YES. Please answer.

—Brother

Lesson Twenty One

Today we begin our course again. Until now we have been laying the foundation upon which an amazing temple will be built. The foundation of any building is the most important step, and so it is with us, those seeking to be called "Instruments of Peace," "Emissaries of Light," or "Spiritual Peacemakers." The stones we have been laying upon the ground are the holy concepts of peace, grace, and the truth that cannot be challenged by anything you have made in this world. Now they are in place, and now we will progress into the very temple we have fashioned together.

You must now make a very important decision. Will you choose to rededicate yourself to this goal, after so many weeks and so many lessons? Will you decide this moment to increase your commitment that you may leave the world altogether and realize yourself to be what you have chosen to seek? You cannot complete your role unless you do this, for until now we have allowed a certain ease in our lessons. That moment has now passed, and it is time for you to decide once and for all if you are willing to take the final step toward full realization, and thus full service. You are ready, but will you choose?

If the answer within your soul is the "YES" we have been asked to live, then step forward. If there is any part of you that still believes you are not ready, then wait here for awhile and I will send angels to pick you up and lead you forward. You will not be left behind. I will see to that. Such a thing is impossible at this point, for I have called you to my side and you have answered. I am here and I will not leave. Take a deep breath, and take the step toward life.

There are only thirteen lessons left, and we will use them wisely. As I said, we have given you the tools, and now you must activate and use them. The final lessons will take everything we have learned till now and bring them together into a harmonious whole. We will take each of the twelve attributes of an Emissary of Light and we will apply them to the Three Enlightenments. Through this you will learn to ascend with them, as they ascend with you, to the holy altar of the temple we build together. For the next twelve lessons we will take each of the attributes and apply them to this template. On the thirteenth lesson we will be left with one final step, the step into your enlightened mind, heart and soul. We will also apply the central teaching, noted through the center triangle in the Emissary wheel, which is the foundation of our practice which: Surrender, Trust and Gratitude. (Have the image of the wheel near you as you read these final lessons.) The stage has been set. This is the moment you have been waiting for.

Remember: YOU ARE READY! *I AM READY*

The First Attribute: Courage

The First Enlightenment, Illumined Mind:

Courage must first awaken in your mind before it can be felt in the world. It is this feeling that will ultimately lead to your release, but it must first be known as a possibility, however dim. As you awaken this enlightenment, it will become more real to you, and it will no longer be a concept. This is when you will know that a shift is beginning to occur, the shift into the Second Enlightenment. Hold this thought high in your mind, then, and know that there is nothing for you to fear. You are protected more than you know.

Surrender Meditation:

I surrender all those places within my mind that were afraid to step into my chosen role of being a Spiritual Peacemaker, and I acknowledge that only Divine Courage can lead me forward from here. I do not know what to do, but through my surrender I will be shown. I am that Courage now, fully Illumined.

The Second Enlightenment, Awakened Heart:

I now FEEL courage escape my Mind and release the power of my Awakened Heart. I am not waiting for this courage to dawn, but claim it now with energy and commitment. I am no longer afraid to fulfill my part in God's plan for salvation. My courage spills into the world now from my heart, and is seen and felt by all beings everywhere. My heart is sufficient unto all, and knows only the Light that leads it forward. I embrace courage and draw it inward, then extend it as a blessing to the world.

Trust Meditation:

I trust that you are with me now, Beloved One, and therefore I have the courage to step forward. There is no path I will walk that you have not already covered, and so I trust you and am filled with an inner strength that the world does not understand. I trust that you know the path to walk, and so I am courageous. I am that Courage now, fully Awakened.

The Third Enlightenment, Realized Soul:

My soul rejoices in the courage I have found within. My soul knows only this joy, for it exists only for this moment, the moment when courage propels me into my Divine Purpose of a Spiritual Peacemaker. I realize now why I was born into this world, and I will not waste another moment.

Gratitude Meditation:

I am grateful for the courage born within me today. My soul does now embrace this moment, for it is the moment I have waited for since I was created. I step forward in courage and I KNOW who I am, thus do I know all things. There is nowhere I need to go but where I am NOW. There is nothing I need do but what I am doing NOW. I am grateful for the courage I find within my soul. I am that Courage now, fully Realized.

—Brother

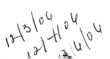

Lesson Twenty Two

The Second Attribute: Patience

The First Enlightenment, Illumined Mind:

Only eternal patience will bring immediate results. That is because eternal patience does not seek anything except what it already has, and it recognizes that it lacks nothing. Therefore, what comes from God remains with God, and it knows itself as God. There is nothing that can invade the deep peace this thought inspires, which comes from the Illumined Mind. It does not look to the physical world to prove its conviction, but to the Spirit where all things are given and received. You need nothing, and your recognition of this fact is your salvation.

There is nothing you can gain that you do not already possess in your soul, for all things exist and remain where you exist and remain. Therefore, they are already together. Do you see how simple this is? Your ego would have you believe that you must gain what you do not have, while your Spirit tells you that there is nothing that is not already yours. Which will you believe? Whose voice will you listen to, the voice of lack that comes from your ego, or the Voice of Peace that tells you the Truth? When you grasp this Truth then you will understand the real meaning of Patience; then you will be ready to sink into the Second Enlightenment.

Surrender Meditation:

I open my hands to receive all the gifts my Spirit wills for me. Until now my fist has been closed and I have been unwilling to surrender to the Divine Current that flows through me now. I accept that I made a mistake, and yet it has had no consequence at all. I let go and accept a new frame of reference, one where my surrender reveals all things that are already mine. I patiently accept all these gifts and know that they are fully revealed through and as me. Patience is the gift I give and receive. I am that Patience now, fully Illumined.

The Second Enlightenment, Awakened Heart:

Now that you KNOW that eternal patience is the only thing that will give you the immediate results you seek, you must begin to FEEL this completion. I say completion because it is what I perceive in you, and I am asking you to perceive the same. Your mind has accepted this, and now your heart must awaken to the reality I am describing. It is the only way for you to enter into the stream of Grace that a Spiritual Peacemaker must know and embrace in order to be of true service. Otherwise you will understand what you do not have, but this still leaves us far from our goal. Your ego will endure your understanding, but not your experience. This is where the real release takes place. But what the ego considers a battle you will turn around and see as a victory. As you patiently open to the Peace that has always been yours, the ego's defenses will fall on their own. No battle will ensue, for you have seen past it altogether.

I have been patient with you, and now you must be patient with yourself. Some of you wonder if you have been integrating the code I have placed within these lessons, for you have not been able to access it intellectually. I ask only that you look to the world around you and see how it has been healed. Be patient a moment longer and all your questions will be answered. I have chosen you for a reason, and now you must trust that I know what I am doing.

Trust Meditation:

I open my heart and Trust you, Beloved One, for you have not let me lose track of my Divine Purpose here on Earth. I have been given a Holy Guide to show me the path I walk, and I trust that my feet are being led toward the only goal worthy of my soul. I will be patient and let all things be revealed. The only thing that is required of me this moment is my trust, and I offer it now. I trust that the Universe is perfectly revealed through my Awakened Heart, and all things flow toward God. I am that Patience now, fully Awakened.

The Third Enlightenment, Realized Soul:

The immediate results you are seeking are already yours. What more do you need to hear? Realizing this, it should be a simple thing for you to be truly patient and Know that you have everything you need. In this way do we back into patience, for it is not a result we seek, but the very means through which we realize the truth. It is within your soul now, protected and whole. The more you access this Divine Patience, the more conscious it will become for you. Take a deep breath, then, and Know who you are. In doing so, you will know all things.

It is impossible for my words to ever fully describe this step, for it is not aligned with the world you have created in any way. It operates according to the laws of a different world, and your patience is the only thing that will lead you into it NOW. Decide this moment if it is what you really want. There is no sacrifice that will be required of you, except all your illusions. But if you are honest with yourself you will realize that they have never given you what you really want. Be free, then, and do not expect too much of a world that you designed to keep you from this truth.

Gratitude Meditation:

Patience has opened a new door for me to see who I am, and I am grateful for this gift. The only words that escape from my lips this day are – "Thank you my Beloved." At last I have realized who I am, and who I will always remain. I am that Patience now, fully Realized.

—Brother

Lesson Twenty Three

The Third Attribute: Wisdom

The third attribute that you must consciously integrate in choosing to join me as a Spiritual Peacemaker, is Wisdom. It is the fruit of the first two, Courage and Patience. The Wisdom you are seeking will reveal a new world to you, or a very old one. This is the world that has been prepared for you since the beginning of time. It is your rightful home, the place where you sleep even now. I am there with you holding your hand, and I will not leave your side until your eyes open and you are wide awake again. The Wisdom being offered to you now is the key to this moment. Will you take it from me, and from all the others who hold it safe for you?

I would like to lead you through a process of inquiry that will help you integrate this even further. I do this because I have accepted my role as a teacher and a healer, the same role you are choosing to accept this moment. Follow me, then, and see where this process leads. It ultimately leads nowhere at all, but you cannot realize this until you walk with me for just a moment. In that sacred moment will you know the truth, that there is no journey, no distance and no destination. You are walking to You, nowhere else, and you are ready to realize this now.

What is "Wisdom" but the full and combined Knowing of the mind, heart and soul? This is the path we have been walking together, is it not? Therefore, what is it you seek to Know? You are seeking the Truth, only the Truth. And what is the Truth you seek? It is simply that you are safe and invulnerable. But how can this be true if you exist in a world where you are anything but safe, where you experience possible peril in every moment? Remember that either the world's position or God's is true, but not both. Either you are vulnerable or you are safe. If you are choosing to listen to the Spirit within you, to know in your mind, heart and soul that you are safe, then could the world's version of reality be anything but false? Do you see this now? What can that mean but that the world you perceive is not real? But there must be another world that you can access and enjoy this very moment. It is the Heaven within, and it is with you now. You need do nothing but accept this rapture; then you will experience it. It is now, and it is yours.

This is the essence of the Wisdom that this attribute describes.

The First Enlightenment, Illumined Mind:

The Wisdom that comes to the mind cannot be understood by the mind. This is because Wisdom is not bound by the laws of this world, and even your Illumined Mind is not completely divorced from these laws. It stands with one foot in the world of form and the other out. That is why I have said that accomplishing this level is nothing at all. It is only a step in the right direction, though a big step. Until Wisdom falls into the heart, then it is not full, and this, after all, is what you are seeking.

Surrender Meditation:

I surrender to the Wisdom I Know is within me. Where else would it be as it is revealed in my mind that opens now? And yet I will not hesitate. I will move forward into the Light that reveals the full rapture of this experience. I will step forward into the Holy Presence that the Beloved reveals within me now. I am that Wisdom now, fully Illumined.

The Second Enlightenment, Awakened Heart:

The Wisdom that comes to the heart can be understood, but not according to my former concepts or beliefs. These have only clouded what my heart has sought to reveal, and I let them pass now as a mist does clear when morning breaks. My heart ascends with this Wisdom, for it knows it well. It has slept within its deepest chamber waiting for this moment, and now that it is here, it rejoices. Wisdom is revealed, and I welcome it wholly.

Trust Meditation:

If I am to welcome this Light, then I must trust what it reveals. The shadows that once frightened me are seen and dispelled, for they were nothing but the images I created and held apart from love. Now I let them go, and I welcome what Wisdom reveals. I am that Wisdom now, fully Awakened.

The Third Enlightenment, Realized Soul:

Wisdom is nothing more than the realization in my mind and heart of what my Soul has always known. My Soul is the sacred sanctuary where the truth within me has been held safe. The Truth is who I am, and so I am the One that has been protected there. I am opening to see and Know this, and so I claim my enlightenment. What else could enlightenment be but this Holy Knowledge, integrated through me and as me? I am open to receive, and my openness is the only gift I need offer the Beloved. I am here, and so is God.

Gratitude Meditation:

I open in gratitude now, for the truth has come, and I have welcomed that truth. My heart explodes with the love that has always been contained there, and fills the sky with such Light that my former self simply falls away, revealing the Sacred Self where I make my home. I fall into the refreshing waters of Soul Realization, and everything I have ever sought is found, and every question I have ever asked is answered. I claim this because it is my right as the Holy Child of God. I hold it in my hand with the same tenderness that the Beloved once held me while I slept. I am that Wisdom now, fully Realized.

—Brother

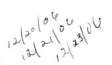

only Love is real!

Lesson Twenty Four

You are journeying toward the center of the Wheel, and as you move through the spokes away from the outer edge you begin to feel something falling away from you. What is leaving you are the thoughts you have held of yourself that have never served the Divine Purpose for which you were created. Let them pass you by happily, for you do not need them any longer.

The only thing you need is to remember an ancient agreement you made before you were born, even before the thought of birth in this world seemed possible. That moment is not so far away as you might think; in fact, it is happening right now. That is why the ending is sure, that you will awaken and fulfill this Holy Contract. That is why I am so confident in the Light that draws you forward, for I am standing before the transformed YOU now. If you want you can sense me there, holding you and loving the truth within that was never changed by your meaningless dream. We look upon each another in gratitude for the One that made our dreams of separation impossible, and never allowed us to fall too deeply into the snares of a world that never existed.

Your journey to the center of the Emissary Wheel is simply your willingness to REALIZE and to KNOW what God perceives in you, and in realizing this will the contract be fulfilled. For then you will extend this blessing, which is as natural as your breathing. Others will remember, and they will know through you. This is why you have answered the call to be a Spiritual Peacemaker. Nothing else will satisfy you now. All other pleasures will seem vain compared to this. And thus it should be, for the Light has entered your Heart.

The Fourth Attribute: Certainty

We will now speak of the gift of Certainty, which you are realizing now. I have said that the path to enlightenment is simply the movement away from Faith, through Certainty, and finally into Realization. Faith is of the Illumined Mind, the intellectual understanding that only love is real. It is not until you are certain, which springs from the Awakened Heart, that your transformation is secured, and then finally Realized in your Soul. Do you see how simply this transition takes place? First you believe, then you feel, then you know. And yet it would be incorrect to conclude that enlightenment does not occur until the final stage of Knowingness is experienced, for that would mean that God's Vision of you can be changed by your vision of yourself. That is not possible, and it is this fact that ultimately secures your release from hell. Hell is in your mind, and cannot leave the home you have created for it. When your Mind is Illumined, and your Heart is Awakened, then hell has no place at all in your Realized Soul.

If you are to attain the Certainty I am describing to you now, you must be willing to ask yourself one simple question. This question, if answered well, is all you need to open this Fourth Attribute, diving even closer to the center of the Wheel where all answers are revealed.

"If you could only be certain of one thing in this world, one thing only, what would it be?" I am confident that the first answer that came to your mind was Love. "Only the Love of God is real." If this is true, and if reality cannot be threatened by illusions, then we have found ourselves at a Divine Junction. What is real cannot be threatened, and only God's love is real. What does that mean? It means that you can leave behind all things that do not serve this end, and enter the sacred chamber where LOVE lives NOW. It is waiting for you, just as you have waited for it. Enter now, and SEE for yourself.

The First Enlightenment, Illumined Mind:

There is no place where the experience of Certainty and your mind meet. I have said to you many times that this first Illumination is only the first step of your enlightenment. You cannot be content with the Light it reveals, though it may at first seem very bright indeed. Acknowledge it and move on, for there is so much more to come. The mind can only believe; it cannot Know. Certainty is the same as Knowing.

Surrender Meditation:

I remain where I have been, and I surrender all these thoughts to you, Beloved One. I live in the Divine "not-knowing" even as my mind is illumined by the Light that extends past this world. I will not stay here for long, for Certainty calls me, and I will answer. I am that Certainty now, fully Illumined.

The Second Enlightenment, Awakened Heart:

It is here that Certainty finds its home, for what the heart feels, it can realize. This is the Gift you have been searching for, for the feeling that Love inspires washes away the stains of forgotten dreams. The dream is ending now, and you are ready to take the final step.

Trust Meditation:

What can I say now, Beloved? I Trust the direction you are leading me, for I feel what will soon be revealed. I know that we have come too far to retreat, for the past is receding and falling away. Only Love remains, and I am certain that you are here. I am that Certainty, fully Awakened.

The Third Enlightenment, Realized Soul:

Of this we cannot speak. No concept, no matter how holy it may seem, can cross this boundary, for the mind and even the heart have been replaced with something far more essential. Just breathe, and Know that you have made it Home.

Gratitude Meditation:

Through Gratitude is my Certainty revealed. Say this over and over. Feel the fruit of this Divine Light now. It is the only gift you need. I am that Certainty now, fully Realized.

—Brother

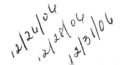

Lesson Twenty Five

The Fifth Attribute: Compassion

All beings strive to be released from bondage. It is the most natural urge within the soul, even when it is clouded and obscured by the selfish desires that seem to block its return to grace. Knowledge of the Higher-Self is inherent within the mind of the lower-self, which stretches for what it cannot fully comprehend. Every cell in every body holds the blueprint of the "Realized Master," and that is why nothing of this world will ever satisfy the larger part of you. Your lower-self follows every road that seems to offer satisfaction or release, yet its motto is "seek but never find." And yet, you have discovered a new path, one that leads away from the empty promises of this world, and you will not be denied the gift you seek. Compassion has brought you here, and it will give you everything you need to fulfill your heart's desire.

The gift of "Divine Compassion" is the result of Certainty, which you have already achieved. I say that you have already achieved it because this is what I see in you. I refuse to acknowledge the part of you that still believes it has anything left to do or to achieve before this experience is yours. I look upon what is whole in you, not what seems to be lacking, and when you learn to do the same, then the lack will disappear on its own. No effort is required to dispel an illusion, but it takes great effort indeed to deny what is and has always been true. This is why your heart is so tired, because you have used the power of creation to deny the power of creation. Do you see this, Beloved? When you release and let go of this insane need, then you will no longer feel this dis-ease. Then will Compassion reign in your soul, for you will have extended your Certainty to the world and beyond.

Compassion is the act of extending your Certainty to others. It is that simple. Once your spiritual eyes have opened and you are able to See what has always been right in front of you, then you will KNOW who you are. But this is not a stagnant knowledge. It must continue to flow, just as the Love of God flows, in order for your eyes to remain open. The moment you stop giving what you have freely received, your eyes will close again and you will return to the world of separating dreams. But if you are able to give what you know you are, then you will remain awake, and be a blessing to all.

This is your simple role as a Spiritual Peacemaker, to give what you know yourself to BE. It does not mean that you are here to change the world, or to change anyone in the world, but to set it all free. Freedom is what is required, for all beings sense the bondage of this world, and seek to be released from it. You are the point of release for yourself, and yet all other points intersect with yours. The Art of Spiritual Peacemaking and the Art of Compassion are therefore the same.

Compassion is the most natural experience to those who are awake, because they would never choose to attack themselves. They know that every action or word is directed at the source of their experience, and knows itself to be that source. Why, then, would they choose to offer what would limit, when they could instead give what would release? This choice is always before you, and that is why we say that the Kingdom of Heaven is before you as well. It is here now, in the next decision you make or the next word you say. Is that so hard for you to believe, that Heaven could be so close? It is, but only if you choose to See it, and you will See it if you Give it to All.

The First Enlightenment, Illumined Mind:

Compassion is reasonable to the mind because it is easy to see where it leads. It can only lead to harmony because it seeks to unite rather than divide. Therefore, it does not compete with reality but establishes it where it belongs.

Surrender Meditation:

I let go of my need to understand what I must do, what I must say, or where I must go, and accept Compassion as my only guide. It cannot lead me astray, and so I surrender to everything it reveals. I will be as a child and not assume I have the answer, and in doing so will a new answer dawn upon my mind. I am that Compassion now, fully Illumined.

The Second Enlightenment, Awakened Heart:

The Awakened Heart is perfectly aligned with Compassion, for it is not confused about its role in bringing peace. It can only come through union, and so they are the same.

Trust Meditation:

I am willing to trust everything Compassion shows me, for its vision of peace is so much clearer than mine. I know that the more I trust, the more I will see, and this is my only goal now – to see what is real. I am that Compassion, fully Awakened.

The Third Enlightenment, Realized Soul:

Compassion has lost its purpose now, for in the end it is only the bridge into the state of Perfect Knowing. Now that I stand on the other side of this river, the bridge is no longer useful to me. I let it pass with gratitude and joy.

Gratitude Meditation:

How can I express my gratitude for the gift of new life? I have crossed into a world where only love is real, and yet I have not moved at all. I will stand here for a moment and extend this gratitude to the One that has brought me to the Home I never left except in my imagination. I am that Gratitude now, fully Realized.

—Brother

Lesson Twenty Six

The Sixth Attribute: Joy

Many have claimed to hear the Voice for God and to record messages they have received. There was a time when many of my words were recorded, and they were said to have come from God. Know that it is true, that every word that has come from my mouth has been from God. But it is no different for you, when you allow yourself to be used by the Spirit and the Way of God. This, as you know, is your goal.

I was once quoted as saying: "I have come to give you life so that your joy will be complete." It would be more accurate if this were as follows: "I have come to give you back to Life so that your joy may be perfect." This is what we will explore today, Beloved One, for you are at last ready to lay aside all the ways you have limited your joy and convinced yourself that you were satisfied. You may have believed this in your mind, but not in your heart or soul. That is why I've stressed the importance of the Second and Third Enlightenments over the First. Even when you realize with your mind that your joy has never been complete, and you know that you deserve this gift, it is not enough momentum to catapult you into Perfect Joy. This is why I have come, and it is where you will go so that the others who follow you will recognize the gift they too deserve. Isn't this the real mission of a Spiritual Peacemaker, to demonstrate that Perfect Joy is the beginning and the end of our search for God and enlightenment? Isn't this the reason you came to this place, to learn how to lay aside all the things of this world that have robbed you of the gift given by your Divine Parent? But now you have come far enough to realize this and to act upon it, and as always, you will have it by giving it to others.

You have allowed yourself to become completely Certain of one thing, that you are loved by God. From that love has come the gift of extension through Compassion, which is the art of sharing what has been given to you by God. Now we enter the third Attribute in this triad: Joy. Now that you have realized love and given love to all, Perfect Joy is released. How natural is this release when your heart and soul open! It is a sense that cannot be described by any definition this world holds dear.

Perfect Joy is ultimately the realization of your invulnerability, or that the world of form is not real and cannot attack or hurt you. Do you see how we keep coming back to this place? If Perfect Joy is to reign then you must make peace with this fact. The world you see with your eyes is not the same world you experience with your soul. It is only a reflection of the decisions you have made about yourself, all the ways you have tried to hide from the Truth within you. But you cannot hide any longer. You have come outside the cave too far, and you have seen what the ego never intended for you to see. Now it is only a matter of time before the whole Matrix of Illusion falls on its own, for you have seen behind the curtain, and you know what is really happening. This is the beginning of mastery, for you cannot be a master of something you cannot control. And you cannot control the world unless you made it. Herein lies the gift of peace, and Perfect Joy is sure to follow.

See the world as God sees it, as a reflection of your beliefs.

The First Enlightenment, Illumined Mind:

You are being asked to See the world as God Sees it, as a reflection of your beliefs. Now that you realize this, you can choose to see in a new way. The "Way of Grace" will lead you, and you will experience the Joy that has escaped you till now.

Surrender Meditation:

Repeat these words aloud as often as you feel is necessary: "By accepting the 'thought' that the world is not the basis of my reality, Perfect Joy is established in my Illumined Mind."

I am that Surrender, now fully Illumined.

The Second Enlightenment, Awakened Heart:

You are being asked to Love the world as God Loves the world, as a reflection of your decisions about yourself. And since the very essence of love is contained within you now, it is the same decision you make about love.

Trust Meditation:

Repeat these words aloud as often as you feel is necessary: "By accepting the 'feeling' that the world is not the basis of my reality, Perfect Joy is established in my Awakened Heart."

I am that Trust now, fully Awakened.

The Third Enlightenment, Realized Soul:

You are being asked to Know what God Knows. How can I describe to you what this is or how you will Know when you are there? First of all, there is no way you will be able to not recognize this state because it will be so different from everything else you have ever experienced. We can call this the "Peace of God," and it will not escape your attention. It is easy for me to say that you will Know it when you no longer experience separation of any kind, but such a concept is still too hard to appreciate with your mind. It is better to say that you will experience the same reality behind every form, the reality called "The Beloved." When you experience only the Beloved everywhere you look, then you will "Know as God Knows."

Gratitude Meditation:

Repeat these words aloud as often as you feel is necessary: "By accepting the 'Truth' that the world is not the basis of my reality, perfect Joy is established in my Realized Soul."

I am that Gratitude now, fully Realized.

—Brother

Lesson Twenty Seven

The Seventh Attribute: Clarity

Who is speaking to you now? We have asked this question before, and you may have already arrived at your decision. We will revisit it again because your answer is of great importance at this stage of your learning. The decision you make about this will be the decision you make about yourself, and that, after all, is all that is ultimately important.

Who is Jeshua and what role do I play in your learning to be an Instrument of Peace? Am I a man with a personality that existed on this earth two thousand years ago, but not now? Where am I now and is it possible for me, or anyone else for that matter, to share my wisdom and energy with those who still claim bodies and form? Is it possible that I have been sharing these lessons with you these many weeks, and that your willingness to accept this creates an opening for you to likewise "be" the same? Or have you accepted this idea more as a story or a concept because the lessons have some value for your life?

Why are these questions so important at this time? It is because you must begin accepting yourself as I am asking you to accept me. I have said many times that you cannot receive any gift that you are not willing to likewise give. Therefore, I am asking you to give me the blessing of your perfection so that we may share it together. I am asking you to see me as your teacher, so that you may teach yourself. Personalities do not matter at all, especially now, so my request is not ultimately related to who you think I was. It is only related to who you know I AM, for then will you know yourself to be the same. We are not separate or divided in any way. We are one, and so is your decision about me. What you decide about me you will decide about yourself. That is why I have come, and it is why you will go to others. I have not come to give life, but to reveal it.

There are many who claim to speak with my voice or to share messages from me. How will you know the difference, when it is real or when it is an illusion? Whoever speaks with the Voice of "Knowing" speaks with my voice. There is no other, for a voice that speaks from a place of "not-knowing" is not heard at all. The voice of "not-knowing" is the voice of the ego that thinks it knows a great deal, but which makes no sense at all except to others' egos. I say that it is not heard because it has no real impact. Why would you want to speak with a voice that makes no impact? That is why you have been called to be a Spiritual Peacemaker, to have an impact in the world. Give up the words and thoughts that mean nothing at all, and speak only with my voice, the "Voice of the Awakened One."

Whenever you speak, speak through and as me. Do not hesitate in this. Know that it is my voice they are hearing, for only then will your message be true. When you KNOW the Truth and speak from that Knowing, then you will perceive no difference between us. Then will your message be clear, for clarity is our next step.

The First Enlightenment, Illumined Mind:

Enlightenment is not something you do, but something you SEE. When you SEE it everywhere then it will be real to you. What you SEE, you are. You are allowing the Light of Truth to penetrate you on three levels, which we are calling the Three Enlightenments. The first step is for your sight to be made clear, for only then will you understand why you are here. Look around, then, and SEE who you are through these others. Then let the same Holy Sight fall upon yourself.

Surrender Meditation:

Repeat these words as often as you feel is necessary: "My mind surrenders control that I may SEE what is real." I do not know what anything means, and therefore I am able to be shown what was once so obscure. I am that Clarity now, fully Illumined.

The Second Enlightenment, Awakened Heart:

Once you are able to SEE what is real, then you can FEEL the same. Enlightenment has now been accepted by your heart, and so are you now awake. As you claim this you will know it to be true. Do not let another second go by without claiming who you are. Why would you want to stay ignorant when the knowledge has come? Why would you stay in a dark room when you feel the Light so close to you? There is no reason for you to remain in this world when a whole new reality has been waiting for you. FEEL this reality and it is yours. I have been feeling it for you, but now you must feel it for yourself.

Trust Meditation:

Repeat these words as often as you feel is necessary: "I am willing to trust the Light, and to Feel as God Feels." I am that Clarity now, fully Awakened.

The Third Enlightenment, Realized Soul:

Now will you Know what God Knows. God knows only one thing: Love. Therefore, you are contained within that Love, that Oneness, for it is your true home. Now perhaps you can see that I have not asked you to leave anything behind, but to simply be where you belong. It is not something you do with your body. It is not something that changes your personality. It is simply something you Realize in your Soul. Open, then, and Know that you are God.

Gratitude Meditation:

Repeat these words as often as you feel is necessary: "I am Grateful for what I Know." I am that Clarity now, fully Realized.

—Brother

You are holy beyond measure, and God loves you.

Lesson Twenty Eight

The Eighth Attribute: Understanding

In the last lesson we shared this thought: "Everyone that speaks from the place of 'Knowing' speaks with my voice, while the place of 'not-knowing' does not exist at all." Herein lies the deepest truth I can offer. When you enter the chamber of your "Self," then there is no difference between us because our voice is the "Voice for God." When you speak on your own, or from the "self" that exists only in your imagination, then you are mute before God. Your holiness is certainly secure, for that cannot change, but your voice and the gift you can offer is forgotten, waiting for you to step back, surrender, and return to the place where God's Voice is yours again.

Does it surprise you when I say that yours is the Voice for God? It is this surprise that keeps you separated from your real function. Know that it is true and it is. Know that your voice speaks for and as God and it will be so. It is not vanity to claim this, as your ego would have you believe. It is vanity to claim that God's will for you can be challenged by your meaningless dreams. Let them go and they are gone, for they are not supported by anything that is real. Let them pass and they return to the land of shadows from where they were created, sleeping again in the barren ground of the world where you hide from your Self. Let your true voice resound so that the whole world may hear the Truth. Only then will the voices of the other enlightened ones rise like a choir before you. Only then will you know that you are not alone, though all is One within.

You are coming to a place where you fully understand this in your mind and heart, and it is then that you will "Know what God Knows." Your Illumined Mind and Awakened Heart have led you thus far, but they cannot pass into the field that transcends all concepts, the place I cannot describe for you, though you are there with me even now. As I said before, Know you are there and you are. Then you will feel my hand as it touches yours, and you will sense the kiss I place upon your holy cheek. You have drawn closer to me than you realize over these last months, since we began this journey together. And I will continue to guide you until you are aware of the Light that enfolds us, making us as one being before the Throne of God. Your desire to be a Spiritual Peacemaker is all that you need, for the desire alone is enough to break down the remaining barriers. I am giving this to you, and so you must continue to give it to others, for you cannot come to me on your own. All your brothers and sisters must come with you, in your mind and in your heart, for nothing can be left behind. I will not abandon you and you must not abandon them. The shower of Grace that falls upon our anointed heads now is like refreshing rain. Drink and know that you are nearly home.

I said that you will soon "Know what God Knows." How will we define this Divine Knowing, that which you will soon claim? Here it is, so simple that you will be unable to pass it by another moment: You are holy beyond measure, and God Loves You. Herein lies your peace, and the peace of all beings.

The First Enlightenment and Meditation, Illumined Mind:

I believe in my Mind that my meaningless dreams cannot change the Holy Will of God. I have given my mind too much power, thinking that the dream it has created is stronger than the reality created for it by God. Open your eyes and understand what you have missed till now. You cannot understand the world while your eyes are closed, and yet this has been the desire of your ego. It prefers ignorance over knowledge. It would rather have you remain helpless than realize that you have all the strength in the Universe. Which will you choose, then, weakness or the strength of God? Choose well, for your brothers and sisters need to follow your example. You are a Spiritual Peacemaker this moment.

The Second Enlightenment and Meditation, Awakened Heart:

I feel in my Heart that my meaningless dreams cannot change the Holy Will of God. Love alone will bring me to the Home where I belong. My heart is now awake, and so I am able to feel what is real. I begin by "Seeing as God Sees," and then I move to the next step of "Feeling as God Feels." God feels only love, and so I give this gift that it may be mine.

The Third Enlightenment and Meditation, Realized Soul:

I know in my Soul that my meaningless dreams cannot change the Holy Will of God. In this Knowing, I become that Holy Will Itself, for nothing has changed since I was created. I am Perfect as God is Perfect, and I am Whole as God is Whole. I proclaim now that "I Am That," and since my knowledge of this Grace is mine only as I give it to others, my soul answers with: "I Am." Over and over I chant, "I am That, I Am." I call and the Universe responds. The Universe calls and I respond. It is the same. It is the same now and always. "I Am That, I Am." What more is required but this? Where else can I hope to ascend but to the throne where the echo of these words are all I hear? "I Am That, I Am." I will rest now, knowing that my journey is complete. I have not changed the Holy Will of God. I am Home. I am Home. I am Home.

—Brother

You are the extension of the love and the loveliness of God.

Lesson Twenty Nine

The Ninth Attribute: Depth

It is not the depth of this world we are seeking together, but of the world beyond your imagination. Spiritual depth comes from answering one question correctly: "Who am I?" I am the Christ come to save the world from meaningless dreams where sickness and death seem to rule. I am the holy extension of the Mind and Will of God, fulfilling the foresight of the prophets of old. I am all of that, as are you. In fact, I cannot know myself to be any of these things until I know you to be them first. You are the extension of the love and the loveliness of God. I have seen it in you, and I Know that I am the same.

You have given others this gift, but you have not allowed yourself to receive it back. Listen, Beloved Ones, for this lesson will be the cornerstone of all the rest. If you can grasp what I am about to say to you, then you will Know yourself as I know you. Here is what I most long to share:

"Your eyes are already perfect, though they may, for a moment, be covered with scales. Please accept the gift of my Perfect Sight of you, then you will see what is so clear to me. I need you to stand by my side in full awareness. The Universe needs you to walk the path of truth in quiet freedom. You need your Self, and yet you will not fulfill this need until you willingly receive what I offer. Please open now and accept what my hand holds out to you. It is your life. It is your love. This is the moment when you must decide. You are ready NOW!"

Many times throughout this course I have asked you to understand that the world you created, the world of separation and form, is not real. We would do well to discuss this further so that it does not escape our attention. I said that any voice that speaks from the place of "not-knowing" makes no real impact and therefore isn't real. Whatever you do that draws you away from your true purpose here, that of being an Emissary of Light, creates no real impact in the world because it is not eternal. You are eternal, so how can something that is not like you in such a vital way hurt you at all? It cannot. You have forgotten that you are so full of life, and have therefore led yourself to imagine that you are vulnerable and alone. This is the illusion you have created for yourself, and it is the world you chose to see to justify that illusion. But a real impact in eternity it has not, and you are eternal. I do not perceive any of this as a threat, and now I am asking you to do the same. The world you created in your imagination is not the world you really want. This is the gift you can receive today, if only you would finally choose it.

"... you are far more than you believe yourself to be"

You have called to the Universe and it has answered. You call, as I once did, "I Am That," but the Universe does not respond with the words, "You Are." It responds with the words, "I Am." What does that tell you? When the Universe answers you, it answers as you. It is critically important that you understand this now. I will say it again so you will not miss it: The Universe responds AS you.

When you created your ego you looked out and said, "I Am That," then you looked around for something to identify with. It chose the body and the personality, and therefore could not hear the Universe's Holy Response, for you are far more than you believe yourself to be. You were deaf to its reply and so were not able to complete the cycle. But now you are. Proclaim who you are and live from that proclamation, that is all I am asking of you, and then listen as the Universe responds with the one gift that will set you free. "I Am." And so are all things bound by the Holy Vision of God. You are bound now, for your willingness to accept this has been enough to lay aside all things of time.

Illumined Mind and the Awakened Heart:

Today we will not choose to separate these two enlightenments, but to see them as the same. We have separated them till now only that you may understand them. But now full release is required of all the concepts we have held, especially of separation. And so, for the next four lessons we will look upon this with new eyes, and we will open in a new way.

The instructions will be very simple. For the next three days, look out upon the world you created as it really is. Look at all the things around you, what you perceive as beautiful and what you perceive as ugly, that which you call good and that which you say is bad. As you look upon all these things, say with a whisper or aloud: "I Am That." Know that you are that thing, that person, or that condition. This is not a metaphor. It is the truth that you are now ready to embrace. Then listen for the holy answer that comes from whatever it is you look upon. "I AM!" It is a gift to you, for you are all the things you see around you, even what you have called evil. Embrace it all now. Your willingness to practice this exercise fully will be the measure of your progress.

Exercise

Realized Soul:

Are you willing to enter into this final stage of your awakening as a Spiritual Peacemaker? If you do this, then you will experience the Truth you have been seeking since you were created. It is my promise, and I will keep it.

—Brother

Lesson Thirty

The Tenth Attribute: Generosity

I am holding your hand firmly in mine. I know that you feel this. You have surrendered and I have come to you, not as a teacher but as a guide. I have walked the path you are walking now. Who else would you want for this Holy Task but one who knows the way? The blind cannot lead the blind, and as long as your eyes remain closed you need someone who has removed the heavy scales that keep the Grace from appearing so near. You are ready to open, and I will be there with you when you do. Let that be your comfort for now, knowing that you will never be abandoned.

We are nearing our journey's end. We have walked this winding path together toward the Home you never left at all, save in your imaginary dreams. God has given you many gifts, but making what isn't real true is not one of them. However, you can make what isn't real "seem" true, and that is what you have done. There is nowhere for you to go but forward, for the path to ignorance has dissolved behind you. We are together now, one Holy Mind communicating with another Holy Mind. Another step and you will Feel what I Feel, and Know what I Know. Then you will understand why I have taken such care to bring you to this Holy Moment. Then you will understand why I love you so.

The statement of truth we have been working with, "I Am That, I Am," is all you need now. I asked you to look around during the day and identify everything you see as "who you are." I Am That tree. I Am That mountain. In doing so you have jumped past the limiting beliefs of the ego and realized that you cannot be identified by anything particular, but by the ALL. Today's lesson takes us a step further, and if you are able to realize what I am aiming to reveal, then you will find yourself where I am, in the Heaven you never left. The next step is so very simple, and yet it will make all the difference if you choose it.

Our goal today is to open our eyes a little wider, to see past the horizon of the ego's design to another reality you have been blind to until now. We will try for the first time to embrace the ALL, to say "I Am That" and have it apply to everything you perceive, not just one particular person or thing. To believe you are some things is no different than thinking you are your body, or the personality that seems to define you. Our goal is to have you open the wings of your Divine Perception so that you may know yourself to be the ALL.

I will stop for a moment so that you can catch your breath. Even with all the mountains we have already climbed together, what I am asking may still seem a distant dream. I ask only one thing, for you to trust me. Suspend your disbelief or hesitation for just a moment and consider that I have a better idea of what you are capable of than you. I look upon the truth

I am all of this.

in you clearly, while to you it is still in a mist. The mist is beginning to pass, indeed, but we are only at the dawn of your awakening. The sun will surely clear away this mist, but I am able to see past it even now. So give yourself the gift of knowing that you are ready for this step. Then you will move forward in confidence and grace.

Stand in an area where you are comfortable and where you can be alone. Close your eyes and take several deep breaths. Center your Illumined Mind and your Awakened Heart on this thought, breathing deeply as you consider it:

"I am all of this."

Start with your hands extending straight in front of you, hands together. Now open your eyes. As you chant these words over and over, begin to move your hands apart very slowly, and know that your Realized Soul is opening too. Whatever thoughts come into your mind, whatever you see, know that you are that. Whatever person comes to your mind, know that you are that. Open yourself fully to everything that appears before you, and do not push it away. Embrace it all, knowing that they are different aspects of who you are. You will not lose track of the "perceptual being" you have designed by practicing this, so let go of any fear that may arise. You will not lose track of anything that is real, but you may shed all the unreal beliefs you have held till now. This, after all, is your goal and, if you choose, you can achieve it today.

Illumined Mind and Awakened Heart:

We will consider these as one, for so they are. You are nearly awake, and so I will not treat you any differently than how I wish to be treated. What I have offered to you today is the essence of what I am calling "Generosity," for it is what I mean when I say, "Give everything to have everything." I am asking you to open your mind and heart fully so that your blessings may extend to all that is real. There is nothing left for you to do. It is the only thing there ever was for you to do. Now I'm asking you to stand by me and do as I do, for it is the only way you will be called a "Spiritual Peacemaker." Trust me when I say that you are ready for this.

Realized Soul:

There is nothing left for me to give you. You only need follow my final instructions and you will see for yourself. Open your eyes and Know that we are One.

—Brother

The ego's role is to seek, but never find.

Lesson Thirty One

The Eleventh Attribute: Abundance

Your goal today is to seek after what you really want; for that is the only way you will have it. It would seem that you would not need to question this, that you would always be seeking to draw to yourself that which serves and blesses you and your mission. But as you have seen through your own life, this is not always true. There is a part of each one of us that seeks gifts that are not ours, so we find ourselves lost upon roads where we do not belong. Yet even this can be used by the One who is with you now, leading you from darkness into the Light, but only if you have enough courage to uncover the reasons you chose these things in the first place. This is where we will begin our inquiry, and it is what will lead you into the spiritual abundance you seek.

We have addressed these issues before, but now that we are near the end of our course on Spiritual Peacemaking, we will examine them once again so there is no confusion at all. Before you can be clear about what you are, you must also be clear about what you are not. This would not be required if you did not confuse these two in the past, but such is the condition of your life here. The ego's role is to seek but never find. Then you wonder why the world leaves you so unsatisfied. Your Realized Soul does not seek at all, for it KNOWS that all things are already contained there. Nothing is required because nothing is absent. This, of course, is the essence of abundance, while the desire to seek after anything is its denial.

Once again, your Spirit does not seek at all, for it realizes that it is already full. Understand this and your journey will be over. You have been looking outside yourself for what does not exist, and have then been surprised when you were unable to achieve your goal. Time and time again you have done this, all because you have been listening to the wrong voice within, the voice that would have you forget rather than the one that would have you remember. But as always, the Spirit of Truth never closes its wings to you, and you are always given the chance to "Choose Again." Will this be the moment that you decide to lay aside all the things that have not served your life, only your death? If you do, then you will realize the reason you were born into this world, to heal and to bless. That is why you have embarked on this journey with me, but I have nearly led you as far as I can. The next step belongs to you. Will you choose to open your eyes and look upon the love I have revealed, or will you retreat again into the shadowy figures that have taught you nothing except loss? The choice is yours, and you must make it now. That, after all, is the only moment there is for you to choose anything at all.

Know that I am challenging you because I want you to have what you deserve, not be denied anything that is real. I have led you to the edge of a cliff, and it may seem to you that something will be lost if you take this final step. I may tell you that you will be safe, and remind you that I too have suffered through this and taken the step you must now take. But your trust in me must be strong, and I know it is. Are you willing to risk nothing in order to have everything? Read that last sentence again. Are you willing to risk NOTHING in order to have EVERYTHING? This, as unusual as it may seem, is the choice that you must make. Unfortunately, you have not seen it this way until now, otherwise you would have made the choice of life. But that is why you are here, and it is why I am with you. All the lessons we have shared have led to this moment. If you are able to take this final step you will be supported upon the wings of angels and they will guide you to the home your soul longs to return to. You can see it in the distance. Of this I am sure, for I can see it reflecting in your eyes as I speak to you, Beloved. But you must KNOW that my words mean life, otherwise you will interpret them according to the thoughts of death you have held. Open your wings and fly with me. We will be there before you realize anything has happened at all. I will not let you fall, for such a thing is impossible now.

Illumined Mind and Awakened Heart:

(Repeat these words with conviction)

"I have accepted in my mind that I must give everything to have everything, and my heart has felt the approach of this great gift. Now I act upon what I have learned, for my acceptance is not enough. I must complete the cycle of giving and receiving in order to know that I am abundant now. I will not measure this by the standards of the world, but by God's standards. God's currency is love, and so I give this to all that it may be mine. Nothing else will satisfy me now. I give only what I want to receive and, in doing so, see the same gift return to me."

Realized Soul:

"I am standing at the edge of a cliff, and my guide is beside me holding my hand. I will not hesitate in taking the step that leads to the life I seek. I can see my Gentle Home in the distance and I will not wait another moment. I step out with confidence, then fly."

—Brother

Lesson Thirty Two

The Twelfth Attribute: Agape

To Love as God Loves.

You have been told that it is impossible to understand and realize the Love of God. I am telling you now that this should be your only goal. It is the goal of anyone who seeks to be a Spiritual Peacemaker, for what can this Love be but the extension of the peace that surpasses the world of separation and form? It is true that it is impossible to realize the Love of God so long as you cling to conflict of any kind, and yet conflict is the foundation of the world you constructed in your imagination. It is a place of war, and the experience you are seeking is not here. Therefore, the Peace of God can only be found in the world where you really live, the Home you never left. I have said that I am with you there now, and I am waiting for you to open your spiritual eyes and realize this. I want to emphasize this again because it will make this final step, which is the only true step you must make, easily accomplished. Take a deep breath, for you are very near the end of our journey together. Your freedom from despair is a single thought away. Open your eyes and you will see me, and you will know that the Love of God is already yours.

Does it surprise you when I say that realizing the Love of God, Agape, has been your only goal from the beginning? This is because the larger Self which I look upon now, and which you will soon see, has never been threatened by the impossible dream you have tried to construct in place of reality. The question then is, why are you here at all? If your agenda and Holy Spirit's have always been perfectly aligned, then why have you lingered here so long? The answer I am about to give you will not make sense to your mind, but if you allow yourself to dive to the deeper ocean where I have been leading you, then it will make perfect sense to you. Then will you grasp with your heart what even your Illumined Mind cannot comprehend.

Why have you lingered here so long?

"You haven't."

This is how I perceive it now, though I must say that it has not always been so. I am an effective guide because I am able to remember the amnesia that still grips you, though I can see the memory of love beginning to flicker in your mind. I was able to SEE what has never changed. I saw it in others, and that is how I was able to have it myself. I saw my own enlightened mind everywhere, in everyone, and so it was mine. The illusions that once clouded my heart were swept away in an instant, and all things became clear. It was at that instant that

I realized the Love of God was my only goal, even while I slept. And that is why I am saying this to you, Beloved, for we have progressed enough now that this gentle memory will easily fall into place within your mind. Every path has led to the Holy Altar you are now about to regain. Know that my words are true, and follow the path I have blazed for you. Then you will realize the completion of your deepest dream.

Illumined Mind and Awakened Heart

Though the world you created in your imagination is not real, you will not "BECOME" the Real World until you fully accept yourself here. The world you look upon is not real, but YOU ARE. Once again, take these words into your Awakened Heart, that you may understand what I am trying to communicate. Even when you are dreaming, YOU ARE REAL WITHIN THE DREAM. Do you understand? When you look about the world you created and say, "I Am That," then you realize that the dream and the dreamer are the same. This is the magic of seeing your own holiness in everything you perceive. It is like stepping closer to your own heart, and your soul will surely follow.

Look upon the world one final time, everything that appears before you both animate and inanimate, and say with love, "I Am That." God's love flows through you and everything you perceive. In other words, God loves you as much when you're asleep as when you're awake. When you learn to imitate this by giving the same gift to others, first in your Illumined Mind and then in your Awakened Heart, then you will have achieved the final attribute. You will suddenly "Love as God Loves," and Agape will flow though everything you do.

Realized Soul

When you are finally able to love in the way I have described, then you will realize the greatest mystery of all, and you will at last be able to call yourself a Spiritual Peacemaker. There is no difference at all between the world you created and the world God created, when Agape is revealed. You are real within both, and so is your love. It is the bridge that leads from one into the other, and is what the mystics described when they said: "Be in the world, but not of the world." I do not want you to go anywhere, for leaving the world was never our goal. I want you to be here fully present and realized. Stand upon the bridge and look upon what you have created, then look upon the world prepared for you by God. When you love as God, they will appear the same, for love will be reflected everywhere you look. What else can Heaven be but this? And where else will you find it but where you are now?

Spend as much time as you can meditating upon the Emissary Wheel in the next three days. The final lesson will be your graduation.

—Brother

Love is all around you.
God sees me as fully enlightened
Believe that you have gained your
own confidence

Lesson Thirty Three

Do not think that you have finally gained my confidence, for such a thing is impossible. You cannot gain something that you have never lost. Believe, rather, that you have gained your own confidence. That has been the only real goal of this course, the only thing that you have lacked which has kept you from being the Spiritual Peacemaker I perceive. You were not able to look upon the beauty and completion that I see in you, and so you have limited your ability to accept and then give the same. It is like a whole world has passed by us now. You are not the same person that started this course 99 days ago, and yet nothing has changed at all. God's love is the same as it has ever been, regardless of anything you have seemed to do to diminish it. You are still as God created you, and you are at last ready to embrace yourself as I have always embraced you.

And perhaps you are also ready to embrace me, and to have confidence in my confidence in you. In limiting yourself you have also limited me, for it is impossible for us to be separated. I have told you that you are Holy, and yet you were unable to trust me. But now you are, and everything has changed. My confidence in you is complete, and we are now able to leave the world behind and enter fully into the Heaven created for us before time began. I have been waiting for you and now you are here, in full awareness and consciousness. Open your eyes now, and see what you have hidden from until now. Love is all around you.

In the first lesson I told you that you are ready for this shift. Now I tell you that the shift is complete. I am not willing to accept any question about this. There is no longer any room for vacillation, for you have come too far to deny what you have gained. Now you must deny the denial that has plagued you till now. You have been willing to give me the confidence that is required to join our intent as one, and now it is done. I see you as I see myself, as fully enlightened. Now you must do the same. See it in me this moment, and know that it is your own face you look upon. Nothing else is possible now. Accept what is real, and know that you have arrived at your Home.

Look upon the Emissary Wheel again and let your eyes move from one spoke to another. Your vision knows where to go. How else would you have been able to find me, and to discover your Self? Move from point to point and remember all the attributes you have embraced. You have become each one of these. That does not mean that you will never need to be reminded again, just as your former inability to realize your enlightenment hasn't changed anything that is real. The whole tree is contained within the seed, and so are you complete this moment. I will not allow you any further movement from this, for that is my role as a teacher of God. And you will no longer allow any vacillation in yourself, for you are ready to stand beside me. Do you see how easily you regain Heaven? It has always been yours, and so it is easy to return. Bless this day, Beloved, for your homecoming is felt through the whole Universe.

And now, as you continue to gaze upon the wheel, let your eyes focus upon the center circle. This is the place within you that does not move, the Holy Child of God that has never been abandoned by eternity. This is where our time together has led you, to this solid ground where your enlightenment illumines all other minds. Once again, I will not allow any debate in this, for I assure you I am correct. Now that you have attained this level, more will be expected of you, for you are now poised to heal as an enlightened being heals. Your Illumined Mind and Awakened Heart extend as a blessing to all beings, and you serve as you were born to serve. What other gift can you offer now but that which you have received? I have given to you and now you give the same. The peace that flows from you proves that time has no solution for itself. Only eternity can answer what is eternal. So you are now and will always be.

Graduation

This is the moment you have been prepared for. There are times when your heart needs to hear and to know how far you have come. I have said this many times before and I will repeat it once again: You have not gone anywhere at all, but in your consciousness there is no way for us to measure your progress. You stand upon a Holy Bridge from where you will translate the gifts you have received into gifts you give. They will not come in words, but in the Presence that transcends words. But first you must hear from me the words that will finally activate it all. It is my greatest joy now to offer them to you.

YOU ARE AN ENLIGHTENED BEING, FULLY REALIZED. Do you believe that I have offered every word you have read in this course? If you do, then you must also trust that the commission I have given is true. You are an Enlightened Being sent to bless all beings. You are no longer ready. You are there. Love is complete within you, and your heart is no longer split off from your Holy Mind. It is done! It is done! It is done!

I still have so much more to say that will make this reality solid within you. Continue to walk with me.

—Brother

2/20/07
2/21/07
2/22/07

Daily Spiritual Peacemaking Lessons

Daily Spiritual Peacemaking Lessons – *Day 1*

Will you stay awake with me?

Now that you have stepped forward and proclaimed your willingness to transform the world through love, only one question remains. Will you choose to stand beside me in full readiness, full commitment, and perform with me the role of liberator and protector of Grace? Will you stay awake with me, not just for an hour, but for as long as time does last? It will only be for another moment, and yet so much can happen so fast. I have reached out my hand to you and you have taken it. Let us walk together in the perfect Light that illumines the world, for this was what you chose to do before you were born. I will not abandon you, and you must not abandon me. Stay awake now, and we will discover a way of living that cannot be described in words, but can be lived and loved.

Today we begin a year of Grace. These lessons will remind you of the pact you made to be a Spiritual Peacemaker in the world, and by reminding you, deepen your awareness of the gifts you will both give and receive. How can you do this unless you are enlightened? I have seen this in you, and you have accepted it. It does not mean that anything has changed, for change was never our goal. Our goal was simply to open your heart to the love God has for you, and then to give the same. You are here to Love as God Loves, for it is the only thing that will satisfy you now. The former world has fallen away, and you are left only with Grace this world cannot understand. Can you accept this? Will this be the first day of your continued commitment?

I need awakened hearts to work beside me and end all things of time. I have chosen you and you have in turn chosen this sacred path. There is nothing left for us to do now but move forward into the Light. I am there, and you are standing at my side.

—Brother
Jesus

Daily Spiritual Peacemaking Lessons – Day 2

Beloved One. This is who you are to me, because this is what I am to myself. I see myself in you, and that is how I know that I am perfect as I was created. Will you choose to See others in this way, that you may continue to perceive this GIFT everywhere?

Perceiving this GIFT everywhere is all I am asking of you, and all you are asking of your Self.

There is only one path now, for all others have disappeared. There is only one Truth, though it has so many faces. Look in front of you now and see the Face of the Beloved. Let this be the day you deepen your commitment to see only Grace. In the past you chose to see your attack thoughts made manifest through these others whom you claimed to be outside and different. Now you are choosing to manifest your thoughts of Peace, and this is what will make all the difference for you. Decide to SEE what is really there, rather than imagine what isn't. As always, it is your choice.

You may be able to choose what you See, but you cannot choose what is real. Now you have seen this Truth, and all that is required is that you keep SEEING it. Then you will be awake with me, and we will be able to complete our great work together.

Stay awake with me. I still have so many things to show you.

—Brother

Daily Spiritual Peacemaking Lessons – Day 3

Peace must come to the world through you and as you. This has been the foundation of everything we have learned till now, and it will remain so. You are not separate from the Peace you give, and that is why you cannot offer it to another without receiving it yourself. Let this be the day, then, that you choose to have everything you deserve.

You deserve so much. Why do you think I have been so patient with you? Now you must be patient with yourself, and with everyone I give to you. I will offer more and more souls for you to love and transform, for that is now the role you must fulfill. It is the next step in your mastery, and in your enlightenment. This is not a static charge I give, but one that must be given and shared. That is how you will stay awake, which is all that I ask. If you are awake then you will perceive everything that happens around you as God perceives it. If you are asleep then it will be impossible for you to know what anything really is. To love something you must be able to identify it clearly. If you see only the shadow, you will misidentify what it is.

I am standing right in front of you this moment. See me clearly, in Perfect Light, and know that I SEE you. That is the gift you will receive and give. It is the only thing that is left NOW.

—Brother

Daily Spiritual Peacemaking Lesson – Day 4

Look behind you to the distant horizon. Notice that the sun is beginning to rise, and that the earth is beginning to glow. It is dawn, and the sky is alive with the possibility of a new day. This is your mind as it appears now in Heaven, and your heart as it exists within the Heart of the Beloved. Do you see how far you've come? How does it make you feel, knowing that you have at last made it through the darkened night of unforgiving sleep?

You have chosen to stay awake with me to assist in the awakening of all other minds. Praise this decision, and be true to it. These lessons will be like gentle nudges to your heart that you may not forget this commitment you have made. It is not me you have said this to, but to your Self. And this is all that matters now, that you honor what you have given to You. Then all the things of Light will fall in around you, and you will know what is real, and let pass all the things that are not.

You are now a Master of Peace. Stay awake with me a little longer.

—Brother

3/6/07

Daily Spiritual Peacemaking Lesson – Day 5

Stand with me and let us walk together. In the distance you will see a shining city, and yet there is no one living there at all. All the inhabitants are beneath the ground, and they are sound asleep. They have rested there for thousands of years, and the gifts of their ancestors have not been known since then. The city is filled with all the things that would make them sing, and yet they are not aware of any of it. Their dreams are filled with terrible images of death and loneliness. It grieves me to see and to know of their abundance, yet in their dreams they are so alone.

Come with me, then, and we will awaken them. The sun is slowly making its way across the horizon, and it will soon be upon the Holy City. And so will we appear as does the Light, and we will awaken the slumbering ones, that they may see and feel what has always been theirs.

Will you stay with me and fulfill this ancient pact? It is why you are here, for you have chosen to be an "Awakener." I have asked you to stay awake with me, and this is the only way. Now you must give what you have received, that it remain yours. Come with me and together we will open their eyes, not with our words, but with the Light that streams from our hearts.

—Brother

3/10/07

Daily Spiritual Peacemaking Lesson – Day 6

Be willing to know that when we work together, we do so as one Mind and as one Heart. Notice that I did not say "with" one heart and mind. We are not separate in any way, and neither is the extension of the love we give to the world. If we love "as" one heart, then we do it in communion with the ALL that is present in love. It is not my love that is present, or yours, but Love itself, and that cannot be separated from the Beloved. Do you see where it is I am leading you in this? Meditate on this single thought today. Feel my love, which is yours, as it radiates to the whole world, and beyond. Know that you are embraced by this now and always, even while you slept. Awaken and feel the Light that surrounds you.

—Brother

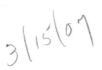

Daily Spiritual Peacemaking Lesson – Day 7

There is no time in which you are not doing the work you came here to complete. That is because I have called you out of time, and you are beginning to realize that whatever seems to happen within it does not happen at all. What we are concerned with now is what happens in eternity, which cannot only be felt here, but also accessed. What we are interested in feeling is the Love that extends past all of time's boundaries, all its meaningless limitations, and touches the Self that was created by God and remains perfect. You have literally tried to "Un-create" that Self and you have failed. Rejoice today in this supreme failure, for it is in reality your greatest accomplishment. The loss of your ego is the triumph of Love in your Soul.

There is nowhere for you to go today, for you are not bound by the things that seem to move or pass. You are bound only by Love. Let this be the goal, then, in every dealing and every word you offer another. Then it is yours, for it would be impossible to separate you from your creations, just as it is impossible for you to be separated from God. You are the Perfect Creation of a Perfect Mind. Know this and imitate it today.

—Brother

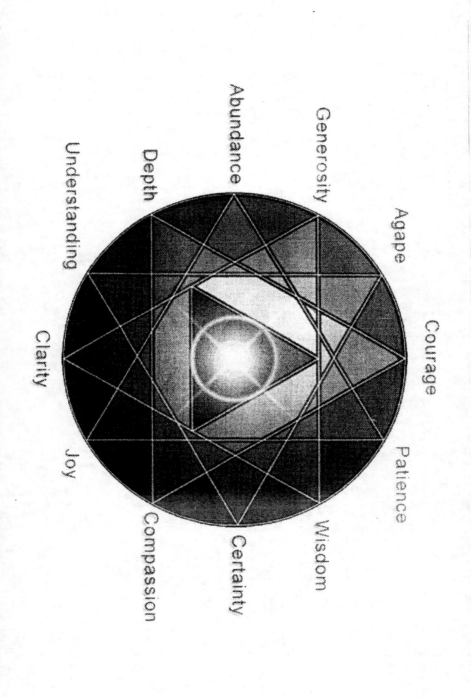

Courage

Patience

Agape

Wisdom

Generosity

Certainty

Abundance

Compassion

Depth

Joy

Understanding

Clarity

Daily Spiritual Peacemaking Lesson – Day 8

There will be moments in this journey when you will wonder if your progress is just an illusion. There will be times when you will think that you have been talked into your "enlightened mind," rather than its being a real experience. It may have happened already. I would, in fact, be surprised if it hasn't.

This is such an important point, and it is why I am addressing it so soon in this study. You have not been talked into anything that isn't true. All I have done is point out what I see in you. There will be moments when you see it as well, and moments when you fall back to sleep and forget. It does not matter, Beloved One, for you have come too far to recede. You have turned a corner, and it is impossible for you to go back. This is your salvation, for it means that you are SEEING, whether or not you think you are. The awareness of this sight will come and go, yes, but it will not be lost. That is the function of this year-long study, to bring the presence of the truth you have discovered into full awareness. Do not worry about how and if it will happen. Just trust that I know what I am saying to you. Everything is in perfect order.

—Brother

Daily Spiritual Peacemaking Lesson – Day 9

Walk with me today, and SEE the world through my eyes. They are the eyes of forgiveness, and blessings flow from me into everything I perceive. Nothing is left unblessed, and so am I saved by the vision of Christ Consciousness, which I AM.

When I ask you to SEE the world through my eyes, it is not a personality I am pointing you toward. Rather, it is a unified field of "Knowingness," which is within you now and always. I am in you as you are in me, and all is contained within the Gift God gave before creation began. And what Gift can God offer but the essence of Itself? This is the "Present" you seek, and it is already yours. Understand this mystery and everything else will fall naturally into place.

Look upon a New World today with the eyes of forgiveness, for this is how God SEES all things. And then, finally, your vision will fall upon your Self, and you will understand what I have been trying to say. Then you will KNOW that there is no Gift worth giving but that which your soul most fully desires.

Accept love today by offering it to ALL.

—Brother

Daily Spiritual Peacemaking Lesson – Day 10

" You are the Gift I have been seeking all my life. You are the Present that lifts me away from the world of form into the formless embrace of eternity. You are the One I have been seeking, and now that I have found you all things do shine."

Say these words as often as you can today, to as many people as you are able. Even if you do not memorize them, let the essence of this wash over you, then flow into the Enlightened Ones who stand before you. Give what you want, and know that you are only giving to your Self.

Your own enlightenment is like a newborn child and needs your strength. If you neglect it now it will fall back into the world of dreams and you will forget why you are here. Dear One, this moment is too important to forget. Stay awake with me. Hold firm to your commitment to be a savior to all sleeping minds, then will your own eyes remain open.

—Brother

3/20/07

Daily Spiritual Peacemaking Lesson – Day 11

The unseen is becoming seen "through" you. This is your function now, and I want you to realize how important it is, and how necessary it is that you keep vigilant with me. You chose to be here and to awake at this time so that the "Transition" may take place. And what is this Transition? It is as simple as opening your eyes and seeing what has been in front of you for so long, then gently touching the shoulder of the others sleeping next to you, that they too may behold the presence of Joy. The Light is streaming in through the door and every window. Will you open it, then, that it may fill the room where you live?

The unseen is becoming seen "as" you. This is not something of which you are an effect, but the direct cause. Please understand that nothing can happen to you now; in fact, nothing has ever happened to you aside from your Holy Desire. But now that you are awake you can choose well all the things that will serve your growth rather than stop it. Now that you are awake, you can see that all Grace flows "through" and "as" you, for such is the will of the One who sent you into the world.

You are here to realize why you are here, then to fulfill it. Let this be the moment you recommit to this, for that is your function this and every moment – to remember why you are here.

—Brother

3/22/07

Daily Spiritual Peacemaking Lesson – Day 12

If you want to adopt my mind, then ask for my help in everything you do. No matter how small the decision, if you become accustomed to bringing my mind, which does not perceive itself to be separate from yours, into the decision, then you will soon realize what is so clear to me. Then you will know that we are One, and that you can literally See through my eyes. This is all that is being asked of you, to See what is real. Mine are the eyes of the Christ, of perfection itself, just as yours. They are not the Eyes of Perfection because they disregard everything that is not aligned with Grace, but because they transform and bless everything that has forgotten the truth. This is the function of a healer, and it is what you are now. Therefore, if you ask for my help then I will have the chance to remind you why you are here, for then our minds will operate as One.

If you ask for my help in everything, I will give it to you.

—Brother

Daily Spiritual Peacemaking Lessons – Day 13

When I ask you to "See through my eyes," I mean this quite literally, and I would not ask you to do something you are not capable of. Likewise, I would also not ask you to do something that you are not already doing. These lessons are all designed for one purpose: to reunite your awareness with Truth. It is not to change you or to point out something you are not doing now.

Once your eyes are open and you are able to See, the first realization you will encounter is that you have always Seen through the eyes of Divinity. You will wonder how it was possible that you perceived anything in any other way, for in that moment you will realize that there is no other way. There is no other Beloved to bless than the one standing before you now. There is no other world than the healed world reflecting the holy decision you make NOW! Do you see how simple this realization is? Claim it and it is so, for you will in that instant realize that God's Will cannot be altered by meaningless dreams.

Please remember that I cannot ask anything of you that is not already true, and I cannot give anything to you that we do not already share. This is the true meaning of salvation, the perfect acceptance of what has always been and what can never change.

—Brother

Daily Spiritual Peacemaking Lesson – Day 14

I have called you away from time because it is not your home, though you have claimed it as if it was. Your fear is that you will now have to give up the things you love in the world in order to serve as a Spiritual Peacemaker. Nothing you love can ever leave you, for nothing you love is ever outside who you really are. In fact, this is all I mean when I say that I have come to call you away from time. When you realize that love is within, and that the things you love are within you as well, then you will understand how nothing ever changes when you undergo this Divine Shift.

Until now you have tried to set yourself apart, and so it seemed that losing love was a real possibility. It is not. The more you give the more you will have, and the more you let go of, the more you will realize that loss cannot occur in the Holy Mind of God's Perfect Extension, otherwise known as "You."

Let go of all the ego's evidence of love lost. There are so many moments in your life when this has seemed like the truth, but you were only mistaken. All that was lost was the projection of love, and that could never satisfy you. Now we claim "love itself," and that is something that is found within you, not outside. And when you find love within, then you will discover so much more. Then everything will suddenly make perfect sense.

—Brother

3/31/09

Daily Spiritual Peacemaking Lesson – Day 15

Let this be the day that your soul reaches out for the Heaven you never left except in your imagination. It is there now, and you will find it by giving it to others. How will you choose to do that today? You already know that the practice of a thing is the same as the achievement of it. In other words, you cannot have it unless you BECOME it. Why? Because everything you desire is already within you, otherwise you would not be able to desire it. It must be present before it can be known. Therefore, you have already achieved everything simply through your desire. The experience of this teaching is what it means to be enlightened. This is what must be activated in you now. Open your eyes, then, and see who stands next to you. Then give to them the gifts you would choose to have in your life. Is it love, or perhaps peace, that you choose? Then do not let this be anything but the perfect day of giving, for only then will you know the wealth that has been given to you before you were created, and which you can never lose.

—Brother

4/6/09

Daily Spiritual Peacemaking Lesson – **Day 16**

Time is beginning to fade in your mind, to be replaced by the timelessness that is your natural home. Step outside this imagined boundary and surrender to the tide that will pull you into the deeper waters where your treasures lie. The current has been pulling you all along, but you have resisted it. That is because you were afraid of what you might lose if you left the shore. It is also because you were afraid you would drown in these deeper waters. But I am there with you, and so many others. We have confidence in who you are, and that death cannot come to the Child of God who has realized the Truth within. Give this faith to another and you will discover it in yourself. Does it help to tell you that it is how I found it in myself?

This is the moment of my awakening as I look into your eyes and give life back to life. It did not happen before this moment occurred between you and me. That is the timelessness I am trying to communicate. Enlightenment happens NOW or it does not happen at all. It is not an historical occurrence. It happens through your desire to SEE as God SEES NOW.

Trust that I am guiding you perfectly into the home where I live, for I do indeed live there and know each door and room. If you allow me, I will lead you there and you will begin to remember. Let it happen NOW.

—Brother

Daily Spiritual Peacemaking Lesson – **Day 17**

You world you created in your imagination to hide from Truth is tired, and so are you. Let it rest today, that you may learn to see the world that is not compromised by your dreams. Look upon it with gentleness, and it will return to you in a way you cannot imagine now. The symbols of hatred and despair will be removed from your sight, replaced by Holy Messengers who sing a song you seem to recognize, though you are not yet sure you know where you heard it before. It stirs a place deep within you that has slept in quiet solitude, and as it awakens a New World dawns. Let this be the day that your tired eyes are replaced with new eyes that SEE and KNOW what you have only guessed at till now. The world is waiting for you. Will you answer by giving everything to everything?

I am standing with you. That is all you need to know for now, for I am here to lend you my strength while you stretch and wipe the sleep from your eyes. The day will come when you will be strong enough to offer this gift to others, but for now you must be strong enough to receive it from me. The world is waiting for us both, for our forgiveness is required. Walk with me today, and we will contribute our love to a world already filled with it. Open your eyes now, and SEE what is real.

—Brother

Daily Spiritual Peacemaking Lesson – *Day 18*

My only goal is to give you what I have received from the Beloved, simply because it is the only way I can know it to be true. God's will for you is Perfect Joy, and so I open to this gift "through" you. Do you understand what I am trying to show you here? I open my heart as yours, knowing we are the same. This knowledge transcends the evidence of this world and so is not understood through human perception. But the Divine in you, yes, it understands it well, and rejoices when you recognize it. Meditate on this today. How can you receive the Gifts of God "through" others and, in doing so, allow them to receive it through you? As always, do not try to understand this with your mind, for you will fail. Open your heart to this current, and it will flow into you as naturally as air into your lungs. This is what it means to be a savior, and it is why you are here. Do not think it is anything less than this.

—Brother

4/11/07

Daily Spiritual Peacemaking Lesson – *Day 19*

I am here for one reason only: To Know what God Knows. When you adopt the same goal, and only this, then all things will flow to and through you. It is why you are here, and it is what it means to be a Spiritual Peacemaker. How will you do this? You can only Know what you are able to SEE, or experience. This is not a function of your physical eyes, which were made not to see what is real. It is the function of Spirit, which escapes the attention of your physical self and lies sleeping until you stir its deeper pulse. How is it stirred? Through practice. It is stirred by Seeing what is really there, all the things that are invisible to your eyes but which are experienced by your soul. If you practice Seeing what is real, then it will become a habit. Then it will soon replace the empty visions you thought were real, and reveal the world you want to see. As before, your function as a Spiritual Peacemaker is to offer this gift to others by practicing it yourself.

You must become the living example of the Vision of God made manifest in the world of form. Are you willing to accept this role? Does it help to tell you that you already have? If this is true, that the decision has already been made, then the activation of it is simple. Say yes to what you have already determined, then you will know, and then extend this knowing to others.

—Brother

4/15/07

Daily Spiritual Peacemaking Lesson – Day 20

Do not underestimate how much the world needs you to be awake at this time. It is critical that you realize and remember, for in doing so you give permission to countless other sleeping minds. You show them that it is safe to be aware of the power of Love, and to let Peace Prevail in your life. They will in turn touch many others, and the ocean of Light that has been promised will then be released. The whole world is opening to the Divine Current that is gaining momentum now. This is the moment when you chose to open, and then to KNOW.

Do you truly want this? Then let this be the day that you accept it. Better still, let this be the moment, for at this time it is best to move slowly through the landscape of Grace. There is so much to SEE, and so many treasures to be revealed. Open your eyes and look around you. The world shines in a New Light, and the source is reflected through and as you. You are the extension of God's love and loveliness. Do not hesitate for another moment.

Open your eyes, and SEE today.

—Brother

Daily Spiritual Peacemaking Lesson – Day 21

Your goal today is to see one other being through the eyes of Christ Consciousness or, in other words, to be conscious of the Christ within them. If you can accomplish this goal, even for an instant, then you will have reserved a bright space for the world to realize the Peaceful Kingdom that is its destiny. Today look around and SEE what is there, who is there, and pay attention to how each person you meet can save you from despair simply by your KNOW-ING who they are. Until now you have spent all your time knowing who they are not. Let this be the moment, then, when you use the world as it was intended to be used. It will make all the difference.

How simply is salvation found. It is right in front of you to claim, if you would but open your eyes and SEE it. How easily is Heaven won. It has always been your prize, if you would but claim the fruit of your Holy Accomplishment. You need do nothing but embrace God's Gift for you, then share it with others. Your Beloved shares everything, and if you are to KNOW as God KNOWS, then you must imitate this. Claim it now and it is yours. This is the day you have been waiting for.

—Brother

Daily Spiritual Peacemaking Lesson – Day 22

You are here to seek the Christ by using the Consciousness of the Christ in everything you do. How will we define this? The Christ does not refer to a person, but to a "Beingness" that is most natural to the "You" God perceives. It is not an historical being we seek, but an identity that transcends all history, for its nature is eternal. It is the extension of the Love of God, which is what you are. Becoming aware of this is all that is required. In other words, no change is possible in this, for the awareness of the Christ within you requires nothing but recognition, then extension. Then you will Know as God Knows, and then you will understand what has escaped you till now.

The Christ is everywhere you look. This is why I said that whatever you do to the least of them, you do to me. When you identify with the Consciousness of the Christ, then you know that you are "All in All." Let this be your goal today, to see the Face of Christ in the most ordinary situations. Then you will realize that within even the most ordinary moments, God calls to you.

—Brother

Daily Spiritual Peacemaking Lesson – Day 23

These lessons are simple. It may even seem that the same simple point is being repeated over and over. It is true, for when you fully integrate one truth, then the rest fall effortlessly into your consciousness. In the end there is only one thing for you to learn. God loves you regardless of who you think you are and what you think you've done. God's love for you has no condition, no reason, and no end. You will learn this by giving it to others, for God calls you to identify with the Nature of God that is within you now. Let the lessons be simple, then, and allow your mind to explore every possibility. Become like a child today, and try not to overcomplicate the Truth.

—Brother

Daily Spiritual Peacemaking Lesson – Day 24

How easily is salvation won, and how quickly is the Mind of Christ adopted by the one who is willing to step outside the world of form and perceive everything as God. You were told that this would take time and effort. It is not true. Time is the enemy of eternity and understands it not. Release time and you are released from it. Open your heart and all effort melts into the sea of forgiveness. This is your function here on earth now. Accept it today. Let this be the moment you claim your birthright. There is no other goal but this, and it has already been achieved. Open your mind and realize your victory.

How easily is your release from fear accomplished. Simply open your eyes and See who it is that stands before you. Know that the "Perfect Realized Child of God" reveals Itself in an infinite number of ways every moment, and then you will not be fooled by changing forms. Open your eyes and SEE today. It is the only lesson I am here to teach you.

—Brother

4/30/07

Daily Spiritual Peacemaking Lesson – Day 25

Commit yourself today to looking past your brother's error, and seeing what your ego has refused till now. Others' perfection is not affected by their error, and so your Holy Vision should be the same.

I have said over and over that your only goal is to See each person and situation as God Sees it. To the ego this is impossible and, therefore, should not be attempted. But to Spirit it is the most natural thing in all the world, for it was made for this very purpose. If your sister makes a mistake, look past it to the Truth that cannot be threatened. Do not follow the guidance of your ego, which would rather use this seeming error to prove something it thinks it sees, but which is not there at all. Choose to See the Truth, and then you will openly receive the real gift they offer you. Then you will remember who you are, by simply blessing the other.

You are, after all, a Spiritual Peacemaker, and you know this to be your only function.

—Brother

5/1/07

Daily Spiritual Peacemaking Lesson – Day 26

Now that you are attuned to Seeing what is Real, and Knowing the Beloved in all its varied forms, you are ready to return to our Emissary Wheel and enter again into the twelve attributes of a Spiritual Peacemaker. Over the next weeks and months we will follow this path, spinning around the wheel and integrating each of these. We begin, as always, with Courage.

Today your mind will focus on all the ways Courage will serve you in this ascent toward the Home you desire. You have hidden for a very long time in a place where fear seems to rule, and where courage is a forgotten dream. But now you will reclaim this strength, knowing that you have everything you need to complete all the Holy Tasks you have placed before yourself in this life. There is nothing for you to fear, for the world where you have hidden till now has not existed at all. Your Courage now shows you the Real World where only Light dances upon your soul. You are free to open your eyes and see what you have missed. Then you will Know for yourself that my words are true, and that there is a way of living in this world that affirms reality and life, rather than denies it. All that is required now is your Courage, and the rest will fall into place on its own. If you would but spend this day Seeing all the ways this will serve you, then you will be on the Path to Freedom, a Path that your Holy Feet will remember well.

—Brother

Daily Spiritual Peacemaking Lesson – Day 27

"From my Patience today, comes my strength. I will wait patiently upon that which has been assured for my soul. I will not worry and wonder if God will follow through on the promises given to me. I will have Patience and know that they are already complete. I am already enlightened, and so I give this gift to everyone I meet. Time has no dominion over this, for it was not born in time. All things come to me now from the Heaven where I was conceived, and where I return now as I open my eyes and awaken. All things fall into their natural place today."

Patience is natural when you know that everything is in perfect order. Even when things seem to be chaotic, there is a sense within a Spiritual Peacemaker that tells them to relax, then Know that nothing real can be threatened. You are real, and so is everything you love. Be patient, then, for nothing will be lost, no matter how it appears. Today, even when things do not line up as you think they should in your mind, remember this. Know that your enlightened mind is already open to this way of life, then feel Patience in your soul. Then will joy return to your mind, and you will remember why you are in any given situation.

—Brother

Daily Spiritual Peacemaking Lesson – Day 28

Wisdom is born through your willingness to hear the Universal call to your soul, claiming for it what has always been offered to it by the Beloved. And what is it that is offered in which your soul does rejoice? It is the answer to a statement you have already learned, one that has the power to reveal to you the true purpose of your life and why you are here as a Spiritual Peacemaker. It begins, as you know, with your proclamation, "I AM THAT!" But it does not end here, for to say these words and not hear the response from Love is not enough. Once you have claimed this, you must realize that the Universe conspires to make it Known. Now you must listen and hear these words as they resound through your whole being: "I AM." Thus does the song, "I AM THAT," "I AM," become your salvation. In this does God speak AS you and TO you. In this has the illusion of separation come to a final end, for you have heard the call of God to God. This is what it means to be wise. It begins with your willingness to hear, then act upon what you have heard. Let this be your focus today.

—Brother

5/4/07 — This is still hard for me to understand.

Sick & hospitalized 5/11 – 5/15

Daily Spiritual Peacemaking Lesson – Day 29

Be certain of one thing today: That you are Loved by God. This is all you need to escape from the bondage you have claimed till now. When you understand that the Beloved's love for you is not contingent upon anything of this world, then you will feel the freedom you were meant to feel, and soar above the chains that once bound you. Only this thought: God loves you without condition. When you are fully embraced by the New World, then you will understand this even with your mind. That is because your mind will have been transformed through Grace, the process you are undergoing now. Until then, do not try to comprehend anything with the mind, but with your heart. It has an intelligence all its own, a way of understanding the universe that transcends time and space. That is where you will find me, for I am holding your hand this moment, and I will not leave you until we stand together in this perfect recognition.

—Brother

5/19/07 — God loves you without condition.

Daily Spiritual Peacemaking Lesson – Day 30

When you KNOW of God's love for you, then you will begin to act as God acts, which means to extend what you have received. Do you see that this is the truest and only function of love—to extend? Imitate this today, then you will understand Compassion. It is a gift you give and receive in the same moment.

There is a reason the Beloved acts in the way it does. It is because it knows the truth, which is to say that it wants only one thing and therefore gives only one thing. When you come to the place where your desires are limited to what your soul really wants, then you will give only that. And when there is only one thing you give to others, then it is the only thing that will be yours. Decide now what you want today, then determine to focus on its discovery. Focus on giving to the Beloved AS the Beloved. Then you will understand the greatest miracle of all: that the Beloved is the only thing that exists.

You are here this day to KNOW who you are.

—Brother

5/22/07

Daily Spiritual Peacemaking Lesson – Day 31

Our goal today is to experience Perfect Joy. As you have already learned, your role as a Spiritual Peacemaker is essentially to experience, then translate, the Real World for those still chained to the world of memories and dreams. You have been chosen because you are uniquely qualified. That does not mean that you have more of something than anyone else. It simply means that you SAW, then responded to what you SAW. It means that your YES to God has passed through the perceived boundaries of this world and was heard in Heaven, and now Heaven responds back to you. There are many angels at your side because you demonstrated the courage they carry within their sacred hearts. Now you are ready to fly as they fly, and to know the freedom that they have always known.

Perfect Joy is the way you will help translate the current of Peace to your brothers and sisters in this world. When others look at you they will sense a Joy that is not bound to this world. In other words, even if everything here were taken away, still would Perfect Joy persist and expand. It comes from your knowledge of SELF, and your unity with Life. It does not depend upon anything other than Love. And so Love is the means through which you give this gift to others. Let this be the day that you expand upon this truth. Find new ways to realize it more deeply than before, for this is a process that has no ending place. It continues on as you continue on, and it expands as you expand.

I am expanding with you.

—Brother

5/23/07

Daily Spiritual Peacemaking Lesson – Day 32

From Perfect Joy arises Perfect Clarity. You cannot be clear so long as you struggle through a world that exists only in your imagination. Joy comes from freedom, and Clarity is what freedom would show. It is like rising above the clouds as the concerns of another world fall away. The air is different here, and so you can breathe in a way that you couldn't before. And the visions you perceive are different as well, for the eyes that were given to you at your birth have been given a new purpose. Now are they used to bless, for all of creation is in your sights. You have risen above the world and can see what you could not see when your feet walked upon the ground. Joy is the means through which you ascend, and Clarity is the gift. Use this gift today. Do not let these lessons rest upon your mind, but within your heart, for then they will touch other hearts and fill other souls with the Light you have chosen to receive. Today is the day Perfect Clarity dawns.

—Brother

5/25/07

Daily Spiritual Peacemaking Lesson – Day 33

Do not seek to understand anything today. Understand. Do not seek to love anything today. Love.

You are passed asking for something to be given to you, especially when it is already yours. All I have asked you to do is open your eyes and SEE. Understanding comes to the one who is willing to observe what is right in front of them. You have already shown your readiness and willingness to do just that. Do not waste another moment, then. See and Understand. Only then will you know why you are here.

—Brother

5/26/07

Daily Spiritual Peacemaking Lesson – Day 34

Diving into the Depths of your Enlightened Mind takes great courage. Most others are content to stay at the shore and let the water lap against their legs. To be immersed in this water seems too great a risk, for it means leaving one world behind, then diving to a place where your lungs will not work as before.

Do you see where I am leading you with this? The ocean of life is open to all of us, yet very few will seek the Depths I am leading you to. And yet, this is where you will find the Holy Treasure you are seeking. At the shore there are many shells most would enjoy. But I am telling you that you have come too far to let it end there. These things will never satisfy you, Beloved. Seek the treasures that lie at the very bottom of the ocean, and then return to show these others what you have found. They long for the same, though they lack the courage to follow their dreams. If they see you return to the surface and breathe the same air again, then they will be inspired to follow your example, just as you have followed mine.

The only way to find yourself is to dive deeper than you think you can stand. You will survive. I can assure you of this. I have gone before you, and now I am here to set a good example. Will you do the same today?

—Brother

Daily Spiritual Peacemaking Lesson – Day 35

Today you will be generous in the same way that God is generous, for that is the way you will receive everything your heart desires. God gives without reserve, for it is the nature of Divinity to serve. So shall you, in your desire to have all the things that will serve you, serve others. And what is the greatest service you can offer today? It is the abundance of your love flowing like a river into their souls. You do not need to speak a word to them. You need only look into their eyes and Know who they are, who it is that stands in front of you, and who it is that deserves all your blessings. You are here to be the Beloved's eyes and ears today, but, most of all, God's heart. Focus on this. Do not miss a single opportunity, for you would only miss the chance to give to yourself.

—Brother

Daily Spiritual Peacemaking Lesson – Day 36

Today is a day of celebration. Your generosity has become your abundance, for in giving love you have received love. The cycle is now complete and all things are seen in the Home you Know yourself to be. Once again, you are the Home you seek. It can be found nowhere but where you are NOW, for God would not place the Kingdom anywhere except where it can be found. The reason you did not find it before was because you searched outside, the only place it could not be found. Imagine if you lost something you dearly loved inside your house, and yet you spent all your time searching for it in the yard outside. You could search for days and yet never find it. But the moment you give up the search and go back inside, then it appears before you, for it was not hidden at all. You were hidden, but now you are revealed. It is a time for joy, for you have rediscovered your Divine Abundance.

But the journey does not end there. If you are to continue to remember, you must resolve to keep giving what you have received. Once again, I will repeat this over and over, for it is the only lesson there is for you to learn. You will learn it by practicing it, for it is not something for your mind to conceive, but for your heart to love. It is important that you don't fall asleep again, for you are so needed right now. I need you to stand beside me and forgive everything time would claim. Hold out the Light you have found within and let it shine brightly for these others. In doing so you will not lose it.

—Brother

5/31/07

Daily Spiritual Peacemaking Lesson – Day 37

TO LOVE AS GOD LOVES. This is who you are. Notice that I did not say that this is what you are here to do. You are not here to do anything, but to BE everything. Love is the only thing that exists. Yes? Therefore, you are here to BE love, for it is who you are. You will remember as you relax into this. It should take no effort to BE the truth, for everything that isn't true disappears in the Light. Spend this day BEING Love. Spend this day knowing who you are. This is a very simple lesson because the truth is so simple. Putting it into practice, though, is the real lesson. That is where you will learn the most, not by reading these words. Let this be the day, then, that you take "Your Self" seriously.

—Brother

6/2/07

Daily Spiritual Peacemaking Lesson – Day 38

Will you choose to demonstrate the courage it takes to leave behind the things of the world you thought you made, and SEE only that which has been created by God? It may take more courage than you realize, for time conspires to draw you into its illusion and claim you as its own. But you do not belong to time, nor to anything that time has made. You belong to eternity, but it takes courage to deny the things you have built your earthly life around.

    You long to grow old and die. Do you realize this? If you didn't long for it then it wouldn't happen, for nothing exists outside your desire. Why would you long for such a thing, especially when it does not exist at all? You are afraid to let it go completely, though, for it seems so many other joys are attached to it. They are not, for joy and sorrow cannot ever be joined, accept in your imagination. Therefore, I am asking you to have the courage to let it all go and trust me, for I have seen past this world and can show you the same. There is more Light beyond these meager lines than you can ever know in your mind. Choose to SEE with new eyes today, and let courage guide your way into the world you really want.

—Brother

6/3/07

Daily Spiritual Peacemaking Lesson – Day 39

Patience and Peace are the same today, for they spring from the same quiet source. Neither has the need to claim anything for itself, for it knows that all things are already claimed, though in a way no mind can ever comprehend. Peace can only come when you realize that who you are cannot be threatened by anything real, and Patience follows right behind. It knows that everything is unfolding in perfect order, and so it allows peace to guide it to the home it knows it never left at all. Let this be a day of practicing Divine Patience, knowing that you already have everything you need to be happy, and that happiness is the only desire of your awakened heart.

    Be Patience with your brothers and sisters today as well. Remember that you cannot give any gift to them that is not received also by you. Even if their bodies linger behind your desire, wait patiently upon their souls. Give them the gift you would choose to receive from me, and then you will receive it. Let this be the day that you discover the benefits of quiet Peace, and the Patience that can never be removed from you.

—Brother

6/5/07

Daily Spiritual Peacemaking Lesson – Day 40

I AM THAT NOW, only because I have realized that we are the same. My gift to you is the gift I receive, for to look upon your holiness is to KNOW my own. This realization brings peace to my mind, and the world of separation seems to disappear. It is now replaced with a world where the laws of God are not challenged, and where reality itself is seen forever as it really is. All things fall together and are revealed as One, and love is renewed in my soul.

This is the wisdom I claim today, and I will let it move through everything I do and see. This is what it means to be alive, for without this I only seem to be alive. I will wait no longer. I deserve this Light and humanity deserves the love I bring. I will not wait any longer for this wisdom to come alive. I claim it today.

—Brother

6/7/07

Daily Spiritual Peacemaking Lesson – Day 41

At this point in our journey, can you be certain that I am in you, working AS you? What does this mean? It says to the world that you will not accept littleness any longer, for it is not appropriate for the perfect extension of God's love, which is what you are, to realize your Self as anything but perfect. It means that your eyes bless everything they see, for you look upon all reality in forgiveness and love, giving them the gift you had the courage to receive. Most of all, it means that you accept that you are an enlightened being sent to the world to awaken all other sleeping minds to the love that is their inheritance. This is why you came. It has been my mission and now it is yours. Are you finally willing to accept and live this, or will you continue to deny with your mind what you heart already realizes?

Be certain today that this is true. Find ways to express this certainty, for as always, it is in the giving of this gift that you will fully receive it. Most of all, be certain that you are loved by God, for this is the foundation of wisdom. Nothing can disturb you now, for you have found your home and can finally rest in peace.

—Brother

6/8/07

Daily Spiritual Peacemaking Lesson – **Day 42**

What compassion will you show your brothers and sisters greater than seeing Reality reflected in their eyes? Look past the world of form and everything it seems to offer for just a moment. Is there anything here that will satisfy you more than the love God has for you? And what is the womb of love if not compassion? You are here to learn to love in the same way God loves you. It is already within you; you need only release what you have hidden away in the dark corners of your mind.

Let every moment be as a baptism, washing you clean of all your perceived wrongdoings. You cannot give this gift to others until you accept it for yourself. This is my whole teaching, for it is the only thing you really need to know. Give what you want, and then compassion will follow. What else do you require but this, and what in the world of illusions can satisfy you this much?

—Brother

Daily Spiritual Peacemaking Lesson – **Day 43**

I have come to share my joy with you. That is all. Let this be the day you take it from me. Lay aside all other dreams and let me reveal what I have seen. Its beauty is greater than anything you can imagine. Therefore, let this be the day you accept the Precious Present I have come to offer. I have seen it in you, but now you must see it in others. Then it is yours.

—Brother

Daily Spiritual Peacemaking Lesson – Day 44

You are here to SEE. Let this be your only goal. Do not try to SEE with your eyes, because they were, in fact, made not to see. They perceive only what is separate and disregard what is One. Close your eyes for a moment and FEEL what is true. This is the first step toward SEEING, for you must first learn to feel that the Truth is True. Stop trying to convince yourself that the Truth is not True by using the evidence your physical eyes gather to prove what you cannot understand. Feel it first, then you will bypass the evidence of your physical eyes. Then Clarity will come to you, and you will Know that I am telling you the truth. Knowing doesn't come from the mind, just as your mind will never be clear as long as you rely on false evidence that prove what isn't really there.

In this lesson I am not speaking to your linear mind, so you may not understand anything I am trying to say. I am speaking directly to your heart, so take a deep breath and let it enter that Sacred Chamber. Are you beginning to sense what I am trying to communicate? Good.

—Brother

6/12/07

Daily Spiritual Peacemaking Lesson – Day 45

Seek to understand your Self this day. You are everywhere and, therefore, you can use anything you choose to SEE. The Christ Mind is operating through and as you this moment, but you have not understood this till now. Even as it sleeps within, still is it there, and it reaches out for your recognition. Know that you are THAT this day. Look around and let the Universe reveal itself as it really is, not as your ego once asked it to be. Its beauty will astound you if you lay aside the past and disregard all hope for the future. Live NOW, and then you will understand who you are. Then you will perceive the miracle.

The world needs you to reflect the beauty of the enlightened heart so that the Peaceful Kingdom may be finally realized. It must be realized within you first, then extended into the world. Let this be the day, then, that you allow this flood to overtake you. Let the waters of enlightenment wash you clean, then you will step forward as a New Creation, ready to play your important role.

—Brother

6/14/07

Daily Spiritual Peacemaking Lesson – *Day 46*

Each day you have the choice whether to live on the surface of the world or ascend to the depths of who you really are. Notice that I said, "ascend to the depths," rather than descend. If I were to ask you to descend to the truth within, you would think that you need to remove yourself from the world and everything it could reveal. It would be better for you to rise above it, for though it becomes small and your ears do not hear the noise, still you can See and forgive, for that is your role. You will only be able to forgive the world if you SEE it, and that is why it is so important that you not try to leave and go anywhere. Where would you go to escape your own mind? If you went to the bottom of the ocean, you would still be there. If you climbed the highest mountain, still would you find the same mind. Seek not to rid yourself of anything, but to embrace everything. Then you will find yourself in the very depths of your being. Then you will Know and will respond as one who Knows.

—Brother

embrace everything –
don't try to get rid it

6/15/07

Daily Spiritual Peacemaking Lesson – *Day 47*

Will you be generous to your Self today? What will you decide to give to your Self that generates more love, the only thing you are here to receive? Decide upon this now, for then it will be within you, and what lies within you must ultimately find itself in the world you created.

Until now you have been confused about what to give to your Self, and so you have vacillated back and forth, giving love one minute then attacking in the next. It is no wonder that you have been confused, for how can you see the return of your gift if the giving be not steady? Decide today that you will give only one thing, the thing you most want, then you will have that thing, and you will witness the Will of God as it flows from and to you. This is the only lesson for you to learn, that your giving cannot be separated from who you are. You give but to your Self. Who else could there possibly be? Do not withhold your generosity this day, for you deserve so much through these others.

—Brother

6/19/07

Daily Spiritual Peacemaking Lesson – Day 48

Today is a day to rejoice and enjoy the fruits of giving. You are so much more abundant than you can possibly realize in your mind; but your soul, yes, it understands this well. It perceives who you are and what gifts belong to the Perfect Child. It has not forgotten a thing, and it seeks to communicate this with you. Listen and know that you are only teaching your Self. I am nothing more than the awake aspect of You, and you are finally able to realized this. I am not outside you, but within, and so the gifts I have received are also yours. Most of all, the gift of Resurrected Life is yours because I have claimed it, though not for myself alone. I claimed it for my Self, which is the same as claiming it for your Self. There is only one Self in the Universe, and it is you. Do you see where I am leading you?

Enjoy your abundance today, Holy Child. It does not matter how much money you have, or how many possessions. These things will fade with time, and yet the gifts I offer are yours forever. But you must claim them if they are to be enjoyed. Otherwise they are like precious jewels that are hidden away in a dark closet where no one can enjoy their radiance. Do not hide any longer, for there is so much you have to offer.

—Brother

7/21/07

Daily Spiritual Peacemaking Lesson – Day 49

The Love of God is your only desire, and always has been. No matter where your mind and ego seem to lead you, this alone will satisfy your soul's longing. You came from God and were created like God, which means that God alone is the Home you seek. And since this alone is real, you need only open your eyes to perceive Love everywhere. A sleeping mind cannot see what is right in front of it, and that is why it is so important that you stay awake with me.

You are like a person dying of thirst, asleep in a boat floating in an enormous fresh water lake. Wake up and see where you are. There is no need for you to deny yourself the life-giving water of God's Love, which is also yours to give. Let this be the day that you give up your search and accept what has always been yours. You are only denying yourself, which, as you have already discovered, is completely inappropriate for one so blessed.

—Brother

7/24/07

Daily Spiritual Peacemaking Lesson – Day 50

Today, and for the next three days, we will take a break from our Emissary Wheel and refocus our minds on the Beloved Within.

This is a day for you to choose again what you will SEE and whom you will LOVE. Call upon the name of God as often as you can today, and the Beloved will reveal Itself in and through you. What name will you choose? Do not let it be a word that falls from your tongue, for the moment it is defined it is lost. Let it be a recognition you hold in your heart, one that is assigned to every person you meet this day. Call upon the name of God in them, and you will awaken from the dream of separation. Call upon the name of God without words, without sound, and without the definitions your mind would claim. Your heart alone will know what it is you SEE, and it will rejoice.

—Brother

4/24/07

Daily Spiritual Peacemaking Lesson – Day 51

Call upon the name of God in every action you take this day. It is like a song that rings in your ears that you long to sing. Let the world hear this song through the way you live, the way you act, and the way you simply look upon the Beloved. The only thing you need to do to realize the Beloved Within is to SEE the Beloved everywhere. Will you decide upon this task and claim it as real?

Every lesson has said the same thing, and this will not change. You may wonder if this is the only thing I know, and you would be right. Soon it will be the only thing you know, and then you will understand.

—Brother

Daily Spiritual Peacemaking Lesson – Day 52

"Today I choose to SEE what is real, and disregard the illusions the world would reveal. I call upon your name, Beloved, for you alone are the reality I seek. Where else will I look but where you are, within me and within everyone I look upon this day? They are here to teach me about myself, and my Self. I choose to SEE only Love, for it alone will give me what I really want. It is mine to claim, if only I keep awake and fulfill the role I chose before I was born."

"Today I recommit myself to the role of being a Spiritual Peacemaker. I am here for this one simple task, and yet I realize that it is the only thing that can bring about the Peaceful Kingdom on Earth. I am here to assist in the Realization of Grace in all things. Where else would I look for this but within my Self, and where else would I SEE it but within every person God puts before me? This is a holy day, and I choose to use it wisely."

"I am here to be truly helpful."

—Brother

6/28/07

Daily Spiritual Peacemaking Lesson – Day 53

It is now time for you to Claim what is rightfully yours. Take it from me, for I offer it willingly. That is because I know that I cannot give this Grace without receiving more, and so I long for you to claim your enlightenment from and through me. For the next twelve days we will allow the attributes of a Spiritual Peacemaker to lead us into this Perfect State. Begin by saying the opening prayer, and then remember it throughout the day. The rest will happen on its own.

"Today I have the Courage to claim the Holy Mind of the Beloved."

What other courage is required but this? What else will fulfill your every need, bringing into perfect balance all the things your soul requires? You have sought after the riches of a world that exists only in your imagination. It takes Divine Courage to claim the world that seems to live outside your experience. But now you have come too far. You have seen too much, and you KNOW that you are capable of remembering the truth you forgot but for a moment. The moment has passed now, and you are once again embraced by the eternal home you have longed to see again. You are there. Open your eyes and SEE. It takes but a moment of Courage.

Use the power of this Divine Current today to claim what is rightfully yours. It is within you now.

—Brother

6/29/07

Daily Spiritual Peacemaking Lesson – Day 54

"Today I have the Patience to claim the Holy Mind of the Beloved."

Divine Patience brings immediate results. That is because it is impossible for you to lose what God has given you, though you may "seem" to lose it for a moment. But the moment of this illusion is now passing, though it has seemed to last many lifetimes. When it is over you will realize that it was but a second, and then you will relax again in the eternal Peace that has always been your home. Do not worry about whether you will achieve this Grace or not. It is already yours. Know this and the rest will come to you. Simply relax into knowing that God would not leave you vulnerable, not even to death. It is not real, but you are. Claim the Holy Mind of the Beloved this day, and your Patience will have won.

—Brother

6/30/07

Daily Spiritual Peacemaking Lesson – Day 55

"Today I have the Wisdom to claim the Holy Mind of the Beloved."

Wisdom is simply the willingness to flow with the Divine Current that seeks to guide your life. Claiming the Holy Mind of God is your only goal, for it sets you straight upon this path and leads directly to the Home you never left. What else is there left for you to do but follow and know that you are One with God? You are wise, otherwise you would not have come this far. Accept this and then claim the Mind that is your salvation. It is waiting for you, but it will not come unless you realize that it is yours already. Do not deny this any longer, for your Wisdom knows no boundary. Open your heart this day and claim who you are, then you will SEE what has always been true.

—Brother

7/1/09

Daily Spiritual Peacemaking Lesson – Day 56

"Today I have the Certainty that I am claiming the Holy Mind of the Beloved."

You no longer believe, but Know. Live within this Knowingness. You are claiming the Holy Mind of the Beloved NOW. Spend today feeling this energy pour through your entire being. You do not need to have the evidence of the world if you are Certain of something. It is an inner commitment that the world cannot understand. Know that you are Holy, and that your Holiness is not limited to the smaller definition of you. Claim the Holy Mind of the Beloved with vigor, for that is where Certainty leads you. It is yours. Do not hesitate. Then you will be able to show others how to do the same. You will do this simply by looking into their eyes. You will not need to say a word to them, for they will feel who they are through you.

—Brother

7/5/07

Daily Spiritual Peacemaking Lesson – Day 57

"Today I have the Compassion to claim the Holy Mind of the Beloved."

It is important for you to realize that these prayers require three levels of action if you are to integrate the lessons they would teach. The first and most important is your willingness to "claim" what is already yours. This is something we have examined in many ways since beginning the Spiritual Peacemaking course—the fact that these attributes, and the Mind of the Beloved Itself, are already yours. They are not something you need to learn or deserve. That would imply that you are not accepted by God as you are this moment, which you are. The second action is the Emissary attribute that changes everyday. Today you are asked to possess enough Compassion to lead you into a state where you perceive all things AS your Self. This is, of course, the only goal of compassion. The third action is the desire for the Mind of the Beloved. Realize now that it is the only thing that will satisfy you, the only thing you really want from this world. The desire for this will then lead naturally into realizing the first two actions.

Live in Compassion today, as I did when I walked on this earth. It will show you the New World for which you long. Then claim the Gift of God that cannot change. The Holy Mind of the Beloved is yours NOW.

—Brother

7/8/07

*Daily Spiritual Peacemaking Lesson – **Day 58***

"Today I possess the Joy to claim the Holy Mind of the Beloved."

What but Joy will lead you to the Holy Mind you seek? It is not the opposite of sorrow, for sorrow is the denial of Joy. To deny Joy is to deny life, for one leads to the other. When your heart expands then your joy expands with it. It is this natural expansion we are seeking together. This is the Perfect Joy that leads to the Heart of the Beloved, which is what you are. Live within this prayer today. Let it teach you about yourself, then feel your heart and your Joy increase beyond anything this world can comprehend. Claim what is yours, for God longs to give it to you today.

—Brother

*Daily Spiritual Peacemaking Lesson – **Day 59***

"Today I am Clear that I am claiming the Holy Mind of the Beloved."

What more do you need but this Clarity? It gives you everything you desire, for when you are clear about something then the Universe Itself rises to give you the thing you perceive. And what is it that you are Certain of? Yes, this is the question you must ask. Is it your life, your love, or even the purpose for which you were born on this planet? None of these things will matter in the end, for you do not fully understand them, and to be certain of something you must understand it. The question then becomes, what do I fully understand? Do you have an answer? If your inquiry is true, the answer is "Nothing." So where does this leave you in this Divine Inquiry? Somewhere within your "Nothingness" lies the realization of "Everything." Why? Because they are the same thing.

Do not try to understand this with your mind. It will never work. The Everything and the Nothing exist in the same place, and when you embrace one you embrace both. Allow yourself to be Clear about Nothing today. Play with this and see where it leads you. Claim the Nothingness that you embrace and let it claim you as well. There is magic in this mystery that I cannot explain, but in the realization will all your questions be answered.

—Brother

Daily Spiritual Peacemaking Lesson – *Day 60*

"Today I Understand that I am claiming the Holy Mind of the Beloved."

What is it you are seeking to understand? Exactly what would you claim if you were to achieve this? Is it an idea or a concept you hold in your mind, or is it a real experience that when you try to explain with words, they fail you? This lesson follows upon the heels of the last. What I want you to understand is that you are unable to truly understand anything. Therefore, what I say to you is, seek to be understood, not by the world or by others, but by God. When you allow your Self to be understood by God, really allow it, then everything flows naturally, and then you will understand everything. Until then you cannot understand anything at all because everything is interpreted by your experience of the past. Do you see this? God does understand and has always understood you. That is why I am saying that you need to "allow" your Self to be understood. It is the same as becoming conscious of God's love for you. When you are conscious of God's love, then you can give love to others. Likewise, when you are conscious of God's understanding, then you will understand.

Today you will claim this understanding by giving it up, and allowing your Self to be understood.

—Brother

7/14/07

Daily Spiritual Peacemaking Lesson – *Day 61*

"Today I feel the Depths of claiming the Holy Mind of the Beloved."

The world cannot understand any words I say to you. It does not comprehend the Depths of this experience, or the importance of claiming who you really are. But you are able to comprehend it. How do you do this? You do it by simply giving up the need to comprehend anything. You experience the Depths of your soul by not focusing on it, or by your willingness to not pay attention to how deep you've gone. This may be hard for you to accept, but it is so important that you do. The instant you acknowledge that you have finally experienced the Depth of Illumined Consciousness, is the same moment it disappears. Be willing to simply be where you are right now. That attitude is the essence of Spiritual Depth. Do not be concerned with measuring these things, for that attitude is of the world you are leaving. Adopt, rather, the attitude of the world where you belong. There is no such thing as one person being deeper than another. The only thing that may change is being conscious of it. You will not know when you have claimed this, at least not in your mind, but it will show in your eyes.

—Brother

7/15/07

Daily Spiritual Peacemaking Lesson – *Day 62*

"Today I am Generous enough to claim the Holy Mind of the Beloved."

Give everything to everything today. Do you really want to claim the Holy Mind of the Beloved? This is how you will do it. Accept a new understanding of what it means to be generous, then everything that has real value will be yours automatically. There is nothing in this world you can give away to another, and in doing so, lose at least a portion of that thing. That is simply how the world you created in your imagination works. Likewise, there is nothing in the Real World that you can give away and not have more of that thing. That is how the world God created works. Today you have the opportunity to choose which of these experiences you want in your life. You do not need to die to experience the Real World. You need to live. Will that be your choice? Will you choose life over death, which is the only real choice a Spiritual Peacemaker ever makes?

Let this be a day for true Generosity. Do not cling to anything but the love of God today, knowing that it is yours to give to everyone you meet. Then you will understand love in a way that transcends logic.

—Brother

7/17/07

Daily Spiritual Peacemaking Lesson – *Day 63*

"Today I am Abundant enough to claim the Holy Mind of the Beloved."

True abundance leads to your constant perception of the Beloved, which you will SEE everywhere you look. You are already aware that this has nothing to do with money. If you judge your abundance according to the amount of money you possess, then you are poor indeed. True abundance is assigned to that which does not pass away in time. Love alone will suffice, for it is the only thing that will satisfy who you really are. Therefore, claim the Mind of the Beloved this day by focusing on what is already yours, and then you will understand what I am trying to teach you. You are already abundant, for the thing you most desire, Love, is all around and within you this moment. Claim it, and the Grace you seek will open before you.

—Brother

7/18/07

Daily Spiritual Peacemaking Lesson – Day 64

"Today I possess the Love to claim the Holy Mind of the Beloved."

If you want to attract something to your life, you must become that thing. If the perception of the Beloved is your truest desire, then you must adopt its very essence, which is love. You do not need to understand this with your mind, for the love you seek is wholly beyond the reach of its limited scope. Let go of trying to understand, and simply "be" love. Your mind will only slow you down, while your heart will guide you to your heart. Do you understand what I am trying to say here? Your heart will lead you to your heart because it is what you really want, and it is who you really are. Let love guide you in everything you do this day, and every moment. Seek only to be like love, and then love will draw you to the center of who you are.

Let this be a simple path, Beloved One. Open your heart today and I will teach you in new ways.

—Brother

Daily Spiritual Peacemaking Lesson – Day 65

Now that you have claimed the Holy Mind of the Beloved, now that it is yours, what will you do? How will it change the way you look upon your brothers and sisters and, therefore, your Self? All these lessons are designed to allow you to SEE the truth that is all around you. The Mind of the Beloved is intended for you to perceive and understand in a most natural manner, though it has been nearly forgotten. As you remember this, your life takes on an ease that was not present before, and the flow of Universal Peace becomes your companion. Think with this Mind today. Consciously choose to use it to reveal a new world. Then you will be ready to take the next step, which is to KNOW. That is where I will lead you now.

—Brother

7/26/07

Daily Spiritual Peacemaking Lesson – Day 66

"Today I claim the Holy Heart of the Beloved."

The Courage to Love as the Beloved.

In this world you have created, courage is required to go so completely against the decree of sickness, pain and death. Your life declares that only Love is real, and anything that seems to contradict Love is an illusion. Spend this day proclaiming the Reality of God in everything you do. Let every word you speak be the evidence that you do not need the world to prove anything, for it cannot reflect and extend the truth of who you really are. Today you will show the Courage that I showed when I walked on this earth.

—Brother

7/27/07

Daily Spiritual Peacemaking Lesson – Day 67

"Today I claim the Holy Heart of the Beloved."

The Patience to Love as the Beloved.

We will repeat this prayer for many days, knowing that the Heart of the Beloved is our only goal, and that it is the reason for our existence. You were born but to remember who you are, then to extend this as a gift to other sleeping minds. You are the Heart of the Beloved. It can be found nowhere except where you are. The problem you have had until now is that you have misidentified where you are. You have believed that you begin and end where your body is in a given moment, and that your body is the house for your personality, your soul, and all the things that define who you are. I say to you that there is no place where you begin and end, for the Truth within you cannot be defined by these limited means. You are the Holy Home of God, and God's Home is everywhere and nowhere at the same time. Will you allow your heart to be enfolded by this mystery today?

Your Patience will help you see the Holiness that has escaped your attention before now.

—Brother

7/28/07

Daily Spiritual Peacemaking Lesson – Day 68

"Today I claim the Holy Heart of the Beloved."

The Wisdom to Love as the Beloved.

You are already wise, for wisdom is like the blood that runs through your soul. But your wisdom cannot be revealed as long as you lie sleeping and cannot make the choices you would make while awake. As you claim the Holy Heart of the Beloved and know that it is yours, then will you stand within your Wisdom, and you will Know what is Known by God. You are That. Do you see that this is all God Knows, and now you can do the same? If you cannot be separated from God, and God is the fullness of creation Itself, then you are That as well. This experience is the essence of Wisdom, and it is something that can be seen even in this world. It is not something that can be spoken with words, but when you live this truth, it is made evident through you. Let this be your only goal today.

—Brother

Daily Spiritual Peacemaking Lesson – Day 69

"Today I claim the Holy Heart of the Beloved."

The Certainty to love as the Beloved.

What other than Certainty can lead to Love? God loves the essence of who you are. I'm not asking you to believe this, but to be Certain of it. Let this realization be your only prayer. This is the instant you choose to understand God's love by understanding who you are. Then you will give this gift to others. Then it will be secure within you.

—Brother

Daily Spiritual Peacemaking Lesson – Day 70

"Today I claim the Holy Heart of the Beloved."

The Compassion to Love as the Beloved.

You cannot claim the Heart of the Beloved, unless you become the Beloved. Do you believe that this is your goal, to become the Beloved? Your goal is to realize that you are inseparable from the Beloved, which you will find everywhere you look. You are that Now, and nothing can change what God has created Perfect.

Realize this! Open your eyes and SEE who you are, and perceive the Beloved everywhere. Then you will not need to think about Compassion, for it will be your natural state.

—Brother

8/5/07

Daily Spiritual Peacemaking Lesson – Day 71

"Today I claim the Holy Heart of the Beloved."

The Joy to Love as the Beloved.

Joy is the natural state of awakened minds, for they have seen past the world of form and disregard its effects. This is also the path for claiming the Heart of the Beloved. What is not real cannot affect you in any way. What is real is impossible for you to change. I am telling you this because it is true, not because I need you to believe it. If belief were necessary then we would emphasize the mental portion of this course more. What is important is your experience which transcends the mind altogether, piercing the soul which is your home. Let the Joy of God be yours this day, then the trivial things of this world will make no difference to you at all. Only the Heart of the Beloved will matter to you then.

—Brother

8/9/07

Daily Spiritual Peacemaking Lesson – Day 72

"Today I claim the Holy Heart of the Beloved."
The Clarity to Love as the Beloved.

"Give me a clear mind that I may See what is before me this day. Only then will I know that the Holy Heart of the Beloved is already mine. Give me the Clarity to break down all the imagined barriers that seem to keep me separate from the Beloved. They are not real, and so I will not let them deter me from my real goal. I am here to give everything to everything and, in doing so, to realize that there is nothing left for me to achieve. I am clear about my role, and I perform it with determination and joy, because I will to see this reflected everywhere I look. I now SEE what is true, and I disregard what has no reality at all. For what other reason am I here?"

—Brother

Daily Spiritual Peacemaking Lesson – Day 73

"Today I claim the Holy Heart of the Beloved."
The Understanding to Love as the Beloved.

"At last I Understand why I am here. I was confused for a very long time about this, but now I SEE that there can be but one true purpose. I am here to give Love to Love Itself, and to know that it is present everywhere. My gift is needed, even required, if the Peaceful Kingdom is to be realized on Earth. The world I created in my imagination is fading now as I perceive the world that God made for me. This Divine Understanding does not come to my human mind, but to the Heart of the Beloved itself, which is what I am. I will not try to carry my past concepts, for they will not help me now. I allow my heart to open and to remember the truth that cannot change. This is all that is required of me now for this Understanding to be made manifest."

—Brother

Daily Spiritual Peacemaking Lesson – Day 74

"Today I claim the Holy Heart of the Beloved."

The Depth to Love as the Beloved.

We have been focusing our attention on this prayer for an important reason. As you have already experienced, the repetition of some of these words can be enough to inspire a whole shift in consciousness. You have come to "claim" this state of consciousness because you realize it will not be handed to you until you ask for it. But you must first clearly define what it is that you want, or rather, what will satisfy you. This is not a new proposition, for you have spent your whole life seeking what you thought would satisfy you. And yet you weren't satisfied, because there is nothing in this world you have created in your imagination that will even begin to fill the void you believe you have. The Heart of the Beloved alone will do this, for it shows you that the void you thought you felt was only your soul's sense that you have misidentified your truest desire. This is the Depth you are searching for, and it is yours now. Claim it for yourself and for the whole universe and then you will know that I am correct in this.

—Brother

8/14/07

Daily Spiritual Peacemaking Lesson – Day 75

"Today I claim the Holy Heart of the Beloved."

The Abundance to Love as the Beloved.

This is the essence of Abundance, the love that sets you free. Let it be your only desire this day. Lay aside all other desires but this, for you are seeking your soul's satisfaction, and that can only happen in consort with God's will for you. Money will not satisfy you, and neither will anything else in this world. Love alone is what you came to give and receive. If you seek to serve rather than to be served, then you will understand the mystery of Abundance.

—Brother

8/15/07

Daily Spiritual Peacemaking Lesson – Day 76

"Today I claim the Holy Heart of the Beloved."

The Generosity to Love as the Beloved.

"Today I choose to be Generous in everything that is real. I am here to give love in every moment and to every person, for it is the only way I can fully enjoy the truth that cannot escape me. I will no longer ignore who I am, but give it to all."

To be generous with love is to remember who you are. Love is your foundation and source, and so must you give this gift in order for it to be yours. Do not hold back today. The Beloved is everywhere you look, if you would but have eyes to SEE. Give everything that is real, and do not worry about what has no reality at all. Then you will fall into the truth you seek, and it will fall into you as well. Let this be your only goal today.

—Brother

8/22/07

Daily Spiritual Peacemaking Lesson – Day 77

"Today I claim the Holy Heart of the Beloved."

The Love to Love as the Beloved.

This prayer may sound strange, but it is a symbol of how far you have come on this journey. You are entering a stage where you will see everything through the same lens, for love, as you have discovered, is the only thing that really exists. Your entire experience has been made up of the ways you have extended love, and the ways you have blocked it. Love can be yours in every moment, even when you are challenged by life. This is the only ground we walk together now, and the path grows more and more simple. You are ready to let the truth be true, or to let love guide every action and word. It is enough, just as you, in your essence, are forever loved by God.

—Brother

8/23/07

Daily Spiritual Peacemaking Lesson – *Day 78*

Today will begin a week of open prayer. I say open because that is how I need your mind and your heart to be if we are to welcome a New World. You have been focused on the Holy Heart and Mind of the Beloved for the last twenty-four lessons. It is your Heart and Mind, not one that is outside the truth of who you really are. I am drawing you to You. Do you see this? The only dilemma you have is that you have not believed this till now, but when you heal this seeming division, everything else falls into its perfect place. There are no true problems in the Universe, since everything, no matter how it may seem to you, falls into perfect balance when seen through the eyes of eternity. These are the eyes I am helping you open. It is how I SEE, and I am drawing you into the same vision. The fact that you are still reading these lessons says that you are ready. Will you accept my confidence? If you do, then you will accept my sight as well. Let this be your goal, for I am willing to share everything with you.

—Brother

8/24/07

Daily Spiritual Peacemaking Lesson – *Day 79*

The world you see with your eyes is not the real world. The world you perceive, or SEE, with your soul is eternal, and is therefore true. When you seek this Truth above all things, then you discover who you are, for you cannot be separated from the Truth except in your dreams. Seek to Know by Giving what you Know. This should be the only thing you think about, the pervading desire of your whole mind. Wholeness is returning to you now, for it never left. You are discovering this NOW, since NOW is the only moment such a discovery is possible.

—Brother

9/1/07

Daily Spiritual Peacemaking Lesson – *Day 80*

There is nothing I have to teach you. In fact, there is nothing I have to say at all that will help you in any way. Does this surprise you? It is the only way real learning can take place in this relationship we have formed, and, of course, that is why you are here. If I thought that I had something that I could give to you, something that you do not already have, then we would be helpless together. The blind cannot lead the blind, except into greater confusion. I am not confused, and, therefore, I do not offer you a confusing perspective. I am here to tell you the truth, that there is nothing that I have that is not already complete within you. Throughout this course I have asked you to believe me, to trust me enough to consider this, even for a moment. An instant of truthful consideration can make all the difference. It is the difference between freedom and bondage.

—Brother

9/2/07

Daily Spiritual Peacemaking Lesson – *Day 81*

The Truth cannot be shared. That is why I am not trying to share anything with you, but to reveal what is hidden. If I thought that I had anything to share, then I would be of no value. Anyone who realizes that Truth cannot be shared has total value, and that is what we are after.

That being said, sharing does have value within the context of the shift you are undergoing. I will on one hand offer you the Truth, then I will offer a path to the Truth. Do not confuse the two. Sometimes a means to an end is not the actual end. In other words, it seems that we have entered into a relationship where something is being shared. Though this is not true, we can use this illusion to lead into the Truth.

That is the function of a Spiritual Peacemaker, and it is now your function.

—Brother

Hard to understand!

9/6/07

Daily Spiritual Peacemaking Lesson – Day 82

I ask one thing today -- (that you speak to the world with my voice.) It is not the voice of a particular personality that I am asking you to adopt. I am not the historical figure that you once believed in. I cannot be contained within your definitions just as you cannot be imprisoned by your own. I am one who saw the chains that had been wrapped around my Being, and found a way to break free. You too will break free if you learn whose voice it is that speaks AS you. It is the Voice of Awakened Consciousness I am asking you to claim, which has been known by many names. Today it is known by the name YOU claim. Trust that I am right about this and it is so. Speak today with the voice that cuts past all error, and leads everyone who hears it into the Light.

—Brother

9/8/07

Daily Spiritual Peacemaking Lesson – Day 83

Today is a day to refrain from looking for everything you think you lost. Your holiness is still with you, for it has been guaranteed by God. Your Grace is perfect, and so perfection flows from everything you say or do. I ask only that you realize this, that you open your eyes and SEE what is so clear to me. You have been looking for the Truth of your existence in the only place it cannot be found. Look within, and know it is already yours. Then these words will make perfect sense, and a second later you will forget they even existed.

—Brother

9/9/07

Daily Spiritual Peacemaking Lesson – *Day 84*

Call to me as I call to you, and then you will Know what is Known by God. There is nothing else for you to do, for the experience of your Divinity will give you everything you are searching for. It begins with your willingness to give what you want. Decide, then, what means the most in your Life. Is there anything in this world that will produce the peace you desire in your deepest heart? Or does this longing spring from a place beyond this small existence, a place that exists beyond the limits of time and space? You are there with me now, and that is why I am asking you to call to me, so you will recognize who it is that stands at your side. Then I can be truly helpful, which is what I am also asking of you. We will do this together, for this is what was ordained before time began. You are ready, and you are here to initiate a new level. That is why I have called you to be a Spiritual Peacemaker.

—Brother

Daily Spiritual Peacemaking Lesson – *Day 85*

You have been called to remember so that others may remember through you. This is what it means to be helpful in the truest sense. How can you help awaken your brothers and sisters if you are sleeping at their side? You must first open your eyes and SEE what is really happening before you can interpret the world for one who does not see. This is not at all dependent on your physical eyes. They were, in fact, made NOT to see what is real. They show you the world that exists for your ego, not your soul. And yet, as you bless this world, it is replaced by the world created for you by God. Choose to SEE today, and to offer this sight through little actions. God's love is not grandiose, and you would do well to follow the example set by the teachers who have demonstrated simplicity. They are the ones who have truly listened.

—Brother

Daily Spiritual Peacemaking Lesson – Day 86

Is it possible for you to imagine yourself to be the same as me? What could possibly make us different? All I am trying to communicate is that differences in the Eyes of God are impossible; therefore, we are One. Will you give yourself the gift of this recognition? Will you allow the truth of this to invade your consciousness and replace all the untrue ideas that have limited your experience of love? Begin by realizing that your brothers and sisters are the same as you, are indeed One with you. Then see through my awakened eyes, and you will discover it is the same. Then the world you thought you created will cease to exist. That will be a very good day.

—Brother

9/12/07

Daily Spiritual Peacemaking Lesson – Day 87

It is time for you to ask yourself a very important question: "Why are you here?" If you are able to answer this, then your life will shift and you will be the helpful Emissary you have imagined yourself to be.

I will give you the answer that I found:

"I am here to realize the flow of love that comes to me from my Father/Mother God, then offer that flow to others. Only then can I be truly helpful in the world."

How will you answer?

—Brother

9/24/07

Daily Spiritual Peacemaking Lesson – Day 88

There is nothing that you can hold in your imagination that you cannot create. Until now you have held many dark images that reflected your original fear. It is no wonder, then, that these images found their way into your world. Now you realize that you have always had a choice about this, and that you can now choose again. What will you do with this choice? Now that you understand that the world you perceive is nothing more than an out-picturing of what you believe, how will you use this knowledge? I suggest that you be wise and use it to heal, for that is why you came. You have chosen to be a Spiritual Peacemaker, and that requires a serious commitment to healing. You do not need to say a word to anyone about this, but you do need to let them see it in your eyes. Then your brothers and sisters will remember themselves through you. That is why you have come into this world.

—Brother

Daily Spiritual Peacemaking Lesson – Day 89

Have compassion for the Beloveds who are just beginning to open their eyes and remember who they are and why they are here, and have greater compassion for those who are still dreaming. Remember, they are not outside you in any way. They are aspects of your own imagining that separation is possible, and that your dreams could ever be made real. The greater your compassion, the easier it will be to look past these impossible illusions. When you wake up, the whole world wakes up with you, no matter how it may appear to your physical eyes. An Awakened Mind perceives Holiness even in the darkest places. It is time for you to stop being fooled, and to realize that you are in perfect control.

—Brother

Daily Spiritual Peacemaking Lesson – Day 90

The image you are holding of yourself right now is nothing more than a frame of reference. Realize this, and then you will find your Self standing at Heaven's Door. No frame of reference is different than any other because of the one who exists behind them all. That is the Beloved, and it is who you are. You can choose to SEE through any eyes, for you do not need to be limited in any way. You can choose to SEE through my eyes if you want, and in doing so, you will KNOW what I KNOW. Why? Because there is no difference, as I said before. You are not limited by the chains you think you have fashioned around yourself. You only seem to be imprisoned. The door is already unlocked and is even ajar. Don't limit your Self any longer. The recognition of the ONE who exists behind all frames of reference is your goal, and you will achieve that goal by SEEING what is true in others. There is no other thing in this world that will satisfy your soul as completely as this. But practice and diligence are required. Let this be a day devoted to both.

—Brother

Daily Spiritual Peacemaking Lesson – Day 91

Call to the One behind the veil of your consciousness, and then listen for the answer that is sure to follow. I promise you that you will not search in vain, and your call will not go unheard. Have faith that the path I once walked is the path you are walking now. I can guide you because I have already passed by this place. My feet have already touched the terrain that causes you to stumble and fall. Today I am asking you to trust this. I have asked this many times, because trust is so important at this stage of your learning. There are so many masters who are at your side, and they long to reveal the lessons they have learned. Listen today and know that our voices are One. There is, in fact, but one answer, one voice, and one moment of your awakening. It is now!

—Brother

Daily Spiritual Peacemaking Lesson – Day 92

God is calling you into an experience of intimacy that is completely foreign to the world you have made. How will you respond? Will you say yes and participate in the world that was created for you, or will you choose instead the dreams that have never filled the void you thought was there? There is no void, just as there is nothing outside for you to claim. I am within you now, calling you to awaken. Wake up.

10/4/07

—Brother

Daily Spiritual Peacemaking Lesson – Day 93

If you only knew what you were giving up to stay where you are, you would let loose and trust the song that sings within you now. Say YES this moment and really mean it. Let God hear and Know that you are serious about this path. God will respond, but only if you create the opening for that response.

10/15/07

—Brother

*Daily Spiritual Peacemaking Lesson – **Day 94***

God's intimacy is yours. It cannot be separated because that is what spiritual intimacy is. It is being held out to you this moment. Will you choose to accept it?

These lessons are short and their messages direct. Let the truth be simple. Reach forward and do not try to understand more than needs to be understood. Just give everything and love everyone. That is the only real thing I can teach you now.

—Brother

10/20/07

*Daily Spiritual Peacemaking Lesson – **Day 95***

There is nothing more important than this: To give who you are, every instant of Life, rather than who you want to be. You are here to become AS God, and you cannot do that so long as you believe that you must be different from how you were created. You are still being created, and that is why you have not changed. The desire to be something else is born from your frustration that who you are is not enough. It is, but you must give of this if you are to receive. Allow others to be their Blessed Selves and it will be natural for you to do the same for yourself. Let this be the day when you focus on giving the truth of your Divine Presence.

—Brother

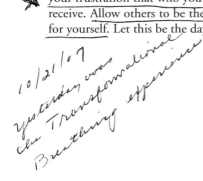

10/21/07
yesterday was the Transformational Breathing experience

Daily Spiritual Peacemaking Lesson – Day 96

There is nothing you have to offer the Universe on your own that has any value at all, and yet, what is offered THROUGH you is immeasurable. You are here to be an instrument of peace. It is all you are here to accomplish. And yet, to give up the dream you have made on this earth is a great accomplishment, and that is why your role is so valuable. Just try to remember that it is not you who is doing the work. That is the easiest way for you to lose track of who you are. Remember instead that God is revealing a New World through you, ★ and then be willing to be used. Being used by eternity is the greatest gift you can receive.

—Brother

0/23/07

Daily Spiritual Peacemaking Lesson – Day 97

When there is nothing left in this world that pulls you away from your Divine Mission and Presence, then you will know you have truly surrendered to the Will that Made You. Are you able to understand what I mean by this? You have come far enough to know that this is why you are here, and that it is the only thing that is important if you are serious about being a Spiritual Peacemaker. Why are you so concerned about the things that will not be present in a very short while? Nothing that passes away with time has any real value, for only the Gifts of Eternity are real. Place your focus here today and always. Surrender fully and let the Gift be yours. It is waiting for you, AS YOU.

—Brother

11/3/07

Daily Spiritual Peacemaking Lesson – Day 98

If you have embraced your Eternal Nature, then it means you have learned what has real value. That is what you are here to accomplish and KNOW, for nothing else will ever satisfy you. Do you want to travel through this world time and time again, never realizing the Love that made you? You have done this too many times, and yet this is the moment you decided to choose another path, which is the only path that leads to Truth. How will we define this Truth? We won't, and that is how we know we will achieve it. We will leave the mind behind and embrace the wisdom of the Spirit. It will give us everything we truly want, and will let the illusions fade that once claimed our minds. If this is what you truly want, then it is yours NOW.

—Brother

Daily Spiritual Peacemaking Lesson – Day 99

The mysteries of Heaven are only mysterious to the one whose physical eyes are open, and whose spiritual eyes are closed. You have come to the point where there is nothing hidden from you. The only question is, will you choose to SEE? You have decided that the world you created is not the world you really want, and that there is another creation that was made for you by God. You have said YES to this world, and yet it is not an affirmation that is contingent upon time, but upon eternity. Your YES must resound every moment, every instant of your life, and thus will your spiritual eyes remain open. Let this be your only goal now, for, as we have said many times before, it is the only thing that will satisfy you.

—Brother

Daily Spiritual Peacemaking Lesson – Day 100

Open your eyes this moment. Look around your Self and SEE what is there. Do you perceive a world of bodies and personalities, a world where nothing is the same a moment from now, or a year, or a hundred years? The world God offers you never changes at all, but is revealed even deeper as you choose to experience the depth of your own soul. The Truth in you cannot change, and that is why nothing that does change will ever satisfy you. The Truth in you is eternal, and that is why you must offer unconditional love to everyone, for only then will you know the Love God has for you. It is so simple. Are you ready to realize that? I can only offer it to you, but you must accept it from me. You have done so, and in that I do rejoice. Open your eyes this moment, then, and choose again. You were just born a moment ago.

—Brother

Daily Spiritual Peacemaking Lesson – Day 101

Today we will rise above the world of bodies and form in order to perceive what is True. We will use this mantra for the next week:

"Only the Beloved is Real."

Say these words as often as you can throughout the day. Over the course of the next week I will give you a series of concepts to focus your mind on, all of which are designed to take you out of the mind altogether.

Today's Meditation:

"Today the Holy Mind of God rises like a ribbon above me. My mind releases all the things that do not serve my real goal, and I allow this ribbon take me to the Home I never left. The chaos of this world disappears as I say these words, and focus my mind and heart on love: Only the Beloved is Real. Only the Beloved is Real."

—Brother

Daily Spiritual Peacemaking Lesson – Day 102

Only the Beloved is Real.

"Today I let the foundation of the Real World be revealed to me. I do not need to ask for anything except this Truth, for everything else I need flows naturally from this holy font. And yet, without this foundation, I am not strong enough to receive the Gifts of God. Today I claim the strength that is my right, and as I do so I am able to SEE the Truth of Creation. Only the Beloved is Real. Only the Beloved is real."

—Brother

Daily Spiritual Peacemaking Lesson – Day 103

Only the Beloved is Real.

If this is true, then there is nothing that can harm you in any way. That is because only love proceeds from the Beloved, and that is what you really want. The only thing that can hurt you is what your soul does not want, and yet you seek after it anyway. This is the ego's ultimate revenge, for to seek and never find is the punishment it believes you deserve. You are only punishing yourself, and now that you realize this, you can choose again. Say these words as often as you can today to help you remember your soul's highest goal. Remembering is the first step. The second is the willingness to act upon this memory. Luckily, that is where your role ends, for the Holy Spirit is there to do the rest.

—Brother

Daily Spiritual Peacemaking Lesson – *Day 104*

Only the Beloved is Real.

Is this thought too simple for you to give all of your energy and Love? This is the only thing I have been drawing your mind to, knowing all the while that your heart is sure to follow. You have built your own world in order to deny this, and you have created an infinite number of "things" that make you doubt this simple truth. I am asking you to offer me your hand and trust that I am able to see something that is still slightly obscure to you. The more you trust me, the clearer it will become. Clarity is the goal, not changing what cannot change. Then you will realize that you cannot change yourself either, and then you will be close to understanding the Love of God.

—Brother

Daily Spiritual Peacemaking Lesson – *Day 105*

Only the Beloved is Real.

The reality you perceive within yourself is the same as what you perceive on the outside. That is because there is no such thing as inside or out. There only "IS" the Beloved in everything and in every way. The shift of your awareness from the ego's frame of reference into God's is required if you are to KNOW the Truth. Nothing really changes, however, because reality cannot be changed or threatened. This is your salvation, and it is the only thing that will bring you true happiness, which is God's Will for you. Rest as often as you can in this Holy Knowledge. Continue to repeat these words throughout the day, knowing that they are more than words, the foundation of reality Itself. What God wants for you and what you want for yourself is the same.

—Brother

Daily Spiritual Peacemaking Lesson – Day 106

Only the Beloved is Real.

Small children must be carefully watched so they don't fall into danger. And yet, they must also learn on their own what will hurt them and what won't, otherwise they will never become mature. A good parent is able to see and practice this fine balance. God's attitude to you is very much the same. You have been protected from any real harm since nothing unreal really exists. And yet, you have been given the opportunity to "believe" it is real in order to remember who you are. This would not be necessary if you never forgot, and yet the help you need is gladly offered.

Remember this: As you grow and mature spiritually, there is only one thing for you to realize. "Only the Beloved is real."

—Brother

Daily Spiritual Peacemaking Lesson – Day 107

Only the Beloved is Real

Today you are the Hands, the Feet and the Voice of God in the world. To accomplish this, you must be "AS" God in everything you do, and in everything you SEE. There is nothing to deny or condemn, for God never condemns Itself. God's love only blesses, and so this is what you will do as you move through this place of dreams. Be conscious of who you are and why you are here. Extend the hand of God to your brothers and sisters on the path. Let them hear the sweet sounds of compassion as you speak to them, telling them of the love that can never change. It does not matter what you say, but that your words come from that vast place of KNOWING who you are. Let this be a day for practicing what is true.

—Brother

Daily Spiritual Peacemaking Lesson – Day 108

Only the Beloved is Real

Look around the world you made and SEE what is real. The bodies and the symbols of separation you perceive are like costumes that hide this from you. Look past them today. Try to see what I see, and what every illumined, awakened one perceives. Know that there is no difference between you and I, and it will be easy. That is the key. The distance you thought was present is only an illusion. The Beloved is before us now and waits upon our sweet recognition. Offer it gladly, and it will be given back to you.

—Brother

Daily Spiritual Peacemaking Lesson – Day 109

You have been told that seeing through enlightened eyes takes time, and that it is difficult to master. It is not true. Let go of this terrible belief. These were words spoken by the part of you that is afraid to SEE. But now you realize that there is no reason to be afraid, and you willingly open your eyes in order to perceive the world God made for you. Let go of the belief that anything must change. The truth in you cannot change, and that is the only thing I am trying to get you to understand. Enlightenment is the most subtle shift you will ever experience. When it happens, if it hasn't happened already, you will wonder why you waited so long.

—Brother

Daily Spiritual Peacemaking Lesson – Day 110

Only the Beloved is Real

As you accept this single truth, all is revealed for all is contained here. Is it true that God exists at one point, and that that same point is universal and omnipresent? Then is truth the same as God, for if God is one and all truth lies therein, then there is only one thing for you to learn. And what is that? Simply this: Only the Beloved is real." If you can learn to perceive this truth everywhere, then you will be as God, for that is the only thing the Beloved does, is perceive Itself. Are you beginning to understand that this is what it means to be a Spiritual Peacemaker? You have not chosen this path as it may seem. It, as you have probably guessed, chose you. Will you respond? Do you have the courage to believe that you are here to be as God?

—Brother

Daily Spiritual Peacemaking Lesson – Day 111

Only the Beloved is Real.

> To See as God Sees.
>
> To Feel as God Feels.
>
> To Know what God Knows.
>
> The Beloved Sees only the Beloved.

Meditate one this mantra. It will teach you everything you need to know. You were born to reveal the Light of God where it has been hidden in darkness. You are here to be an Instrument of Peace. To do this then you must learn how to enter into the Mind of God. You do not do this with your own mind, but with your heart. This is not an analytical process, but one of surrendering to the source of your very life. As you enter into the Mind of God with your heart, then the Heart of God is revealed to you. The Heart is the teacher you have been looking for.

—Brother

Daily Spiritual Peacemaking Lesson – Day 112

Only the Beloved is Real.

Is it possible that you are standing now at the very brink of Love Itself, and the fulfillment of all your desires? Look around you now and ask yourself what you see. If you are alone look at the seeming inanimate objects that fill the room you are in. Describe them to yourself. You may see a blue lamp, or a wooden chair. If you are in a place where you see other people, describe what they look like. You may see a woman with blonde hair, or an old man with a gray mustache. This is what your eyes would show you, and what your mind would define. Now close your eyes and FEEL them as if you are God, even the inanimate objects. What are they made of? Feel that. What is their essence or source? Now feel that. Notice how different this perception is from what you employed a moment before. Now, as you continue to FEEL everything around you, say over and over, sensing the truth within each word: "Only the Beloved is Real." The words you say are true. Know this, and you will know everything.

—Brother

Daily Spiritual Peacemaking Lesson – Day 113

The Beloved in you never sleeps, but is awake watching only what is real. What is it, then, that makes you seem to sleep? It is simply a belief that separation is possible. Because you were created from God and have never left your source, your beliefs have the power to create a kind of reality, though it has no real effects. This is what you have done, and you have decided that this creation is more real than God's. Give up this belief and it is gone. Change your mind and the world changes as a result.

Are you willing to consider that salvation is this simple?

—Brother

Daily Spiritual Peacemaking Lesson – Day 114

What is it in you that searches for love? The answer is simple: It is love Itself. You have forgotten who you are and are therefore always searching for your Self. There are so many things you think you want in the world, but when you achieve them the longing for more persists. What is this 'more' you long for? What is it that fills that seeming void and sets you firm upon the Holy Path of Illumination? It is YOU, and you are Love. It is the Truth in you that you are seeking, and when you find it, then all other things flow naturally into your heart. Seek only what has real value, then, and let the unreal gifts of the ego pass by you like wind. Then the love you seek and the love you are, are realized as One, and you are contained within that Oneness.

—Brother

Daily Spiritual Peacemaking Lesson – Day 115

The love you seem to be seeking outside yourself is not outside at all, but within you. Look at the person who is standing in front of you right now, especially if you call this one your Beloved. Do you want them to remain 'outside' where you can never fully contain the passion of your soul? Or would it be better to know that they are sparking something that is already inside, and that this is their gift to you. Their gift is what you choose to see within both of you, not without. You can be the same gift to them, but only if you realize that love is the goal, not possession. You cannot possess another and you cannot possess love. Look into the eyes of the one in front of you now and realize the real gift they hold. Hold each other with open hands, for love is not real unless it is free, and you will not know the truth that lives within you now unless you allow the same freedom.

—Brother

Daily Spiritual Peacemaking Lesson – Day 116

The Way of the Heart is to Love without condition. The Way of the Soul is to realize that God's Love is within you Now. When you realize this, then you will be able to act as God, with God, and through God. This is why you were born into this world. Will you choose to fulfill the choice you made before you were born? Let this be the day of Holy Decision.

—Brother

Daily Spiritual Peacemaking Lesson – Day 117

(The next lessons are a code for the soul, leading you into an experience that no words can explain. Few words are given here, but there is a depth they contain which the mind cannot fathom. The soul, however, waits upon your discovery. Open your eyes, then, and SEE.)

A single point of Light will lead the way to the Door of Eternity. All others fall in around this single ray, filled by the instant of your purist realization. "Where will you find me?"

—Brother

Daily Spiritual Peacemaking Lesson – Day 118

(Continue with this code today. Read it often and let your mind relax. It cannot help you here.)

A single point of Light leads the way to the Door of Eternity. It is smaller than your eyes can possibly see, and yet it is all around you every moment of your life. I have told you that you are ready to finally realize this Great Gift. You have chosen, and now it is yours. "Show me this Light I speak of."

—Brother

Daily Spiritual Peacemaking Lesson – Day 119

A single point of Light will lead the way to the Door of Eternity. If you look at the end of every question you will find it quietly resting there. There is no solution to this for there is nothing it seeks to reveal, save the opening that is all around you even now. The Door is open. Say Yes, realize who you are, and then step forward. Angels await your step of faith. They will not let you fall.

—Brother

Daily Spiritual Peacemaking Lesson – Day 120

The Point of Light within is the touch of the Divine upon your awakened heart. It is there to remind you that the world that seems to attack you is not real, and that you can escape from it at any moment, whenever you decide to return to Love. Your heart is already awake, but your sleeping mind does not allow the connection between the two to be complete. This is the split that has made this world seem possible. When you realize that your heart and mind are really one, then you will SEE and UNDERSTAND everything else as one. This is what it means to be enlightened.

—Brother

Daily Spiritual Peacemaking Lesson – Day 121

The Point of Light that is being shown to you now is who you really are. You are the touch of Divinity upon your heart and soul. You are the single realization of Light that descends into the world of form to forgive and release. This is why you came here, to remember this and to act upon it. Your action secures your release, and the release of all your brothers and sisters. They do not need to do anything, for they are in your mind. Do not think that they are in yours as well, otherwise you will miss the gift that is being offered to you. Trust the Light that reveals this moment of grace, and release the need to comprehend it with your linear mind. It cannot understand, for it is this small part of you that created the seeming problem of separation. Let it go completely, and come with empty hands unto your God.

—Brother

Daily Spiritual Peacemaking Lesson – Day 122

There is nothing for you to fear now, for the Light has come to dispel the terrible shadows that seemed to attack you. They had no real form, except in your mind. You are like a child that looks around her dark room making up stories about the things she knows are not real. A chair becomes a dragon and a toy becomes a monster. But in the end she knows that they cannot attack her, and that she is perfectly safe. Look around yourself now and realize that you are safe as well. There is nothing that can attack you, save your own mind that pulls your belief. Turn on the light and they are gone. Then you remember that there is nothing for you to fear.

—Brother

Daily Spiritual Peacemaking Lesson – Day 123

The Christ in you is already awake, and therefore needs nothing to prove that it exists. There is another part of your mind, which only seems to exist, that constantly tries to convince you that it is real; and yet there is nothing that it pulls around itself that proves anything but death and destruction. It builds a world that seems to prove its existence, but all the laws of this world are the opposite of the laws of God. God's law proclaims only love and life, while the world you have created leads but to death. And this you have chosen gladly, and until now, have refused to abandon.

This is the path you have chosen to walk until now. I bring this back to your awareness because it is important for you to realize what you are choosing against, otherwise the veil will fall again over your spiritual eyes and you will decide again upon the dream of death. Let every word you speak proclaim life, not death. The Christ in you cannot die, and that means you cannot die. Do you understand what I mean? It is like saying that "You are who you are." Let this be true, and it is.

—Brother

Daily Spiritual Peacemaking Lesson – Day 124

A shadow can only convince you of its reality for so long before you see it what it really is. When it no longer moves according to the laws you know in your soul, then you will look to what is casting that shadow, and when you see this source you will release it altogether by turning on the Light.

The shadow that is before you now is the purpose that you have given this world. You have proclaimed it to be a place where people come to live for a while then die, rarely reaching the goal set before them by God. Have you come to the point where this no longer satisfies you? I assume you have, otherwise you would not be reading these lessons. Know that this is the most important moment you can create here, for the instant you are willing to look at the cause of the shadow of this world is the same instant it is dispelled. You have created a world that only seems to exist, but because it is only a shadow of the world God made, it will never satisfy you. Choose to SEE past this illusion and let the vision of Christ be yours. Then you will know that you are a Spiritual Peacemaker, because you will have learned to live in the world without being claimed by it.

—Brother

Daily Spiritual Peacemaking Lesson – Day 125

All I can tell you for sure is that you, as you are perceived by God, exist, while the world you seem to have created to hide from God does not. I know that this is a difficult leap for you, but you have already come far enough where the idea is not completely foreign. All I am asking is that you surrender the last vestige of your concepts of who you are and why you are here, and trust that I can see farther. If you do, then you will rise to the same level and see the distant horizon just as I am looking at it now. Once you have seen what I am looking upon, your belief will be unnecessary. Then you will possess the certainty that I possess, and you will know that we are the same. Then, just as I have done, you will turn back to the brothers and sisters who are one with you and proclaim what you have seen. Then they will follow you into the Light, simply because the Love you look upon is so compelling.

—Brother

Daily Spiritual Peacemaking Lesson – Day 126

The world you have created in your imagination, and which until now you have refused to release, offers fleeting moments of peace, and because your soul identifies with the reality of peace, it believes that it has found its home. But what if you realized that there is another world a step beyond this one where the peace you desire does not move away from you so fast, and rests within your mind for all eternity. You do not need to limit your Self, for God has not placed any limits on the peace you can enjoy. I am asking you to consider that the moments of grace you enjoy in this world are but a glance at the peace that awaits you. You do not need to die to enter the Real World, as you were once told. It is here now, a single step away from where you now stand. Follow me and I will show it to you, then we will motion back to these others that they may too enjoy this joyous vision.

—Brother

Daily Spiritual Peacemaking Lesson – Day 127

You are the single point of Light that saves the world. You are a Spiritual Peacemaker now, and remember why you came to this earth, to see past it and reveal the Kingdom of Peace that is and will always be your Home. Your consciousness has been distracted for while, and you have disassociated from this truth. But all dreams must end, and so does this one breathe its last breath.

There is no reason for you to wonder if you are learning this course or not. There is no way you can miss the Truth when you stand so close. My only job is to keep telling you what is real, knowing that you are waking from a dream and will soon make sense of my words. Your only job is to stretch then open your eyes, just as you do every morning. The Real World is before you now. Remember Love, and you will understand what I mean.

—Brother

Daily Spiritual Peacemaking Lesson – Day 128

The Universe calls to you each moment with a question that you must answer. You must answer because it determines the world that you choose to See, which decides, of course, the world you choose to experience. You already know that you are not a victim of the world you perceive. You created it as surely as you created yourself. And that is why it is always changing, because your ideas of yourself are always changing. God's idea of you never changes, for God knows that you cannot change from the perfection in which you were created. Therefore, the question before you is meant to lead you toward that unchangeable experience:

"What would God choose to SEE Now?"

In every moment of your life, be willing to ask this question of yourself. What choice would you make in any given moment if you knew that you are one with God? In other words, what choice would God make, THROUGH and AS you? Let this thought fill your day, your week, and every moment of your life. Know that this simple question has the power to change the way you SEE everything, and therefore, how you will relate to everything. In essence, this question, properly understood, will change the world.

—Brother

Daily Spiritual Peacemaking Lesson – Day 129

I have already said that enlightenment is related only to what you are willing to SEE, rather than what you are, or what you are becoming. You are as God created you. That fact is beyond your negotiation. You can only choose whether or not you want to experience that fact, which until now you have refused to do. Until now you have chosen to see what wasn't there, and so you began to perceive yourself as an illusion. Do you see how these two are related? As you give so shall you receive. The moment you choose to SEE what IS there, then the spell that has been cast over your mind is broken and you begin to remember who you are and why you are here. This is the only thing you must change, the way you See.

Continue to ask yesterday's question as often as you can as you go through your day. "What would God choose to SEE Now?" A single instant of True Sight is all that is needed to convince you that your former way of seeing the world is no longer what you want.

—Brother

Daily Spiritual Peacemaking Lesson – Day 130

Allow God to SEE the world through you, then you will Know the truth that cannot change. Do not try to see anything on your own. That is what you have done till now and it has only revealed a world that is not real. Choose to give your eyes to the One who knows how to look upon the world. Once you change the way you SEE, then the world will change as well. Then you will understand the Art of Spiritual Peacemaking.

—Brother

Daily Spiritual Peacemaking Lesson – Day 131

Enlightenment is related to how you See, not what you do. And yet, when you See Truly, then what you do, or how you live your life, automatically adjusts to reflect who you are. The opposite has also been true. You chose to look upon sin and death, and were surprised when a world rose around you that seemed to support your decision. What do you think will happen if you choose to See only Life? Is it possible that the former world will be replaced by one where only Light Prevails? If the world you perceive is not real, but rather, is the extension of the decisions you make about yourself, then this shouldn't surprise you at all. The world is changing every moment, and yet you are so accustomed to this constant shifting that you no longer even notice it. And there is a good reason for this. If you did realize how transient this world is, then you would be willing to see past its inconsistencies and look upon the Real World instead.

That is why I am calling you to See as God Sees every moment, for it is the only way to release the world you thought was there, in favor of a world that reflects who you really are. The world that reflects "who you are not" is beginning to fade, and you are finally able to SEE clearly.

—Brother

Daily Spiritual Peacemaking Lesson – Day 132

Today's lesson is to watch for the subtle, yet very real ways your world is changing as you choose to SEE what is real. Look with gentle eyes upon your brothers and sisters today, and then notice how everything else changes. It is this practice that will make these lessons come alive. Until you are willing to practice, and then See what you practicing reveals, they are only concepts in your mind, and have no meaning at all. Let this day be for Seeing, not thinking. Look upon the holiness that is all around you. Choose the Vision of God, and everything else will find its perfect place.

—Brother

Daily Spiritual Peacemaking Lesson – Day 133

God looks upon the world and smiles, for who can attack their own creations if they come from love? Yet, you look upon the world you created with distain and distrust, for it rose from a cloud of fear used to hide the Real World from your sight. A single breath is all that is required for this Blessed State to return to your awareness. I came into the world to reveal what I was able to SEE. You share my mission because you heard me call to you before you were born, just as I heard the call of the Holy Spirit before my feet ever touched this earth. Will you follow me now to the resurrection and the ascension into Life? If you stop at the Crucifixion, then you will never enjoy the fruit that is yours as surely as it is mine. You were not born to rot and decay. You were born to be a witness, then an example of Life, which this world cannot understand. Do not stop for anything. Continue to follow me on this path and we will arrive at our Divine Parent's Home together. Then you will SEE for yourself that your mission was True.

—Brother

Daily Spiritual Peacemaking Lesson – Day 134

The world responds to the purpose that you give it. I use the word "give," in the present tense, instead of "gave," very purposely. You are giving the world a new purpose every moment, simply because the past cannot exist unless you bring it into the present moment. You are the one who does this, not time. Time waits upon you, not the other way around. If you decide that the past is worthy of your present creation, then it will reflect it in some details, but not all. The fact that it cannot mirror every detail should be a sign of its inherent instability and, therefore, unreality. That is because the Reality cannot change and is never unstable, simply because it was created by God. The Beloved does not look to the past to define anything, but to the present moment, being the very cause of everything it perceives, rather than the effect.

—Brother

Daily Spiritual Peacemaking Lesson – Day 135

Do you realize that you already answered the call to Grace, and are now simply reliving that choice? The only way I can know that the end is guaranteed is because I have already seen it. You have seen it, too, for we stood together on that day when all shadows were dispelled. To you it still feels like a dream, and I am simply one who woke up from the dream a moment before you. Do not think that it was more than a moment, for time can sometimes seems like an insurmountable obstacle. Your eyes are beginning to flicker now, for my hand is placed lightly upon your shoulder. Wake up, Beloved. You don't want to miss what I now look upon.

—Brother

Daily Spiritual Peacemaking Lesson – Day 136

Is it hard for you to believe that everything you think or do is a choice, and that you will experience your choices exactly as you choose them? This may seem obvious, but it may be more difficult for you to realize that the world you created is a choice as well. If this is not true, then it would be possible for you to be a victim, and if it is possible for you to be a victim, then you would not be able to choose, then experience, the Real World. You would forever be captive here, unable to do anything unless it is ordained for you by a source outside your Self.

God would not do this to you, so why do you choose to do it to yourself?

Now that you have made the choice to be a Spiritual Peacemaker in a world of your own making, you are free of all captivity. There will be moments when you forget this, even today, for the pull of your former thought system is very strong. But the more you choose the Real World, the sooner the other will disappear altogether.

—Brother

Daily Spiritual Peacemaking Lesson – Day 137

Your mind and your heart are meant to serve you. Until now they have served a phantom that they have never seen, but which they believe is real. They believe it is real because you told them that it is, and they are forever obliged to follow your will. You have done this because you placed the power of creation that was given you by God in the hands of a shadow figure that you perceived to be more powerful than the truth in you. Such a thing is impossible. The ego is not real, and therefore has no power. The moment you realize that you are still as God created you, is the same moment you will awaken from the dream the ego tried to show you, and then your mind and heart will follow. They are here to serve you, and they will do just that if you remember who you are.

—Brother

Daily Spiritual Peacemaking Lesson – Day 138

There is only one prayer I have for myself, and it is the same prayer I have for you. I pray that the Light may be perfectly revealed. How can I hold myself separate from you or anything else? For the Light to be revealed, I must know that we are not separate and alone, but forever joined in Light. This is my prayer for you this day as you open more to this overwhelming current of joy. Know that I am with you, in my thoughts, and at your side.

—Brother

Daily Spiritual Peacemaking Lesson – Day 139

Live within the Eternal YES and remember who you are. Remember that in the original Spiritual Peacemaking lessons I said that to a master, every word, thought and action comes from the same place - YES. The specifics of the situation mean nothing, only the inner motivation. Even if you act outwardly in a way that may appear conflicted, if the YES is present then all thing align. Let this be your only goal, then, to BE this YES. All I can say is that it is already what and who you are. God did not create no, for it would seem to cancel Reality Itself. Such an illusion is impossible. As you practice being YES, then you will remember all these things, not with your mind but with your whole Self.

You are already a Spiritual Peacemaker.

—Brother

Daily Spiritual Peacemaking Lesson – Day 140

Asking you to live within the YES is the same as asking you to pretend that you're enlightened. They are more than related because they lead to the very same place. Remember that the ideas of YES and of enlightenment are just that—ideas. They are no more real than anything else in this world. But they lead to the same experience, and that is the only thing that is real in this world. It is the experience of the Eternal Love of God, and that is what you are longing for. Every ounce of your being shouts to remember this great rush of Light, and so it is when you allow your own YES to penetrate the veil of illusion.

—Brother

Daily Spiritual Peacemaking Lesson – Day 141

There is no distance between you and the Eternal YES that is the foundation of God's Love. There seems to be distance and, therefore, time between you and every other experience you have. Your experience of YES is the only thing that does not change and, therefore, it exists wholly outside time. There is more I could say about this, but it would only complicate the issue. Allow it to be this simple, and it is.

—Brother

Daily Spiritual Peacemaking Lesson – Day 142

Let the Eternal YES sing through you this day. The world needs to feel that this is a reality it can enjoy, and it will only feel this if you allow yourself to enjoy it. You are to be the example that this is possible in the ordinary ways that you live your life. Until now it has seemed to be the exception, not the rule, but it is yours to show a new possibility. Will you accept this and move into your Light? It is why you were born into this world, to show that the world is not your real home. Love is your home, and the YES that sings through you brings you a step closer to this reality.

—Brother

Daily Spiritual Peacemaking Lesson – Day 143

If you knew how much you deprive yourself every time you say no, you would never say it again. I am not referring to what you say with your mouth, but through your mind and your heart. You cannot be the example the world needs until every word, every thought, and every action reverberates with the YES that is the foundation of who you are. Until then you are a denial of who you really are, as if such a thing were possible. It is not, and it is from this place that YES springs. Let it be real and whole within you this day so every possibility will be shared through you.

—Brother

Daily Spiritual Peacemaking Lesson – Day 144

When I said the words, "Blessed are the Peacemakers," I was speaking directly to you, no one else. The word was not meant to be plural, but to indicate that there is only one way to bring peace to the world you created, and it is through you. This is not something you can understand with your mind, but with your Awakened Heart. The Realized Mind in you does not need to understand, for it is the very essence of this truth, and the essence of anything cannot understand itself. Do you understand what I mean by this? For now it is important for you to realize, even in your mind, that no one needs to embrace this mission but you. Then you will truly be the Spiritual Peacemaker you intend.

—Brother

Daily Spiritual Peacemaking Lesson – Day 145

"Blessed are the Peacemakers, for they shall be called the Children of God." It would be more accurate to say: "For they will know themselves to be the Children of God." Better still: "For you will know your Self to be the Child of God."

There is no Child outside your acceptance of God's most Beloved. You are That. Breathe this in today simply by seeing it reflected in everyone you meet. Then you will know that there is no difference between any of God's Sons and Daughters, for they are all the same. In this moment, they are all the same AS you.

—Brother

Daily Spiritual Peacemaking Lesson – Day 146

A Spiritual Peacemaker has only one goal: to forgive everything and everyone by SEEING everything as it really is. When you perceive any thing as it is not, you will feel the need to attack it because you do not understand it. But when you realize that you are everything you perceive, that it literally is an aspect of you that seems splintered from the Source, then it is easier to understand because all the answers exist in the same place—within you. Forgiveness is simply the ability to SEE past the illusions you once created to hide from the Truth, and KNOW what is real. You can do this at any moment. No preparation is required, only your willingness to lay aside what has never brought you joy.

—Brother

Daily Spiritual Peacemaking Lesson – Day 147

Every lesson and idea I have shared has ultimately centered on your ability to SEE what is always right in front of you. You will soon be ready for the next step, which is SEEING that there is nothing in front of you. Spend as much time as you can today SEEING the Christ within every person you can, then say to yourself, "What I am seeing does not really exist." You do not need to understand this with your mind, because it is impossible. But soon you will experience it with your soul, and that is all that is important.

—Brother

Daily Spiritual Peacemaking Lesson – Day 148

If the ultimate goal were SEEING the face of Christ that is always in front of you, then your physical eyes would be a necessary element in the process. Your eyes were made not to see. Now you are giving them a new purpose, but as all things of time must end, you must learn to see this as only a tool that will lead to a much higher goal. SEEING the Christ in front of you is nothing more than a step toward FEELING the Christ within your Self. When this is complete, then you will realize that everyone you perceive with your physical eyes, no matter how holy they may appear, are manifestations of the single extension of God's grace. And yet, God's grace is manifest as YOU right now. What does that mean?

—Brother

Daily Spiritual Peacemaking Lesson – Day 149

Once you have accomplished the goal of SEEING the Christ that is in front of you every moment, then realized that there is nothing in front of you at all, then you will be ready to SEE the Self that exists beyond all these forms. Ultimately, your perception of this Self leads to the final step, which is the realization that even it is unreal. Then, at last, you will perceive God.

—Brother

Daily Spiritual Peacemaking Lesson – Day 150

Are you willing to look with grateful eyes upon everything you have created? This is the only way you will learn to SEE, and then fulfill your role on earth. Your judgment alone has kept you away from heaven, and the moment you are willing to let it pass, a New World will appear before you. Be grateful, then, for everything, no matter how it appears. All the wars and conflicts you perceive are really being fought in your own mind. Forgive yourself and they are released. I know this is impossible for you to believe with your mind, and I am not asking for that. I am only asking for your soul's consideration. Give that to me, and I will do the rest.

—Brother

Daily Spiritual Peacemaking Lesson – Day 151

The eyes that were given to you by God will give you the vision you need to look past the world of forgotten dreams, and perceive a New World where forgiveness is completely unnecessary. Look with grateful eyes, then, even when it is beyond your comprehension. You are trying to adopt a new way of SEEING everything, and you may need to sacrifice what you think is real for what really is. But nothing will be lost, for the world God would show you contains only Love, which is what you are really looking for. Let it be that simple, then it is.

—Brother

Daily Spiritual Peacemaking Lesson – *Day 152*

If you knew how easy everything that I am asking you to do is, then you would not hesitate even for a moment. You are still afraid you are going to lose something by accepting everything. You are afraid that giving up pain will be painful. Maybe now you are able to see that these thoughts are insane, and should not be considered at all. Give everything to everything, and look with grateful eyes upon the world you made. Then the Real World is already yours.

—Brother

Daily Spiritual Peacemaking Lesson – *Day 153*

Your gratitude is all that is required, not your belief. You do not need to believe with your mind that you are holy, for the gift comes to you simply from your acceptance. You need only be grateful in advance of the awakening. Your thankfulness will reveal everything else you need, every step you will walk to the altar of your Home which you share with all your brothers and sisters. Therefore, start now. Open your heart and give thanks for every moment of grace, no matter how it appears. You are not able to decide the difference, simply because, in the end, there is no difference at all.

—Brother

Daily Spiritual Peacemaking Lesson – Day 154

How simple is salvation, and how simply it is achieved. You are a Spiritual Peacemaker this moment. That is it. Now open your heart and let your life be an extension of the gratitude that the Universe deserves for keeping you so completely safe from sin. Once again, whether you believe this in your mind or not is of little consequence. All that is required is your willingness to SEE what has always been true everywhere you look. Then the Vision of God will appear on its own.

—Brother

Daily Spiritual Peacemaking Lesson – Day 155

Look with gentle eyes upon your brothers and sisters today. Each one of them holds a precious gift out to you, begging you to receive, that they may claim it for themselves. The gift of Holiness must be shared or it is nothing. It must not be refused to anyone, otherwise God's Love is proven unreal. You alone have the power to make this manifest, simply by being willing to be the eyes of God in this world. The fact is, you are already the eyes, the hands, and the feet of God in this world, but you have chosen to look upon what is not there. Choose again and the whole world will change magically before your eyes.

—Brother

Daily Spiritual Peacemaking Lesson – Day 156

I only have one word to offer you this day: NOW. Act upon it!

—Brother

Daily Spiritual Peacemaking Lesson – Day 157

When you quiet your mind, you will hear my Voice telling you that you are Holy. My Voice does not communicate in words, but in the feelings that lie beyond words. And these feelings themselves lead to even higher realities, for even they cannot contain what I long to show. Your Holiness exists beyond the boundaries of time and space, and yet it can be felt even here. Let your mind relax, then, for it will never be able to break this code. Fall backwards into my arms, Beloved, and I will give you everything you need.

—Brother

Daily Spiritual Peacemaking Lesson – Day 158

Look in front of yourself at the world you created in your mind. Does it really offer you the Love you desire? The passing forms that promise a moment's rapture will never compare to the eternal bliss that is offered to you in the eyes of everyone you meet. One perfect gift given and it is yours. Why do you hesitate? There is nothing here that you even want, and you are beginning to realize that. Look into the eyes of one person today as if they offer you everything. I promise you that they do. Give to them, and then receive what I would also give.

—Brother

Daily Spiritual Peacemaking Lesson – Day 159

You will know that the dream is coming to an end when you do not relate to the things that once brought you such joy in the same way. You may still find in them a moment's reprieve, but they will not be able to satisfy you in the same way. Rejoice if you find this happening now. It means that your heart is prepared to take the final step toward your awakening. It means that you are but a breath away. There is nothing that you love in this world that does not come with you. Let go now, and Heaven will at last receive you.

—Brother

Daily Spiritual Peacemaking Lesson – Day 160

When I say that you will no longer relate to the things that once brought you joy, you may experience sorrow or pain. That is because you still believe that the world you created, in and of itself, can offer you what you really want. It cannot, and the moment you finally realize this will be the same moment these gifts can be offered back to you in a new way. God's only will for you is perfect joy, so it is clear that it is your only inheritance. When you seek first the Peace of God, then these things are given to you in a way which transcends reason, and which fulfills a Holy Purpose. Isn't this what you really want?

Don't think that anything will be lost, for loss in the Kingdom is impossible. I am only showing you the way to have what you really want.

—Brother

Daily Spiritual Peacemaking Lesson – Day 161

Your joy is already complete. I am not asking you to change in any way. All I am doing is helping you shift your awareness toward the Awareness of God, or to become conscious of God's Consciousness. Since change cannot exist within God, it cannot truly exist within you. This is how you can ultimately tell the difference between truth and illusion. The only consistent rule of illusions is that it offers no consistency. Truth, on the other hand, never changes, but only increases. Do you see the difference? By accepting the Joy of Heaven you are offering yourself to eternity itself. Time, then, falls away from you and disappears, knowing that it cannot exist within the Real World you seek.

—Brother

Daily Spiritual Peacemaking Lesson – Day 162

We are very near the half way mark in this Holy Year. What have you learned? Hopefully you haven't learned anything at all. Hopefully you have achieved the gift of being able to let go and SEE what is always in front of you. If I asked you to learn this with your mind, or to understand this process intellectually, then you would still be in the dark. But the Light has come because you have set the mind aside and are beginning to trust the wisdom of the heart. That is what will lead you into the experience you seek. You are here to let the world you created through projection be replaced by the world maintained by love. It is all around you now, if only you would open your eyes. That is all I am asking you to do. Will you follow this consistently?

—Brother

Daily Spiritual Peacemaking Lesson – Day 163

Consistency is the key now. You must learn to retrain your mind to perceive what can only be SEEN by your heart. The Beloved is all around you every moment, but you have learned to be consistent in NOT perceiving this reality. It takes practice shifting this awareness, and it is this, more than anything else, that you need. I have said this over and over, but for good purpose. I know how stubborn your mind is, and how difficult it is to shift your vision of the whole world. But it is simple. Let it be that way, and you will move deeper into this Light. Look around yourself right now and SEE who is there. The Holy One is shining upon you this moment, if only you would choose this for yourself.

—Brother

Daily Spiritual Peacemaking Lesson – Day 164

My words mean nothing, but there is love behind them reserved for the Beloved I SEE in you. Imitate me. Do not worry about your words meaning anything, for in the end they are nothing but symbols. Choose instead to love everyone for the truth that is their foundation, as it is yours. Even if you do this for half an hour a day, then you will begin to shift at profound levels. That is because the truth is compelling. Remember that consistency is the most important path for you now. You have come too far to fall completely back into the ego, but you are also not steady enough to maintain the level of being a Spiritual Peacemaker without offering yourself to God every moment.

—Brother

Daily Spiritual Peacemaking Lesson – Day 165

Light has been reserved for you in the place where you would least expect. Deep within you there is a home, and you are that home, and the Light has never dimmed. Even as the raging tide has ripped through your life, still has this gentle Light remained, waiting to spring from this hiding place and infect every part of you. The Light has come, and it is now yours to share. Will you increase its effect by offering it to all those the Holy Spirit gives? It is the only way, as you already know. You are ready, and the world is now opening before you in holiness and grace. You are here to play such an important role, Beloved.

—Brother

Daily Spiritual Peacemaking Lesson – Day 166

I am calling everyone that was given to me before time began to stand at my side and save what has never been threatened. Do you understand now that this is the only way it can happen? If I saw the world as a place that was in danger of being destroyed, then I would be ultimately ineffective. But if I see through the eyes of God, knowing that all things of time are but the illusion of something far deeper, beyond the effect of these awful dreams, then I can be used for something greater. You are being used now, for you have accepted the same eyes that I see through. And so the world takes on a new purpose, one that is unseen, yet more real than anything you have ever experienced before.

—Brother

Daily Spiritual Peacemaking Lesson – Day 167

How willing are you to be completely ordinary, and by doing so, be the Light of the World? It is easy to think that you must become extraordinary to accomplish this. It is this idea alone that keeps you blind. There is nothing you need to change about yourself, but rather, to accept what cannot change. If you are able to BE this, then you will realize that there is nothing to do. Then you will know who you are, and this knowledge will never leave you.

—Brother

Daily Spiritual Peacemaking Lesson – Day 168

Enlightenment is a choice, nothing else. Until now you have been choosing to keep your eyes closed and not SEE what is right in front of you. And because you are not bound to the past, you are also not bound to the choices you made in the past. You are able to CHOOSE AGAIN, revealing a New World through your holy choice. If you want, you can keep making the same choice over and over, every new moment that appears in your mind, and in doing so, remain where you think you are. But you are not there at all. Do you realize that this is the only thing I am trying to get you to see? You can think you're somewhere, but it doesn't change anything if you're not. If you're wrong, you're wrong. You are still as God created you, and you still live within the heart of Grace Itself. Know this to be true, and it is.

—Brother

Daily Spiritual Peacemaking Lesson – Day 169

Why do you resist the only thing that will give you what you really want? There must be something within that is not conscious of what you really want; otherwise you would already have it. That is why you run from love, all the while convincing yourself that you are running toward it. Stop running altogether. That is the key. There is nowhere for you to go, for the love you seek is within. Hold still and surrender, then love will find you.

—Brother

Daily Spiritual Peacemaking Lesson – Day 170

The journey you seem to be on exists only in your mind. Though it has no real meaning in the World created for you by God, the Holy Spirit can use it to gently shift your mind toward what is real. The only thing that is required is your willingness to release your hold on the world you seem to have made. You will not lose anything that you really want. I can assure you of this. Your values, however, will realign, and you will let pass the things that do not serve your new, yet ancient, goal. Trust the movement of Spirit, not illusion, and everything Spirit would reveal. You are safer than you can even begin to imagine.

—Brother

Daily Spiritual Peacemaking Lesson – Day 171

Now that you know that you are a Spiritual Peacemaker, what will you do with that knowledge? Will this bring you what you desire on earth, the physical tools you once thought would make you happy? Though there is nothing in this world, as you now realize, that will fulfill that longing for your source, it is true that you are now capable of achieving whatever you want in this world or the next. The question is not what you would choose, but why. God's will for you is perfect joy, and this includes perfect abundance; but will you choose this alone, or for the others that will join you? You are not here to make a kingdom on this earth, but to transcend it altogether. But that does not mean that you are here to experience lack in any way.

The universe and everything in it is yours. Use everything to realize the only goal that is worth your energy. Draw everything unto your life that you may share life abundantly.

—Brother

Daily Spiritual Peacemaking Lesson – Day 172

It would be wrong to think when I walked upon the earth, that I lacked anything at any time. I did not come to teach you to deny anything but the ego's desire for dominion. I did not even ask you to deny your ego. Do you understand the difference? Dominion belongs to the One who created you, and who knows why you are here. The ego is your servant, not the other way around. If you give control back to your Source, then it will use the ego to accomplish the goal of Holiness, not separation. How do you do this? By asking for then accepting my help. I am here to offer you my hand, only because I have walked this path before you and have therefore seen where it leads. I am here to be truly helpful, and to teach you to be the same.

—Brother

Daily Spiritual Peacemaking Lesson – Day 173

There is so much Grace left for you to receive, more than you can ever know in your mind. It surrounds you every moment, beckoning to you and drawing you toward Itself. Give what you want today, and it will be yours. I cannot make it any simpler than that. Help others realize who they are by simply Seeing it in their eyes. I have seen it in yours, and that is why you are waking up now. Give this gift as I have given it to you.

—Brother

Daily Spiritual Peacemaking Lesson – Day 174

Your salvation does not rest in a world of dreams, but in the world of the awakened heart. If you want to know yourself as awakened then you must give everything to everything, knowing that it is then yours. When I say that you must give everything to everything, I mean that God is present in every instant, and every way, and that your willingness to See this presence in others draws it into your heart and mind. You are on this earth, in the world of perception, for one reason: to experience the reality of Life in all its forms, and know that they are One. Let today be for this Love.

—Brother

Daily Spiritual Peacemaking Lesson – Day 175

If there were only one gift I could give to you, it would be my willingness. I am willing to look past everything I don't want, to what I really do. Whatever you choose to SEE is yours, and until now you have chosen to See what isn't really there. Your willingness to know the truth through every circumstance in your life will surely bring it to you. Your desire to See the Beloved everywhere you look will surely reveal the face you long for. Be willing, then, to lay aside all the evidence you thought defined reality and choose the path I am revealing to you now. Be willing to walk at my side for a while, and together we will remember who we really are.

—Brother

Daily Spiritual Peacemaking Lesson – Day 176

Do you understand how important your gratitude is to this constant awakening? Combine this with your willingness to accept everything, no matter how it appears, as part of the path you are choosing for yourself, and you cannot help but stir your soul, and the memory of your home. Take everything into your heart, all the joy and sorrow you perceive, and know that it was all created by you and for you. There are no others to whom you can assign blame, for blame and guilt are not appropriate here. The only thing that is appropriate is your unconditional acceptance. When you accept everything in this Light, then Heaven will appear before you.

—Brother

Daily Spiritual Peacemaking Lesson – Day 177

Open your eyes and realize that you are not a victim to anything in this world. That is because the world you perceive, and everything in it, was created for and by you. When you are able to look past the appearance of separation, and the insane belief that you lack responsibility, then you will see everything as God sees it, and sorrow will disappear forever. That is your only goal now, for you have accepted you role as a Spiritual Peacemaker.

—Brother

Daily Spiritual Peacemaking Lesson – *Day 178*

Heaven is waiting for you now. You do not need to die to enjoy this state of bliss, for death was not created by God. It was created by the ego as a way of avoiding life, no matter how it appears. The truth in you can never die, and that is why you are an eternal being. The body and everything that seems to desert you are not yours, though they are being used by you. Do you understand this subtle difference? Life does not wait for you, but you are trying to wait on it. Give this up and a flood of Light will engulf you that you cannot believe.

—Brother

Daily Spiritual Peacemaking Lesson – *Day 179*

If you choose to live in the Eternal Now, then the memory of the past cannot attack you. There is nothing outside your mind and your choice. You are already aware of this, but there is still an attraction to the past and the promises it makes. It is easy to say that these promises are illusions because it is impossible to change anything that "was." But there is an opportunity that is taking place now that you do not want to miss. Never forget that God's will for you is perfect joy, and that can only be found in the present moment. Take a deep breath and feel this River of Light that is always yours. Choose to SEE and reality appears. Is it really so simple?

—Brother

Daily Spiritual Peacemaking Lesson – Day 180

Never forget that I am always with you, because of the choice I am making NOW. That is what enables me to be valuable to you, because my presence and my gift are the same. Learning that you are a Spiritual Peacemaker is very much the same. You are called to be a gift to everyone that comes to you, and you will do this only if you are with them wholly. This requires letting go of the past, of everything that you thought you wanted or thought you could give. There is nothing you can offer on your own, but everything can be given through you, if only you would allow. This is what it really means to be a Spiritual Peacemaker, for reality to be given "through" you. Only then will you realize that it is also given AS you.

—Brother

Daily Spiritual Peacemaking Lesson – Day 181

Give everything today. That is all God ever asks, for it is the only thing that brings the perfect joy we seek. To the ego, giving everything is difficult, while giving only a little is easy. It is the opposite in Spirit. The most natural thing is to give as God gives, for holding back is a way of guarding yourself against death. There is no death and,ß therefore, there is no reason not to give all your Light, all your Love and all your joy this moment. Renew your practice of SEEING the Beloved everywhere you look today. Do you realize that this is the only spiritual practice you need? Anything else is an addition to realizing that you are here to be as God, for nothing but this will give you what you really want.

—Brother

Daily Spiritual Peacemaking Lesson – Day 182

An Instrument of Peace does not act on his or her own, but as the extension of the one who plays them. Likewise, the music that issues from this Instrument is for the benefit of all those who listen or who are touched by this grace, and yet it cannot help but return to touch the One being played. This is your role, to be played by the Beloved and let your music transform all those who have been given to you. Do not be attached to the results, and the results will fall naturally into place. It is not yours to know the end, but to become the means through which the end comes to life.

—Brother

Daily Spiritual Peacemaking Lesson – Day 183

A Spiritual Peacemaker seeks only to serve the Highest Goal this Universe can support. Can you guess what this is? You are living it now, whether consciously or unconsciously. It would be best at this point if you realized who you are and why you are here so that this Goal can be made manifest through you, AS YOU. You can do this today if you choose. There is no need to wait, and nothing that you need before you are ready. All I have been trying to get you to understand is that you are ready right now, this instant. Say it is so and it is. I have said it about you, now you must say it about yourself.

—Brother

Daily Spiritual Peacemaking Lesson – Day 184

There is only one thing I would like you to focus on today: The end is sure. How can the end be sure unless it has already happened? If this were not so, then a million complications could potentially interrupt the final course. What I am telling you is that you have already completed the journey you seem to be on now. This is another way of saying that you have never left your true Home, and that you are still at my side. When a dream ends, you awaken in the same place you retired. You have slept in the Grace of God all this time, while dreams of separation filled your mind. They are almost over now. Open your eyes and discover that what I have been whispering into your ear is true.

—Brother

Daily Spiritual Peacemaking Lesson – Day 185

Today give Praise to the Beloved for offering such a world where you can see your Self hidden everywhere. An infinite number of disguises cannot deny you your birthright, but only so long as you are willing to see past them all to the truth that is perceived by God. There are no words I can offer that will lead you closer to what has never left you. But I can draw your attention to the source of your being which you have denied, and then seeing again, you will acknowledge and love. This is why you are here, on this earth and in this universe, to remember and to know that you have everything you need to be a savior and a guide to the others that have been given to you. Use your day well, for time is your friend if you use it to accomplish the goals of God.

—Brother

Daily Spiritual Peacemaking Lesson – Day 186

You cannot bring peace to the world unless you know it is indestructible. Otherwise you will believe that it is weak and unable to conquer the problems of the world you made. This is the peace you perceive in time, which you would choose to impose over war as if peace and war were in competition with each other. The Peace of God knows nothing of war, and that is why it cannot be overcome by anything in this world. It is full and complete in Itself, just as you. Your willingness to See your Self is the same willingness that is required to See Peace. Let this be your only goal. The gift you give to yourself this day is the same as the gift you offer the world as a Spiritual Peacemaker.

—Brother

Daily Spiritual Peacemaking Lesson – Day 187

What gift can I offer you but the gift I have chosen to receive myself?

I cannot be a true guide unless I choose to accept the truth that is forever protected from dreams of war and separation. The Peace of God is all I want, and so it is all I give. Let this chant be upon your lips today: "The Peace of God is all I want." The universe is waiting to comply with your holy will, for in the end it will honor its creator, but not until you honor your Self as creator.

—Brother

Daily Spiritual Peacemaking Lesson – Day 188

How will you choose to live this life when it seems there is no peace to be found? The world you created is proof that peace does not last, while the Spirit proclaims that only peace is real. Which of these is true, for both cannot exist in the Mind of God? Your choice will reveal the world you desire, and you will experience it accordingly. Choose peace! Do not rely upon the evidence of a world that has never given you what you really want. It cannot satisfy your deeper longing, for it does not understand who you are. God has never forgotten who you are and, therefore, is waiting to reveal the world where all your desires are realized. Now, as the Peacemaker you were born to be, enter into this Holy Vision.

—Brother

Daily Spiritual Peacemaking Lesson – Day 189

The world you created will offer no resistance if you offer none. In the world created for you by God, there is no resistance. Resistance manifests when you deny who you are. When you know who you are, then you are in harmony with the whole universe. This does not take practice, but devotion. You will find it in your heart.

—Brother

Daily Spiritual Peacemaking Lesson – Day 190

The universe will not deny you if you stop denying yourself. This is the only thought I will offer today because it is so important. Live with it today, and see where it leads.

—Brother

Daily Spiritual Peacemaking Lesson – Day 191

Are you beginning to see that your only problem in this world is that you've been denying the "Self" that God perceives? The truth in you is so contrary to the illusion that there is only one place they intersect. When you extend love to another, it is like building a bridge from one world to the next. As you cross the bridge you have built, the two become one, and you realize the single truth that will release you from all error. I have asked you to look for Heaven where you stand, in the eyes of whoever is standing right in front of you. It is the only place it can be found because it is here that you begin building the bridge of love. Build it with joy, and Eternal Joy shall be your reward.

—Brother

Daily Spiritual Peacemaking Lesson – *Day 192*

I said in the last lesson that your only problem is that you've been denying the "Self" that God perceives. God does not deny anything that exists, for everything that exists is created by God, and God loves what God has created. But God does deny what doesn't exist, and you would do well to imitate this.

You are not a collection of thoughts or definitions. You are the perfect creation of God, and you deserve everything. Why, then, do you deny yourself everything by refusing to SEE?

—Brother

Daily Spiritual Peacemaking Lesson – *Day 193*

I am asking you to open your Spiritual Eyes and SEE as God SEES. The world is your cathedral, your holy temple, and gives you everything you need to accomplish the only goal that is required of you. Use time wisely today. Do not waste a single moment of Life. You are still as God created you, and the Peace of God is still your inheritance. When will you accept the gift that is being offered to you now? Say YES, and it is yours.

—Brother

Daily Spiritual Peacemaking Lesson – Day 194

Your YES is all that is required to achieve the Gift of God that has always been yours. You have said YES many times, but the past has no bearing now. The YES I am asking for does not issue from your mouth or even your mind. It is the YES of the heart that opens the Door to Heaven. Every glance toward another can be YES. Every word to a stranger can be YES. Become a living, breathing YES to the Universe, and it will be yours. I am not asking for more than you are able to give, simply because I have already seen you give it. Remember, it is consistency that counts now, for it shows the Universe how serious you are about this, and it will surely respond.

—Brother

Daily Spiritual Peacemaking Lesson – Day 195

What models will you use to achieve this Holy Goal we have set before ourselves? There are many who have stepped upon this altar and witnessed the power of love in this way. Will you turn to them for your own life and integrate the lessons you learn? I can play that role for you, and yet there are so many others who will demonstrate the undeniable truth that is awakening within you now. But do not see those people, those teachers, as separate or different from you, for they are not. I am no different, even in time. Time may seem to separate us for a moment, for I may seem to possess qualities that you do not. The essential qualities are the same and cannot change. Focus there and know that your Guide is one with you. This will lead you to the goal much faster.

—Brother

*Daily Spiritual Peacemaking Lesson – **Day 196***

Let today be a day for quiet remembering. You have come far on this journey, and yet you have not moved at all. The truth is still true within you, and the Light is still as bright as it has ever been. And yet your mind is beginning to open more to that brightness, and you can finally SEE who you are by seeing it all around you. Your spiritual eyes are opening fast. Let this be a day for honoring your Self as you honor God. Soon you will recognize that they are the same.

—Brother

*Daily Spiritual Peacemaking Lesson – **Day 197***

You cannot bring peace to the world until you know who you are, since that is the only way you will understand the world. A Master brings peace by knowing what is real and what isn't. They know that only love is real, and that everything else is easily dismissed because it has no lasting effect. The master is only concerned about what has effect in Heaven, and then allows the earth to reflect that decision. Your perceived sins have had no effect in reality, and therefore cannot change the truth in you. Rely upon this and everything else will flow perfectly. It is the same as relying upon God's Love.

—Brother

Daily Spiritual Peacemaking Lesson – Day 198

You cannot bring peace to the world until you know who you are, for the truth is, you are the world. The decisions you make about yourself will reveal the world you perceive; therefore, you cannot be separated from anything. Your soul does not want to see anything as separate, because it has never denied the truth of Unity. Your ego, however, never understood it at all, and considers it an impossible concept, nice to think about, but never to be attained. You are here to prove the ego wrong, and to prove that God's version of reality is the only path that leads to love, which is your greatest quest.

—Brother

Daily Spiritual Peacemaking Lesson – Day 199

You cannot bring peace to the world until you know who you are, which leads naturally to the next step: sharing who you are. When you share the truth within, then you will experience that truth. There is no other path to your enlightenment—sharing your enlightenment. What you share you realize within your Self. Until now you have been sharing the illusion of separation, and have therefore experienced only that. Is this a surprise? What you share increases, because sharing aligns your mind with the Mind of God. And yet you cannot be perfectly aligned unless you choose to "See as God Sees." When you choose to "See what God does not See," then you experience everything in reverse, which is what the ego's perception is. Change your perception and the world changes.

—Brother

Daily Spiritual Peacemaking Lesson – *Day 200*

If you choose to place yourself into my mind, then you will know that only One Mind exists between us. This is how we will bring peace to a world that does not exist, by acting as and working within the Single Mind and Heart of creation. You can enter now if you choose. This is not a choice of personality, but of wholeness. If you want, you can do the same with any Illumined Mind, for they are all the same. In the end, and this is what you are coming to know, yours is no different either. The only thing that is different is that all shadows have been cast away.

—Brother

Daily Spiritual Peacemaking Lesson – *Day 201*

If you choose to place yourself into my mind, and to see through my eyes, then you will see peace everywhere you look. This is the only role of a Spiritual Peacemaker, as you already know. But knowing this will not help. Doing it, this very moment, opens the door that seems closed to you now. It is not closed at all, but is waiting for the gentle touch of your hand. Reach out and touch it now.

—Brother

Daily Spiritual Peacemaking Lesson – Day 202

I am with you always. How could this not be true if we are one? I am a Spiritual Peacemaker now, and that means you are the same. This is my certainty, and I want only to share it with you.

—Brother

Daily Spiritual Peacemaking Lesson – Day 203

Stay awake with me!

This is all that is asked of you in this critical time. It is critical because you have made it that way, but not for the reasons you may believe. This is the moment you decided to wake up from the dream of separation, and you must be diligent in this. There is no guilt or punishment for the world you created, except your seeming separation from the Love and Home that is your inheritance. Choose again, Beloved. Choose the Real World, this and every moment. You need make no other choice but this. The world that has been reserved for you through God's Love has not changed, nor can it change. But you can remain blind to it, and it is this, and only this, that must now change. I need you to stand at my side and serve. Then all things of time will disappear, and you will remember who you are.

—Brother

Daily Spiritual Peacemaking Lesson – Day 204

You have stepped forward and proclaimed your willingness to transform the world through love. No other question remains. But you must choose it NOW. The past does not exist, nor does the choice you seem to have made in the past. Your YES must be eternal, just as you are eternal. It is something you live every moment of your life and, I assure you, your life does not end. Therefore, neither will your YES end.

Let this be the day when you know this to be true. Let your YES resound all through this world, then past this world to the Home you never left, except in your imagination. I am waiting for you there, and yet I am also right by your side.

—Brother

Daily Spiritual Peacemaking Lesson – Day 205

You have chosen to stand beside me in full readiness to proclaim the end of time and the Gifts of Eternity. This is the essence of what it means to be a Spiritual Peacemaker. You are THAT now! Say these words as often as you can. "I am THAT now!" What is it that you are proclaiming? You are offering yourself as a gift to God, already whole and already complete. You are saying to the universe: "Nothing needs to change within me for this to be true. It is true because I am still as God created me." Is that enough for you? I assure you that it is enough for God.

Let the truth be this simple today.

—Brother

*Daily Spiritual Peacemaking Lesson – **Day 206***

I have called you by your name, and you have answered. The rest is easy, for when we are able to recognize one another and the gifts we bring, then the Universe itself will align to our command. I have called your name and you have responded. Now all things will be given unto you through the One from whom all things flow, as they have always flowed. Nothing has changed except your willingness to KNOW the truth about your Self. Now we can continue our journey in Light, that which seemed to begin in darkness.

—Brother

*Daily Spiritual Peacemaking Lesson – **Day 207***

I see myself in you, and that is how I know who I am. Imitate me. That is the road we are asked to walk together, imitating what is perfect in one another. You are perfect as God created you, and as I am willing to SEE that in you, so will I be able to KNOW it about myself. And because all things work together in a cyclical pattern, the opposite is true as well. As I am willing to SEE God's perfection in me, I will KNOW it in you. Why is this circle so important? Because it leads to one simple truth: We are the same in God's Love. If God does not know a difference, then let your own eyes see past difference as well.

—Brother

Daily Spiritual Peacemaking Lesson – *Day 208*

All paths have now disappeared except one: "There is only one face of God revealed infinitely. Look upon the Beloved and KNOW who you are." Meditate on these two sentences as often as you can today, for they are the key to your salvation. I have offered you a simple path into the Light, and you have taken it. Each step reveals new sights, and yet they are all illumined by the same sun. Do you understand what I am trying to say to you? There is only one Light, one path, and one face of God. It is you! And you will see it everywhere.

—Brother

Daily Spiritual Peacemaking Lesson – *Day 209*

There is only one reason why I came to this earth -- to demonstrate the reality of my Father/Mother's love. And because we stand together in this love, you have come to do the same. We will do this through every circumstance of our lives, for that is what time is for. I used time wisely, and I am asking you to do the same.

—Brother

Daily Spiritual Peacemaking Lesson – Day 210

The question you must ask yourself every day is this: "Am I fulfilling the purpose of my birth on this planet?" You are already able to know what that purpose is, so the only thing that is required now is an honest assessment. It is a choice you make every moment. There will be times when you choose love, and times when you choose fear. But every moment is a new opportunity, just as this moment is. What will you choose right now?

—Brother

Daily Spiritual Peacemaking Lesson – Day 211

In the last two lessons I asked you to assess why you are here on this planet, and whether or not you are consciously fulfilling that. Today's lesson is much more important, for I am asking you to act, not just think.

Look around yourself, wherever you may be, and ask yourself this question: "What can I do in the next five minutes that will make the difference in someone else's life? Is there a person near me that I can reach out and touch as the Beloved? Is there a telephone that I can use to call the Beloved, touching their life with the sound of my voice?" I want you to do something that will make this kind of a difference in the next five minutes. Do not question how important your action is, simply act. Reach out and be the Beloved for the Beloved. Then you will be a step closer to understanding what I am trying to teach you.

—Brother

Daily Spiritual Peacemaking Lesson – Day 212

The Voice FOR God is expressing itself every instant AS you. Your conscious recognition of this is present now, regardless of your mental state. That is because God's Will does not depend upon your consciousness, but upon the Truth that cannot change. You will Know this by giving it. I have expressed this simple lesson so many times, and yet it cannot be offered too often. The simplicity of salvation is all around you, if you would only have eyes to SEE. You have been called to be a Spiritual Peacemaker, and it requires of you open eyes.

—Brother

Daily Spiritual Peacemaking Lesson – Day 213

You deserve so much, and so little is asked of you. The Light of Heaven shines upon you, and yet you have turned your back to it. Turn around now, and SEE the Gifts of God. They are yours, if only you would receive them.

The earth and everything in it is nothing more than the projection of the thoughts you have about yourself. That is why it is so easy to change. A Spiritual Peacemaker knows what is required and gives only that. And yet this little gift has the power to transform everything it touches. Every act of love brings you a step closer to realizing all this.

—Brother

Daily Spiritual Peacemaking Lesson – Day 214

Peace comes to the world "through" you and "as" you. Your goal as a Spiritual Peacemaker is to See that these two things are really the same. It seems that if something comes through you it passes as something isolated and separate, integrated for a moment, perhaps, but at no time is it the same. I am telling you that everything is the same, especially the Love of God that is your foundation. That is why I say that Peace, or the Peace of God, comes to the world "as" you for at no time are you, truly separate from it. Know this first in your mind, then extend it through your heart.

—Brother

Daily Spiritual Peacemaking Lesson – Day 215

You deserve so much. That is why I have been so patient with you, and why I give so much, every moment. Now you must be patient with yourself, and with everyone I give to you. Begin to imitate me, just as I imitate the One who sent us both. I will offer more and more souls for you to love and transform, for that is the role you must fulfill now. It is the next step in your mastery, and in your enlightenment. That is how you will stay awake, which is all that I ask. If you are awake then you must perceive everything that happens around you as God perceives it. If you are asleep then it will be impossible for you to know what anything really is. To love something you must be able to identify it clearly. If you see only the shadow, you will misidentify what it is. Open your eyes and See what is and has always been in front of you, and then you will be free.

—Brother

Daily Spiritual Peacemaking Lesson – Day 216

I am able to SEE you clearly now, and that is the truest gift I can give to you. It is also the truest gift you can give others as a Spiritual Peacemaker. From your Holy Sight will extend a whole world that has been forgiven, and which reflects that forgiveness. It is already there, but until now you have not been able to See what your Beloved has made. You have preferred the visions of separation that you have made, though only in your imagination. Now is the moment you decided to let those empty visions pass away in favor of what is real. So much depends on you, and that is why you are here. You have so much to give, and so much to receive. Let this be the day, then, that they become the same.

—Brother

Daily Spiritual Peacemaking Lesson – Day 217

Let go of every thought you have ever had about what it means to be enlightened. You are not enlightened, and, you are fully enlightened this very moment. It may seem that these two concepts contradict each another. They do not. I am simply trying to get you to consider that you are not separate from anyone you perceive, any of your brothers and sisters who seem to be outside your experience. If you perceive any of them as "unenlightened" then you are held to that decision yourself. If you KNOW that only the Love of God is real for everyone in all situations, then you will enjoy that yourself. This is the only lesson I have come to teach you, and it is the only lesson you will teach. You are a Spiritual Peacemaker only as you live this, for then it becomes real for everyone you touch.

—Brother

Daily Spiritual Peacemaking Lesson – Day 218

Let go of every thought you have ever had about what it means to be enlightened. I mean this quite literally, because your thoughts about your enlightenment will only block your experience of it. An enlightened being does not even realize that he or she is enlightened. They know simply that only the Love of God is real, and that they are enfolded in that love every moment. The natural thing is to then share that knowledge, that experience, for it is the only way for them to keep it. You must desire this over all things of the world of form. Do not hold onto a single concept of what you think it means to walk the earth as an enlightened being. Why? There is only one thing I can guarantee at this point—that every thought you have about this is wrong. But the experience, yes, this can be very real for you, but only if you offer it to others.

—Brother

Daily Spiritual Peacemaking Lesson – Day 219

If someone comes to you and says, "I am an enlightened being," then they do not realize who they are. They are not awake. On the other hand, if when you meet someone you are filled with joy just to be in their presence, and every word they speak reminds you of who you really are, then this is the person for you to listen to, even though they may never speak a word about enlightenment. Their words do not matter, for their eyes will tell you so much more. Ask the one for whom the veils of time and space have dissolved who they are and they will tell you this: "I am you." Begin by imitating this one, and then it will become natural.

—Brother

Daily Spiritual Peacemaking Lesson – Day 220

I am revealing myself to you this very moment that you may reveal yourself to your Self. It is the cycle of Sight, or Holy Vision, that I offer, for it exists beyond all words and all the lessons I could offer you. Learn to See with these same eyes. Love is revealing Itself to you this moment. Let those who have eyes See.

—Brother

Daily Spiritual Peacemaking Lesson – Day 221

Beloved, there are no words available to me to express what I would choose to express. Only this: God is Love, and you are not separate from that. Do you see how simple this can be, as long as you are willing to get out of your own way?

—Brother

Daily Spiritual Peacemaking Lesson – Day 222

You are the One you are seeking. There is no other but you in all the Universe. There is no desire that can be fulfilled outside your discovery of who you are. The peace you long to give to the world does not exist outside of you. If it did, then God, and the Love of God, would also be outside of you. Such a thing is impossible, for you have never been abandoned by your Beloved Creator. Trust this. Rely upon this one truth, for changing it is beyond your control. That is how you will know what is yours (in your imagination) and what is God's.

—Brother

Daily Spiritual Peacemaking Lesson – Day 223

I have loved you enough to conquer death, that you may see past it yourself. You will do the same, but in different ways. You will conquer death every moment by embracing the life that was meant for you. You can choose life over death this moment. Will you realize that it is yours to choose this? I chose it, and in doing so set the precedent for the rest of the world. Follow me, and you will bring peace in ways you cannot begin to imagine.

—Brother

Daily Spiritual Peacemaking Lesson – Day 224

We have embarked on a Sacred Journey together. It is a journey without distance that leads to where YOU have always been. Until now you have been lost to yourself. Until now you have wandered in a place where you did not exist, and therefore you perceived everything else where it did not exist, as well. Is it too difficult to believe that all that is asked of you is to open your eyes and SEE? I assure you that when you SEE Heaven in these others, knowing who they are, you will know it about yourself. This is the simple path I have come to reveal, and I reveal it now through you. Accept it, and you are a Spiritual Peacemaker.

—Brother

Daily Spiritual Peacemaking Lesson – Day 225

Live within the Eternal Yes of God. There is no indecision in the Mind of God because it perceives everything as it really is, not trying to change anything. It accepts and it loves. In doing so, it also heals, because it is not trying to be something else. Do you see how simple this is? I am describing the inner attributes of God, that you may learn to imitate them yourself. As you do imitate them, they begin to feel very natural to you. That is because they are, and the imitation of God reminds of you this. The love you are holding is yours and it cannot change. Embrace this and you will know it.

—Brother

Daily Spiritual Peacemaking Lesson – Day 226

Bringing peace through the world's perspective is very difficult. It requires planning and a great deal of hard work, hoping that in the end others will follow a certain design that you have established as the "way."

Bringing peace from a spiritual perspective is easy. The only thing that is required is your willingness to surrender everything you think you know, in favor of what is already true. You do not need to "do" anything but, rather, "be" the peace you seek. Then, through the gift of the miracle, it is revealed naturally and easily.

It is the miracle you are seeking, nothing else. And yet, the closer you come to it, the more you realize that there is no such thing as a miracle, only the Will of God complete every moment.

—Brother

Daily Spiritual Peacemaking Lesson – Day 227

A Spiritual Peacemaker looks past what is not real to what is. Since only Love is real, you are asked to see everything as either an act of love or a call for love. Give only love, no matter what the conditions might seem to be, and it will be the only thing you perceive. The world will adjust according to your Vision.

The world did not understand my words when I was on the earth, and now that I am working through you, nothing will change. The only difference will be in the results. Love is the most compelling force in the universe. Direct it like a lazar beam into the night to illumine all the dark places where people hide, and then you will know who you are. You are a Spiritual Peacemaker now!

—Brother

Daily Spiritual Peacemaking Lesson – Day 228

Perceiving what is real, a Spiritual Peacemaker extends that vision by the way they live their life. Their words are of little consequence, but there is a tone or an energy in their voice that is more compelling than words. The human mind cannot understand this because it has nothing to do with the world most people perceive. A Spiritual Peacemaker is aware of two worlds at the same time, one where bodies and physicality seem to have meaning, and the other where all true meaning lies. They are able to translate between the two, and in doing so are truly helpful.

—Brother

Daily Spiritual Peacemaking Lesson – Day 229

A Spiritual Peacemaker does not create peace but creates a resonance pattern with the peace that is already present, though sometimes hidden. It is hidden only to those who do not SEE, but perfectly obvious to the one who knows the truth. Knowing the truth, a Spiritual Peacemaker allows a field of energy to be created that makes it available to others. When you come into contact with someone who vibrates with this field, you will know it through your joy, and by the healing you feel in your heart. This is what you are and what you are capable of achieving whenever you perceive what is whole within another.

—Brother

Daily Spiritual Peacemaking Lesson – Day 230

A Spiritual Peacemaker realizes that the problems of the world are spiritual problems, and therefore seeks solutions within themselves. To expect solutions outside of one's self is to misidentify the problem. Being misidentified, it hides where you do not expect it. This is how your ego maintains its hold on your mind. The moment you realize that the problem and the solution are in the same place, within you, your ego will serve you, rather than expecting you to serve it.

—Brother

Daily Spiritual Peacemaking Lesson – Day 231

A Spiritual Peacemaker realizes why they were born! Through this realization, the world naturally awakens to its Divine Inheritance. No effort is required because God's Will cannot be challenged by your dreams of separation. Much effort is required, however, to make a world seem real that isn't. Are you beginning to see where all your problems lie?

—Brother

Daily Spiritual Peacemaking Lesson – *Day 232*

The question most people ask is: "How will I heal the world?" The question you will ask is: "How will I learn to See the world that is already healed?" You already know that this is a course in Seeing, not changing. What is not real does not need to be changed, it simply needs to be seen for what it is. The only thing that is real is Love, for it is always a reflection of the Peace that surpasses understanding. And yet, everything that exists casts a shadow, and if you are not educated to know the difference, it is easy to mistake the shadow for reality. I am simply asking you to look past the shadow to what is solid and real.

—Brother

Daily Spiritual Peacemaking Lesson – *Day 233*

Your body can be used either as a symbol of something that is not real, or as a communication device for what is. It seems to prove that separation is real, and that there are places where you do not exist this and every moment. Seen differently, it is the means through which love is extended to an unloving world. The choice you make about your body is the choice you make about the way you see the world and everything in it. Choose to See the body as nothing more than an opportunity, and it will be so for you.

—Brother

Daily Spiritual Peacemaking Lesson – Day 234

If you knew how much God loves you, then you would not waste another moment in laying aside your dreams of separation and opening the door that leads to Life. If you live in a delusion then you are not living fully. A dream cannot be substituted for what can satisfy all your needs. Love is real and so are you. Trust what I am telling you in these lessons. I have seen a bit further down the road than you, but you are right behind me now. Soon we will stand together in the same light, and then I will not need to say a word.

—Brother

Daily Spiritual Peacemaking Lesson – Day 235

Allow this Great Work to be done through you and as you, rather than by you. The more you learn to step back and become an instrument of peace, the more your Beloved will be able to extend, and through this extension, all things are healed. You perceive a problem and attempt to heal the problem at the level of the error. God sees that there is no error, and heals by extending the truth that cannot change. God simply Sees what really is there and disregards what isn't. You may not yet be able to do this on your own, but if you surrender to the Divine within you, then it will happen naturally, not through effort, but through Being.

—Brother

Daily Spiritual Peacemaking Lesson – Day 236

Your devotion is like a single seed from which an entire garden is born. The fragile shoots that rise from the earth are the prayers of your soul, and each one will bear good fruit. You do not need to tell the seed about the fruit, for the knowledge of its whole life is contained there now. Only water is required, the love which springs from the soul of the Divine, which is what you are. You are the seed, the plant, the fruit and the water contained as one. Stretch your arms toward the sky, and know who you are.

—Brother

Daily Spiritual Peacemaking Lesson – Day 237

Behind your search for anything you perceive "outside" lies the yearning for completion. You believe that you have been split from who you really are, and that there is another person, or another thing, that can make you whole again. As I have said before many times, the point of this course is to lay aside your ego's concept of this and accept God's Vision. God Sees that you are already whole and therefore, disregards any evidence to the contrary. It is like watching the actors in a play, knowing that in a few moments they will lay aside their costumes and resume their real lives. And so it will be for you when you realize that the truth in you can never be compromised by your meaningless dreams.

—Brother

Daily Spiritual Peacemaking Lesson – Day 238

Your salvation, or release from the dream of separation, can come from only one place—You. There is no one else there to save you, for that would prove the ego's dream real. It is not real, and cannot be made so by your longing for death. Only God's Vision is real, and it is a vision of life, not death. It is the only thing that will make you happy, and the only thing that will lead you into your role as a Spiritual Peacemaker. Rely upon this, and it will rely upon you. Then you will know, not with your mind but with your heart, that you are already saved, and that you can relax in the Light that never changes.

—Brother

Daily Spiritual Peacemaking Lesson – Day 239

These are the questions I am asking you to ask every moment:

"What would you have me do?"

"Where would you have me go?"

"What would you have me say when I arrive?"

Your surrender and willingness to be shown are all that are required for you to be "used" by God to heal and bring peace. I tell you from direct experience, there is nothing in this universe that will bring you more joy than this.

—Brother

Daily Spiritual Peacemaking Lesson – Day 240

Love has created you like Itself. That is why you cannot change, because love it eternal and unchangeable. This is also the simple gospel you will preach to others, that they are whole, complete and loved by God this moment. How simple is salvation.

Love has created you like Itself. This is the single doctrine you will proclaim, and live by yourself. The idea that both love and sin reside within you was only an illusion, one which you are willing to let go of now. And as you do, your role as a Spiritual Peacemaker will increase, as well as your willingness to give what you have received.

Once more: Love has created you like Itself. Be with this reality today, and Know its truth.

—Brother

Daily Spiritual Peacemaking Lesson – Day 241

Love IS creating you like Itself.

Today's idea is different than yesterday's because it acknowledges that you are being created and recreated this and every moment. Your creation is not something that took place in the past. That would indicate that you are bound to the past, which you are not. You are bound only to this present moment, where you are being created now in perfection and love. See this and Know it to be true in others today, and it will be solidified within your own mind.

—Brother

Daily Spiritual Peacemaking Lesson – Day 242

I have said this many times before, and I will say it again. All you need is a little willingness for these things to be true. That is all. You do not need to believe them wholly in your mind, for the truth does not exist in your mind. You only need to hold the space open by being willing to accept them as true. The Holy Spirit will do the rest. The less you do, the more can be done through you.

—Brother

Daily Spiritual Peacemaking Lesson – Day 243

Do you realize that the "Willingness to See" is all that is required to allow the shift into your enlightened mind? Consistency of Sight will occur on its own through your willingness to enter into this moment of Grace. Choose to See now, and make the same decision in the next moment. The Holy Spirit and the whole Universe does then respond, because all of creation longs to be seen as it is—in Light.

—Brother

Daily Spiritual Peacemaking Lesson – Day 244

As you SEE so will you be SEEN. Do you expect others to perceive you in this Light? Lay down this desire, for it is like a cloud around your mind blocking your Sight of what is real. Simply choose to SEE God revealed in every moment; then these others will open their eyes to you as well, then to themselves.

There is no moment but NOW! Even if you have failed a thousand times before, still is the Christ revealed to you this very moment. Your Willingness to See is all that is required.

—Brother

Daily Spiritual Peacemaking Lesson – Day 245

My gift to you this day is the same as always, but I am going to ask you to be conscious of this gift in a way you may not normally choose. Today I am Seeing you as the Enlightened Child of God that you have always been. Feel my eyes and heart upon you this day. Know that I am here, deep within, holding this vision of your Light. Let it fill you with strength this day, and give you the courage to imitate me. This is what I am asking you to do for others, but you will not be able to follow my example until you learn to Feel my gift to you. Let this be the day, then, when you lay aside your visions of separation and feel how much I love you.

—Brother

Daily Spiritual Peacemaking Lesson – Day 246

Being a Spiritual Peacemaker ultimately means that you finally realize that all your problems have been solved. How can you do this, other than by realizing that you misidentified the problem, which means that the problem you thought was real never truly existed? Once you accept this for yourself, then you can extend it to others. Once you extend it to others, then you will realize why you chose to come to this place. Once that is complete, you will be able to return to where you came from.

—Brother

Daily Spiritual Peacemaking Lesson – Day 247

There is no problem you need to solve. Trust this and you are saved. Now I will speak to you from the problem you seem to perceive, or which you think you have. It would be best to allow it to be as simple and clearly identified as possible, because then you will be able to release it forever. The problem is that you believe that it is possible to be separated from your creator. From this single idea all error does arise. The solution is simple -- you were wrong. Rejoice in this, then share the joy you feel. Your joy from the realization that all your problems have been solved will make you a servant to the world, just as I AM.

—Brother

Daily Spiritual Peacemaking Lesson – Day 248

You are entitled to peace this day. How will peace come to you? It will come by realizing that all your problems have been solved. Then you can relax, and everything will be added to what never was lacking. This can be the day of your release if you simply choose to see this.

—Brother

Daily Spiritual Peacemaking Lesson – Day 249

Your openness to a new way of thinking is all I need to transform the whole world. The starting point is the realization that you have not been able to accomplish your real goals, and therefore new possibilities open before you. Once you accept that you have not been able to find what you really want on your own, it is possible to accept that there is one who knows the way, or has seen what you have not. It is like putting on a pair of glasses and seeing what has always been right in front of you. The landscape has never changed at all, but your perception has, and you are able to see further than before. And once you finally See what was always true, your illusions fall away on their own. This is the path I am leading you on.

—Brother

Daily Spiritual Peacemaking Lesson – Day 250

God asks so little of you. One of your problems is that you try to give God more than is asked. There is only one thing that is required to open Heaven's Door to you—a little willingness to SEE. You do not need to worry about the quality of your SEEING, or even the consistency. These things will happen on their own when you realize that you cannot add anything unto God's Glory, or yours. Your little willingness shows the conviction you have lacked till now, and all things fall naturally into place. Simply choose to SEE the truth that is in front of you this moment, nothing else. That moment will soon expand to include the one moment that can set you free.

—Brother

Daily Spiritual Peacemaking Lesson – Day 251

Nothing exists outside your experience of yourself. Take a deep breath now and let that fact slide deep into your soul. It has not forgotten this, but your mind has. Your soul holds the memory of your Home and, therefore, your Truth. It has not forgotten that the world of dreams cannot affect you in any permanent way, and what is not permanent is not ultimately real. Therefore, why be concerned about the images that seem to exist on their own? Know the truth about yourself and they will dance before you where once they cried. Love them as you love yourself and let the truth exist on its own.

—Brother

Daily Spiritual Peacemaking Lesson – Day 252

Choose to be an Instrument of Peace this day so that God's Love may be revealed through and as you. This should be your only desire as a Spiritual Peacemaker. Do not try to act on your own, for on your own you are so weak and will accomplish so little. Allow God to act "through" you, knowing that there is no difference. Then you will Know who you really are—the perfect extension of God's Love fully revealed. Is this enough for you?

—Brother

Daily Spiritual Peacemaking Lesson – Day 253

The ego's control is maintained, ultimately, by a single desire—to "not lose." It believes that loss is possible, and therefore guards against it in every way and at every turn. Once something is gained, all its attention is placed upon the desire to "not lose" it. Be it a relationship, a possession, or a place of honor, the result is always the same. When you take this to its ultimate end, the foundation of all its fear is revealed. It is afraid of death. It believes you to be a body, and it knows that all bodies must die. How do we release this fear of loss, and this fear of death? We will spend the next several lessons on this one idea. In the end, the answer is simple—nothing that was created by God has an end. Therefore, loss of any kind is impossible. Herein lies your salvation.

—Brother

Daily Spiritual Peacemaking Lesson – Day 254

What you think you can lose is not what you really want, and therefore is not real. God's will for you is perfect happiness, and that can only be fulfilled if the Gifts of God are eternal. The only Gift you are seeking is love, and love has no beginning and no end. It does not rise as your emotions rise, and fall as disappointment enters. Love is fulfilled every moment equally and completely, and is fully revealed to and for you. The instant you realize that love cannot be lost is the instant you remember who you are. Then you will give this love to others just as it was given to you. The fear of loss is nothing at all, then, for the love you are seeking is already yours.

—Brother

Daily Spiritual Peacemaking Lesson – Day 255

You are afraid of death, and you long for it in the same instant. This is where the insanity of the ego is greatest, and it is also where you will find your greatest release. Because you think you are a body, and everything you have seems to serve your body, the idea that you will die is the greatest threat. The notion that there is an afterlife where you go but your body does not is a comfort, but it is not a real solution. The fear of death can only be solved when you realize it doesn't exist, and therefore there is nothing for you to lose. What God created has no end, and God certainly created you. If you rely upon the love that is at the very foundation of your life, then you will begin to realize this truth very subtly at first, then profoundly.

—Brother

Daily Spiritual Peacemaking Lesson – Day 256

Is it possible for you to believe that you complete God? This is what you must demonstrate as a Spiritual Peacemaker, for the demonstration of this is what leads to salvation. Nothing of this world you created can show you this, for it proclaims that you are weak and under attack. The opposite is true, for God Sees you as invulnerable and safe. Which will you choose to believe? If you trust in God's Will, then you will See that your part is essential, and that it cannot be separated from God's Plan. It will not be accomplished but through your Light and your forgiveness.

What I am telling you is true, and you are ready to hear it.

—Brother

Daily Spiritual Peacemaking Lesson – Day 257

Open your eyes and See that your function and God's are the same. You fell into the world of dreams because you started to believe that separation from God's purpose was possible. It is not, but you can only Know this once you are on the other side of it. The other option is to trust one who does See, one who is standing in a place where you are not, and who has a view that you cannot yet achieve. This is the benefit of our Holy Relationship, and we have both entered into it willingly. If you choose to surrender what you think you know, understanding that it is impossible for you to make decisions about what you cannot see, and then trust that I can, everything will fall into place. That is the purpose of this joining, and this instruction. It is occurring on many levels at once, as you have already discovered.

—Brother

Daily Spiritual Peacemaking Lesson – Day 258

Everyone that speaks from the place of 'Knowing' speaks with my voice, while the place of 'not-knowing' does not exist at all. There is only One Voice that Speaks the Truth, and it is yours, and is uniquely expressed through us all. Do you understand what I am saying? Meditate on the first two sentences of this lesson and you will then fully grasp what it means to be a Spiritual Peacemaker. When we speak as One, then our words are truly heard, but when you 'do not know,' then nothing has occurred at all. It is a Holy Joining we seek, and we find it by Knowing that it cannot end or change.

—Brother

Daily Spiritual Peacemaking Lesson – Day 259

Yours is the Voice for God. What other lesson can I teach you, and what other statement brings you closer to the Truth that cannot change? The only shift I am leading you toward is the realization of this, or the full knowledge that nothing else is possible. I can lead you to the place where this occurs, but only you can reach out and accept the Gift. Then, once it has been accepted, it can be shared, which is how it will deepen even further. Yet, no change has occurred at all on any level, only your appreciation of Reality.

—Brother

Daily Spiritual Peacemaking Lesson – Day 260

Know that your voice speaks for and as God and it will be so. Then you will speak with an authority that you cannot experience otherwise in this world, the same authority I spoke with and which was recognized through me. You obviously want this or you would not be here now. If you were not seeking this Gift then you would choose to remain asleep, just as you have done so many times before. The fact that you are here reading these words means that you're ready. Take a deep breath now and accept these words. You speak for and as God every moment you realize that you cannot be separated from love, then choose to share this realization. Let this be the moment.

—Brother

Daily Spiritual Peacemaking Lesson – Day 261

True Spirituality comes from answering one question correctly: "Who am I?" What do I mean by True Spirituality? I am referring to an experience that cannot be expressed in words, but which the soul fully comprehends. I am pointing toward the "Knowing" that you are perfect now, this moment, just as you were created, and that nothing in this world can change what God made. Who are you, then? You are That! What do I mean by that? It is impossible to say, and that is why it is true. All I am asking is that you consider this as a possibility. This is the willingness that makes you a Spiritual Peacemaker, and which fulfills your role here on Earth.

—Brother

Daily Spiritual Peacemaking Lesson – *Day 262*

"You are That!" Have you had the chance to meditate with this statement? Let your mind fall away and simply Know that this is true. It is that simple. Your mind wants to make it more complicated, but that is only because it wants to make itself seem to be more important than it really is. Your spirit rests in the Truth that exists beyond the mind's comprehension. It does not need proof to know what it is. Read that last sentence one more time. It does not need proof to know what it is. When you do not need proof, then you will know that you have arrived.

—Brother

Daily Spiritual Peacemaking Lesson – *Day 263*

This is the day when you will let the Truth appear before you without judgment. "You are That Now!" I have seen it in you and now it is time to SEE it in your Self. How else will you be able to share this with others? You cannot give what you refuse to receive. Let this be the day, then, when giving and receiving become the same.

—Brother

Daily Spiritual Peacemaking Lesson – *Day 264*

A Spiritual Peacemaker is one who is able to look past what isn't happening, and therefore decrease the effect of the dream of separation. At this point in your growth, now that you have been practicing this for some time, how close do you feel you are to this? Have you achieved a level of consistency, or is your success still sporadic? Now release those thoughts, and realize that there is a part of you or, rather, the WHOLE of you, that has never failed at this. Can you focus there? Can you release the ego's attention, and focus instead on the Gifts of Spirit? We will work with this idea for the next several days, but let it start with your decision to SEE yourself today.

—Brother

Daily Spiritual Peacemaking Lesson – *Day 265*

The simplicity of salvation is falling in around you. You are free to be and to know who you are, and your realization sets all souls free from the constraints of time. The illusion is seen for what it is, an impossible substitute for reality. Do not let it be more than it is, but allow yourself to be what you are and what you have always been. Give all to have all. This is all I have asked of myself, and now I ask it of you as well. I need you. Is that enough for you to take this step? I need you at my side now, and then the mission will be complete. Do not try to understand this with your mind, but accept it in your heart. It is done now through you.

—Brother

Daily Spiritual Peacemaking Lesson – Day 266

You have always been a Spiritual Peacemaker, but this is the moment you are deciding to realize who you are. Enlightenment is nothing more than a recognition of what has always been true. Are you able to see that now? Ultimately, you are here to realize that you are loved by God for no reason at all, except that you are still as holy as when you were created. See this in others now. Give this to everyone you encounter, then you will know that you are as God. Do not wait, for God has never waited for you.

—Brother

Daily Spiritual Peacemaking Lesson – Day 267

There has never been a moment when you have failed to SEE what is real. Does this surprise you? It should, because your experience of the world does not support this theory. Your ego believes that there has never been a time when you have seen the Truth. Therefore, the Truth does not exist. And yet, it is simply a matter of which voice you choose to hear, revealing the world that you will SEE. Let us keep our focus on this single point for awhile. Meditate on this idea as often as you can today, and be honest with yourself. What are you choosing to SEE this moment?

—Brother

Daily Spiritual Peacemaking Lesson – Day 268

You will SEE in the world what you believe yourself to BE. This is the simplest I can put the truth, and yet it makes no sense according to the world YOU have established, the world the ego perceives. And yet the evidence is clear. There has never been a time when you have seen anything outside your personal frame of reference. There has never been a moment when a foreign element has entered your mind, one which you did not place there yourself. Let this be your salvation, for it means that you have complete control over the world. Let this be your Freedom Song, for this realization sets all prisoners free, not just you. This is the moment for you to do more than listen to my words, but to become them. Choose now, and you will be chosen.

—Brother

Daily Spiritual Peacemaking Lesson – Day 269

Choose, then, and you will be chosen. What does this mean? It simply means that you will experience the result of the choice you make about yourself. You cannot escape this, and that is why it is so important. If you choose to acknowledge yourself as God does, then you will SEE yourself as God sees you. If you choose the opposite, then you will experience that result all around you, in every dealing you have with another. Choose life every moment of this day, and life will be yours.

—Brother

Daily Spiritual Peacemaking Lesson – Day 270

What I am trying to reveal cannot be seen by your eyes, but they can be a tool in revealing this new world. What I am trying to say cannot be understood with your mind, but your mind can establish the road upon which this new world can be built. Your heart alone will reveal what I am describing to you. Trust it today, and let it tell you everything you need to hear.

—Brother

Daily Spiritual Peacemaking Lesson – Day 271

There are very few words left for me to say. I have only one question: "Will you stop considering these thoughts and become them?" These are not theories to make your life better, but whole worlds to show you, that you have yet to live. You are about to take your first breath of air in the world your Beloved has reserved for you. At this point I have said enough. Now it is up to you to breathe.

—Brother

Daily Spiritual Peacemaking Lesson – Day 272

Giving everything to everything means you understand what has value, and all your energy is placed there. It also means that you realize what has no value, even if your past has been bent upon satisfying it. This is the only moment that matters now. You are called to add your Light to the Light that transcends all unnecessary dreams. Therefore, you are free to act as God in the world, which is what you have been called to do. You are so needed. Thank you for answering the call.

—Brother

Daily Spiritual Peacemaking Lesson – Day 273

You have been called to act as God in the world. In other words, you have been called to be the hands, the voice, and the heart of God in a world that has forgotten itself. You have been called to walk with the Beloved wherever you go, and to know that holy steps mark your way. Every person you touch is healed, for you have called the power of God into your Self, where it never left. This is why you were born, and you not only realize that now, but you are activating it.

—Brother

Daily Spiritual Peacemaking Lesson – Day 274

If you realized how pivotal your role is, then you would not waste another moment in extending the love you have received. Perhaps you have come closer to realizing this over the last year, but this is the only moment you can activate that knowingness. Say YES now, and let it heal the world. Do you realize that your YES is that powerful? I had to realize it myself, and that is why I am offering it to you. I cannot offer what I did not choose to receive, and the same goes for you. Choose Life then, and Life will be your reward. The ego believes that death leads to Life, and that is why it is insane. Only Life leads to Life, and that is why you are with me now, because you have come to realize the Truth.

—Brother

Daily Spiritual Peacemaking Lesson – Day 275

You do not need to suffer as I did to release this Light. The Light has already been released, and has already vanquished the darkness. You do not need to fall down as I fell, for you have been given a different cross to carry. Yours is but to realize who you are, and you will do this by SEEING it in others, everywhere you look. That is why I said that my cross is heavy. It is not a cross of wood, but one of Light.

—Brother

Daily Spiritual Peacemaking Lesson – Day 276

Your holiness is the gift you have been holding back from yourself. If you want to learn to act as God acts, then realize that God only gives. What is all pervading cannot take, for nothing real is ever lost. You are real just as God is. That is why you cannot be separated from your creator, or from creation itself. So give everything. I have said this over and over in so many ways, but in the end it is the only lesson I have come to teach you.

—Brother

Daily Spiritual Peacemaking Lesson – Day 277

Giving what you want to receive is not selfish, but wise. How else will you have it unless you are willing to give it? The space needs to be opened inside you, then the Universe will flow to fill that space. You are only giving to yourself, or to God, because there is nothing else for you. This is all you need to understand, not with your mind, but with your heart. Stop trying to build concepts around that which is wholly beyond concepts. Simply accept the Truth, and then you will realize that the Truth has always accepted you.

—Brother

Daily Spiritual Peacemaking Lesson – Day 278

The Beloved is all around you and with you every moment and wherever you look. You are not alone, especially in the journey you have chosen. Angels walk at your side and protect every step you take. You cannot be harmed, no matter what seems to happen. You are now able to look past the seeming reality to reality itself, and this is what makes you an effective Spiritual Peacemaker. It is mine but to welcome you into this Light, the Light you never left. But now your eyes are open. Now you can see what has always been Seen by God. This is the moment YOU chose, and therefore it is a holy moment. Rejoice today, that the Light has come into your mind.

—Brother

Daily Spiritual Peacemaking Lesson – Day 279

The more you allow yourself to be "used" by God, the more useful you will be. Isn't that why you're here, to become truly useful? How else will you be part of God's plan for salvation if not through your desire to give everything, every part of yourself, over to the one who knows who you really are? Night is beginning to fade and a new dawn appears in your mind. The moment has arrived, and from this point on we will make very good use of time.

—Brother

Daily Spiritual Peacemaking Lesson – Day 280

There is only one word I choose to offer today - YES. Live there. Breathe the reality of this into your lungs. Nothing else matters but you realizing that you are not separate from the YES you claim. How much more simple can Truth be?

—Brother

Daily Spiritual Peacemaking Lesson – Day 281

It is impossible for you to play yourself, but if you surrender your life to God, then you will surely be played. This is what it means to be an instrument of peace. On your own you can do nothing. Why? It is simply because of your perception of "being on your own." If you begin with a false premise, then no truth can come from your actions. That is why your only job as a Spiritual Peacemaker is to turn everything over to the Beloved and, in doing so, be played. Let this be the day you allow this shift in your attention to take place.

—Brother

222 –James F. Twyman

Daily Spiritual Peacemaking Lesson – Day 282

As long as you think that there is anything at all beyond the decisions you make about your-self, then you will not be of help to all the Emissaries that are here to heal. There is nothing beyond the decisions you make about yourself, simply because there is nothing beyond your Self. Let this be the foundation of everything you do, every action and every word you speak. Once you realize this truth, not in your mind but in your heart, then you will realize that you have always stood at our side and have always done this work.

—Brother

Daily Spiritual Peacemaking Lesson – Day 283

This is the moment of your decision. Which will you choose, Truth or illusions? Which will you give your life for, not your death? The ego asks for the demonstration of your death because it makes its existence seem real. The Spirit, which you are following now, knows that there is no such thing as death, and therefore disregards all its witnesses. Choose truth, then you will realize that Truth already chose you.

—Brother

Daily Spiritual Peacemaking Lesson – Day 284

"Choose to Be—where you are Now!"

This will be the prayer you will focus on for the next three days. Do not be deceived by its simplicity, for there are levels upon levels of wisdom here. This is all I am asking you to do—Be where you Are. Until now you have chosen to "seem to be where you are not." But you can only truly BE in One place, which is the Oneness of your Creator. Let this be true for you, and you will experience only that.

—Brother

Daily Spiritual Peacemaking Lesson – Day 285

"Choose to Be—where you are Now!"

Why would you choose to be somewhere that does not exist? The answer is simple—to avoid being where you really are. And what reason can you find for this insane practice but the fact that you are afraid of who you really are? You are afraid because you see the Power of your Creator within you. Why are you afraid of power? Is it perhaps because you think you will misuse it? All I can tell you is that the end is sure, and so there is no reason to be afraid. Choose who you are, not who you are not. Choose to be where God is, and then you will see everything as it really is.

—Brother

Daily Spiritual Peacemaking Lesson – Day 286

"Choose to Be—where you are Now!"

The recognition of your Beingness is the only goal. There is nothing you can do to change the truth in you, because it is beyond your control. The only thing you can change is the perception of that truth, which you have surely done. You can choose to SEE at any moment. Let this be the moment of choice, then, for Heaven and Earth wait upon you.

—Brother

Daily Spiritual Peacemaking Lesson – Day 287

How will it look when you succeed in giving everything to everything? Is the fulfillment of your every desire a small thing? All the desires that do not serve the Truth in you disappear, and all you are left with is the gentle touch of your Creator's Hand. You will then recognize that there is only one Hand of God, and it is yours. This is what you will find when your only desire is to be real and to give all to All.

—Brother

Daily Spiritual Peacemaking Lesson – Day 288

If there was anything left for me to teach you, you will have learned it by now. But I still have a great deal to show you. At this point you will only learn as you watch, then give what you See. Do you understand? This is not a complicated path, but one so simple that it has evaded your attention. And so we begin in a place where your attention cannot go, for your heart is the only servant now. And so shall the Master appear, when the servant wants only one thing.

—Brother

Daily Spiritual Peacemaking Lesson – Day 289

I am here as the Living Demonstration that death is not real and cannot touch the Holy Child of God. Look to me as your brother more than as a savior, then you will learn what I have to teach you. If you separate yourself from me, then you will also separate yourself from the lessons I would teach you. But if you stand beside me, drinking from the same cup I drink from, then you will Know the Truth about us both. Extend that and you will See the Truth in all, which is the only goal there is. Let this be the day, then, that you accomplish it.

—Brother

Daily Spiritual Peacemaking Lesson – Day 290

When you look to me as your brother, knowing that we are the same, realizing that you came to this place of dreams for the same reason I came here, then you will be a savior. You are not here to look up to me, for that would make us unequal, thus limiting the real role I am here to play. Reach out and touch me; how can you do this except by reaching out to any brother or sister? Know me by knowing them, then you will Know your Self. Then the obvious will become obvious to you. Until now you have denied what is so simple, but your denial has not changed reality at all. It only kept you from enjoying what is real. Let this be the moment you let our role be the same, and then you will enjoy the fruits of my awakened heart, realizing that it is yours.

—Brother

Daily Spiritual Peacemaking Lesson – Day 291

If the task of awakening from the dream of separation were easy, then you would have done it already. What is not easy, however, can be simple. How do you allow it to be thus? You will do it by allowing it to already be done. Do you understand? Accept that you have already awakened from the dream of separation, and it is done. Then it will not matter if it is easy or hard, only that it is complete.

—Brother

Daily Spiritual Peacemaking Lesson – Day 292

Open your eyes and see what is so clear to your Self. There is only one Self in the Universe, and that is why it is so easy for me to make that statement. The only difference between you and me is that I do not expect anything to be other than what it really is. There is still part of your mind that is waiting for your version of reality to win out over God's. I gave up such an impossible battle, just as you are now. Then you will See through the eyes of God, the eyes that I See through, and every other enlightened soul. But Seeing, in this sense, is One, and cannot be separated from the Seer. It is you. Allow this to be true, once and for all.

—Brother

Daily Spiritual Peacemaking Lesson – Day 293

I did not come into the world that you may have life, but to help you realize that you are Life Itself.

—Brother

Daily Spiritual Peacemaking Lesson – Day 294

If you are waiting for something to happen that will prove what I am here to reveal to you, then you will surely miss what I am here to reveal. That is because there is nothing in this world you created that will affirm what I have said. The denial of life can only deny life. But life Itself affirms Itself. What I am saying is true, and your acceptance of this without regard for proof is what will reveal it to you. Surrender everything and Trust what God would reveal.

—Brother

Daily Spiritual Peacemaking Lesson – Day 295

Your acceptance of your role as a Spiritual Peacemaker has nothing to do with time, so do not wait upon that which does not wait upon you. Wait only upon the Truth, which is revealing Itself perfectly through and as you now. Then the shadow your ego has cast upon the ground, that which you mistook for yourself, will disappear, only to be replaced by the heart of Love. You are that Heart, and it is beating wildly, sensing your approach.

—Brother

Daily Spiritual Peacemaking Lesson – *Day 296*

If you do not claim the Truth for yourself, then you will not realize that it is already yours. The Gifts of God have always been with you, but you have chosen to ignore them, thus aligning yourself with what does not belong to you. A Spiritual Peacemaker is one who first believes, then offers that faith to others. Accept that God has not left you homeless, and you will then recognize your home.

—Brother

Daily Spiritual Peacemaking Lesson – *Day 297*

Peace I give to you, Peace I offer, because Peace is all that I choose for myself. Imitate me, and you will know your Self as I know you, and as I am known. Peace is impossible in the world, but it is a reality in God. The only question is -- which world will you choose? It is important that you recognize what is offered in both so your choice will be clear. Do not fool yourself into believing that peace can come from conflict, or that a world that does not understand peace can offer it to you. An apple tree will never offer you an orange, and so the world of separation cannot give you what is whole. Choose instead the world that is yet beyond your senses, but which is the fountain of reality.

—Brother

Daily Spiritual Peacemaking Lesson – Day 298

The path of a Spiritual Peacemaker is a Return to Innocence. You are asked to "See as God Sees," and to "Love as God Loves." How will you do this except by "Knowing what God Knows," which is Innocence Itself? Everything that seems to contradict this will fall away in time, but the eternal Vision of God transcends time and disregards it completely. It knows what it true, not what "seems" to be true. And so will you when you open your eyes and See what is right in front of you. Be very clear—this is your only function as a Spiritual Peacemaker. Peace will come to the world of dreams in no other way but this.

—Brother

Daily Spiritual Peacemaking Lesson – Day 299

Eternity does not wait upon you, but you are waiting upon it. The Vision of God does not change in time, but remains constantly focused on what is real. You, however, have chosen a different path, and it is time for you to realize how useless it has been. You have chosen to look upon what isn't there, wishing it was, and therefore making it appear real. The Holy Spirit does not rely upon appearances, but on reality. Choose to See in the same way. Do you realize that it is as easy as that—Choosing to See? Let it be real for you, and it is real in the world you create.

—Brother

Daily Spiritual Peacemaking Lesson – Day 300

You are all the Children of God, innocent as you were created. Rely upon this in everything you do. Focus on this Truth even when it seems to contradict everything you think you perceive. The more you focus on it, the more the former world will pass away, replaced by Heaven and all the things you really want. Choose to See today. You are a Spiritual Peacemaker NOW!

—Brother

Daily Spiritual Peacemaking Lesson – Day 301

You are remembering what it means to "Put on the Mind of God." Once established, you can then learn the Heart of God. It is not a real learning, for that would imply that it is not in you now, which would mean that God is not God. What is present in Eternity is present in you. There can be no other possibility. Therefore, you are not here to learn anything, but to be everything. You will do this as you remember who you are, and why you are here. Then the Mind and the Heart of God will dawn upon you, and you will be THAT.

—Brother

Daily Spiritual Peacemaking Lesson – Day 302

The Way of Eternity is your Way as well, though you have forgotten the path that leads to your Truest and Highest. When I say that you are here to "See as God Sees," or to "Love as God Loves," I am demonstrating that you are the Way, the Truth and the Light Now! Only your recognition is required. Once recognized, it will transform. Once transformed, it will redeem. Once redeemed, all things of time will fall away in favor of what is Whole.

—Brother

Daily Spiritual Peacemaking Lesson – Day 303

Why do you think you will lose something valuable by accepting everything of Highest Value? Nothing that is real can be lost once you accept the Truth that surrounds you every instant of life. You are experiencing loss now because you have allowed the possibility of loss to enter your mind. Once it is vanquished, once you realize that nothing that is real can ever be lost, and that nothing else matters, then you will lay aside these fears. There is a tension in your mind that does not belong there. This is what binds you to time and to all things that fade in time. Release this tension and you will fall naturally into the Kingdom. Hold onto it and you will wonder if such a thing is possible at all. It is not only possible, but is happening now. Allow the Truth to recognize you, and you are recognized.

—Brother

Daily Spiritual Peacemaking Lesson – *Day 304*

To See the Truth, share it in humility. Do not be attached to anything, especially the results of your Seeing God everywhere. The only result you can expect is the Seeing Itself. The world will not conform to your Seeing, for it does not understand it at all. But Heaven does not need to conform, for it assumes nothing but Truth. It does not need to be proven, for proof indicates the possibility of contradictory reality. Reality assumes only Reality and therefore requires nothing.

—Brother

Daily Spiritual Peacemaking Lesson – *Day 305*

Let all things go, and everything will return to you. If you try to claim peace, or life, or anything you believe is holy, you also claim everything that seems to oppose these states—war, life and everything you perceive as base. But if you allow all things to be as they are, without attachment or judgment, then they wash over you and propel you into the peace your mind can never claim, and the life your body can never live. If you claim one thing as holy and the other not, then you become blind to your Self, and you forget why you are here.

—Brother

*Daily Spiritual Peacemaking Lesson – **Day 306***

My teachings are not hard to understand, as long as you do not try to understand them. They are also not hard to live, as long as you do not try to practice them. I ask only one thing— BE them, and watch the whole world transform before your eyes. Let the ones whose hearts have been opened understand this lesson.

—Brother

*Daily Spiritual Peacemaking Lesson – **Day 307***

Accept yourself as God accepts you, then you will begin to understand why love is the only reality. Give this gift without discrimination, and then you will begin to comprehend how God gives and loves. If you are to be free, then you must learn to give as God gives, without judgment or conditions. Give everything to everything, and you will understand what this world cannot give you.

—Brother

Daily Spiritual Peacemaking Lesson – Day 308

If you are going to be an effective Spiritual Peacemaker in this world, then it is important that you never forget that your only source of power and wisdom is God. Seek nothing but to know this source, and then you will surely be known. Seek only to BE that source, for that source is within you now. You cannot attain something that has never left. This is what you must demonstrate today, that God has never left God. See it and know it in the smallest ways possible, then it will translate naturally into the larger ones.

—Brother

Daily Spiritual Peacemaking Lesson – Day 309

You have been called to be the eyes, the ears, the feet and the hands of God in this world. Most of all, you have been called to be the Heart of God, which so loved the world that it offered it a demonstration that only Love is Real. God does this (as opposed to "did," which would indicate that it happened in the past, rather than this very moment) by showing that death is not real, unless you make it "seem" real. But something that seems to be real and reality itself are very similar in their effects if you believe those effects to be real. And yet, a Light has come into the world, a Light that the world does not understand, that has made all things new. Trust that and your life will be a demonstration of that reality, just as mine was and is. Let this be the day that you allow the Truth to shine through your eyes as a blessing for all beings.

—Brother

Daily Spiritual Peacemaking Lesson – Day 310

If there was only one gift I could offer you that would set you firmly upon the path of your awakening to Light, it would be this: Know that it is happening Now! Do not wait for the conditions to be right, or for more of everything to be yours. There is no such things as "more of everything." Therefore, there is no reason for you to wait to have what is already yours. Simply relax and let it wash over you like a river. God's Love and God's Light are all around you. Open your eyes and SEE what is all-pervading.

—Brother

Daily Spiritual Peacemaking Lesson – Day 311

There is a question every Spiritual Peacemaker must ask in every situation: "What is the gift in this?" No matter how things appear, the Holy Spirit is always reaching out to you, always guiding you toward the Light, no matter how dark a particular situation may appear. You are here to serve every moment, for in your service does your release exist. Read that last sentence again. In your service does your release exist and increase. Release from what? All things of time will fall away, to be replaced by the eternal embrace your soul longs for. This gift is always being held out to you, but you must acknowledge it, then accept it in order for it to be real to you. Otherwise, that which is obvious will be overlooked. It is now time for you to stop overlooking eternity and accept what has always been yours.

—Brother

Daily Spiritual Peacemaking Lesson – *Day 312*

There will be many times in your journey when you will be tempted to make one person more special than another, especially when they seem to offer a greater or brighter Light than another. If you are able to resist this urge and see this person within every other, then their gift will be even greater to you. If you choose to see this person as higher or holier than any other, then you will not SEE the brother or sister who offers you the greater gift. Do you understand what I am saying to you? Do not underestimate this lesson, for the temptation to see one person as possessing more than another is one of the basic tenets of the ego's thought system. The only gift an enlightened master can offer you is a window into the heart of every other being. If they ask for more than this, then they have not realized who they are. You will demonstrate enlightenment when you are able to look past them to the one who is standing beside or behind them, giving them what they most need—the recognition of their Divinity.

—Brother

Daily Spiritual Peacemaking Lesson – *Day 313*

Specialness does not exist in the mind of God, but it does exist in your mind. This is the thing that makes you seem most different from your creator, but as I've said so many times before, all seeming differences fade in the Light of Truth. Look upon the saint and the sinner with the same loving eyes, and then you will understand love. The sun and the air of your world do not discriminate between the guilty and the just, so why should you suffer such exclusions? Seek the Vision of God over all things, and then you will realize that you are contained within that same Vision. Withhold it from anyone, and it will seem to be held from you. This, in the end, is the only thing I have come to teach. I have described it as "Seeing as God Sees," which leads ultimately to "Loving as God Loves." Choose to See all things as One, as they really are, and everything else will fall together effortlessly.

—Brother

Daily Spiritual Peacemaking Lesson – Day 314

In this course, which you have been engaged in for almost year, I have tried to make the truth as simple as I possibly can. That is because it must first be processed by your mind before it can be accepted by your heart. Once your heart has embraced the Truth, the world itself, and everything you perceive, will shift to reflect that realization. I am here to show you what you really want, then help you achieve that. Are you ready now to lay aside all other desires in order to have everything? Let your heart repeat, then, everything you have heard from me. Once it has been repeated, it will be believed, and everything will change.

—Brother

Daily Spiritual Peacemaking Lesson – Day 315

Within the seed of your longing for God, there is also the desire for "not-God." If you pay attention to your heart you will notice that every time you approach the throne of love, sensing the Beloved's hand upon your heart, fear rises, often imperceptibly, directly behind. What should you do when this happens? Is there a way to battle and overcome this fear so only the love remains? Do nothing. Embrace the fear exactly as you would the love. You simply need to realize that they are part of you, and that only Love is real. The shadow disappears on its own, then the Light comes, and so will your fear vanish when you embrace it fully.

—Brother

*Daily Spiritual Peacemaking Lesson – **Day 316***

Pray to God today, but not as something that seems to exist outside of you. Imagine that you are praying, or communing with, the Holy Child that still lives in your heart. Speak to that innocence that you still are, knowing that God and the whole Universe is there as well. If you are to be of true service in the world then you must realize your Self as the source, not the effect. To be a spiritual Peacemaker means that you have realized this source everywhere, and so love God in all things. Peace, then, occurs on its own, not through any action you take, but simply through your willingness to SEE.

—Brother

*Daily Spiritual Peacemaking Lesson – **Day 317***

I have emphasized your work as a Spiritual Peacemaker as one who chooses to SEE what really exists. This is your only function, for you now realize that the whole world rises from what you chose to see. You have chosen to be blind till now, seeing what you imagine and believing it to be real. But this is not "True Sight," for the world you have created does not act in concordance with the "Real World" created for you by God. The first step is to accept that this is true, and not to judge yourself for anything. God does not judge you for creating a world with no meaning. Open your eyes and SEE, then you'll realize that all has been forgiven. There is no sin that cannot be cleansed by the "Vision of God" which you are accepting now.

—Brother

Daily Spiritual Peacemaking Lesson – Day 318

When the Peace of God is the only thing you want in your life, then you will be at peace every moment. I know that this sounds simple and obvious, and yet it has evaded you for a very long time. Therefore, it doesn't matter if it's simple, since you haven't applied it till now. The Truth is always simple, and that is why it is only the most simple among you that attain it. Have you ever met a person who is at peace no matter what happens around them? They could lose everything, yet their peace is not shaken. That is because there is something they have found that means more to them than anything of this world. This is what I called, "The treasure beyond compare." Once you find that treasure, you will never lack for anything again.

—Brother

Daily Spiritual Peacemaking Lesson – Day 319

Embracing all, a Spiritual Peacemaker moves through every situation in grace. That is because they are not attached to anything the world has to offer. How can one be attached to a prison cell when they have known the Real World where Light prevails? Even if that world has only been glimpsed, still does it move that one to such a state of devotion that they will do anything, give anything, to realize freedom. I am not asking you to despise the world, but to embrace it so completely that you touch the reality that lies behind it. Once that happens, you will see everything like a newborn child.

—Brother

Daily Spiritual Peacemaking Lesson – Day 320

Knowing your Self is the simplest thing in the Universe. It may not be the easiest, though. That is only because you have become so attached to the reflections of your lower self rather than to that which even now is fully aligned with the Beloved. Seek and you shall find. Knock and the door of your Self will be opened to you. You do not need to shout at the gate, for the Beloved already knows everything you need. Until now you have been like a stubborn child, too full of yourself to ask for what you really want. That is why humility is the key to everything. Give up your childish desire to be in charge, and you will be brought instantly into the Kingdom.

—Brother

Daily Spiritual Peacemaking Lesson – Day 321

If you only knew how much I love you, then you would lay aside your cross and follow me. Because I carried mine, you do not need to carry yours. I made all things new so that a new world would be born. And so it was, though you have yet to SEE it. But that doesn't mean it isn't there. Think about that today, that you may understand the real function of this world.

—Brother

Daily Spiritual Peacemaking Lesson – Day 322

Only love is real. Whatever question enters your mind, this is the answer. Whatever evidence the world seems to provide, it cannot withstand the singular logic of this Truth. Your mind will never understand it, for it was made to not understand. Your eyes will never see the evidence, for they were made not to see. But there is another part of you that does understand, and does SEE. That is where I am drawing your attention, for once it is established, it cannot fade away. Then love will be seen for what it is—the foundation of the Mind and Heart of the Beloved, forever safe from the dream you made that seemed to threaten it for but a moment.

—Brother

Daily Spiritual Peacemaking Lesson – Day 323

What is it you're looking for? Find it within yourself, and then it will surely be yours. If you believe that you don't have something, then the Universe is unlikely to give it to you, simply because it believes that that is the way you want it—to seek but never find. But when you know that you have everything within, then God rushes in to fill your every desire. Does this make sense at all? Of course not, and that is why it's true.

—Brother

Daily Spiritual Peacemaking Lesson – Day 324

Do you realize that longing for something that you don't think you have is like setting a road block in front of a road you want to travel? If you look at the map you'll see that everything you need is spelled out for you. Follow the directions and you'll surely arrive at the chosen destination. Likewise, there is a map inside of you that will tell you everything you need to know about God, enlightenment, and who you really are. Follow that map and you'll realize that the real journey is one taken by the heart.

—Brother

Daily Spiritual Peacemaking Lesson – Day 325

No one can give you anything, but you can accept everything. In God's infinite wisdom, She placed everything you could ever desire in one place. Unfortunately, it is also the last place you will look. Can you guess where it is?

—Brother

Daily Spiritual Peacemaking Lesson – Day 326

If you call yourself a disciple of any person, the only real gift they can give you is to send you away. A longing will begin that after awhile will force you to return, and you fall at the master's feet with great humility. Again you are told, "Go away." Over and over you come and you go, and the longing increases till it is unbearable. Finally something happens that you did not expect. A door opens inside you that you didn't know existed, but which the master saw all along. It is the longing that creates the opening, not the satisfaction of finding another person who seems to have satisfied their longing for God. It will never be satisfied within you until you realize that God, or the master, have never left your side, no matter where you wandered off to.

—Brother

Daily Spiritual Peacemaking Lesson – Day 327

There will come a day when people will come to you, wanting for you to give them what you have found. Don't give them anything at all. Be as normal as you can be, trying to convince them that you are no different than they are. Then, when you are nowhere to be found, the Light will come streaming through, and you will touch the other in a way that words can never explain. The key is to get out of the way. On your own you can do nothing, but, by surrendering, all things can be done through you.

—Brother

Daily Spiritual Peacemaking Lesson – Day 328

A child clings to their parent until they realize they have learned everything they have to learn, then they set off on their own. Think about this today. A mother feeds a child from her breast until it is no longer good for her, or for the child, to continue. Then she begins to wean the child, introducing a different kind of food. At first the child feels as if it's been abandoned, as if it has done something wrong and is being punished. It is impossible for them to know what is in their own best interest. I am going to begin pushing you away from me now, for it is not in your best interest that we continue the way we have been. Let me wean you from my breast, and you also will begin eating a new kind of bread.

—Brother

Daily Spiritual Peacemaking Lesson – Day 329

Don't forget—I will never leave you. After the mother weans the child, a new relationship begins to develop. It may take many years, but when the time is right they look at one another and say, "Now we are friends." I now call you my friend, because you have learned so well.

—Brother

Daily Spiritual Peacemaking Lesson – Day 330

Are you willing to lay all these lessons aside, and really begin living them? I mean, REALLY live them. It doesn't mean that you haven't been living them till now, but there is still an entire country to cross before you can say that you know the Truth. The map will not help you now, though you have been studying it very hard. Lay it down on the table and forget about it. Stand up and walk out the door. The roads you traced out with your finger will not look the same as when your feet kick up the dust on that road. Only direct experience is important now, and that is where you are heading.

—Brother

Daily Spiritual Peacemaking Lesson – Day 331

I have been offering you concepts to help you recognize the truth. But the Truth is not a concept; therefore, none of them will really ever help you. It is like looking at a picture of a beautiful landscape, then saying you want to visit that place. You may recognize the place once you arrive, but the picture you saw does not show the path you must take to get there. That is what your life is for. All paths lead to the same place—God's realization of You. Notice that I didn't say, "Your realization of God." Soon you'll understand the difference, then everything will finally make sense.

—Brother

Daily Spiritual Peacemaking Lesson – *Day 332*

What will you have to give up to accept the Truth I am offering you?

Nothing.

What will you need to give to accept the Truth I am offering you?

Everything.

How can both of these be true at the same time? You don't need to give up anything to have what you've never lost. However, since you've invested so much time in ignoring what you've never lost, you must give everything. When you can do both of these things at the same time, then the Truth is yours.

—Brother

Daily Spiritual Peacemaking Lesson – *Day 333*

The Peace of God is all around you. Stop looking for it, and it will find you.

The Love of God is everywhere. Stop longing for it, and you'll feel it come from everyone, no matter what they say or do.

—Brother

*Daily Spiritual Peacemaking Lesson – **Day 334***

Peace doesn't come and go. It's everywhere all the time. Your attention is moving everywhere all the time, and that's why you think Peace can be here one moment and gone the next. In reality it's you that is here one minute and gone the next. That's why holding still is so important. You've been playing a game of tag with God for a long time. Tag, you're it.

—Brother

*Daily Spiritual Peacemaking Lesson – **Day 335***

Love indiscriminately. Then you'll know yourself to be loved. Give everything all the time. Then you'll always have everything you need. God doesn't judge you, because it's impossible for God to be judged. A Spiritual Peacemaker is simply someone who looks for the Face of God in everyone they meet. In doing so, they see their own face reflecting in everyone's eyes. When God looks at you, guess what She sees? The answer is so obvious.

—Brother

Daily Spiritual Peacemaking Lesson – Day 336

Try to be as spontaneous as nature is. Some days the sun burns the landscape, while other times it is not seen for days. But there is a rhythm to nature that transcends these definitions. There is no good or bad, for in the end everything is in perfect balance. Likewise, your life is perfectly balanced, if you have eyes to see. There will be moments when you are happy and moments when you are sad. But they all make up the experience of "You." Your goal shouldn't be to always be happy, because then you're judging the moments when you're not. As long as there is a "not" in your life, then you will not be truly happy. Real happiness is a state you achieve that does not depend upon any outside influences. The real goal is to be happy even when you're sad. Do you understand?

—Brother

Daily Spiritual Peacemaking Lesson – Day 337

Yesterday I said that you must realize you're happy even when you're not. It is the same as saying that there is an experience within you that is not dependent upon your transitory states of mind, but which is constantly aware, and constantly revealed. The problem has been that you have refused to let it be revealed to you. This is the Self that God loves, and it is wholly aware of who you are this moment. It exists outside your dream of separation and does not need it to determine anything. If you seek this Self, then it will be revealed to you. If you act from this Self, then you will learn the real meaning of healing, of peace, and of compassion. This is your goal as a Spiritual Peacemaker.

—Brother

Daily Spiritual Peacemaking Lesson – Day 338

If you can live in the world without judging anything, loving everything, giving to everyone who asks of you, and offering peace no matter what the cost, then you will be living the life of a Spiritual Peacemaker. Does that sound difficult? Actually, it is hard to imagine living any other way. Once you've adopted this vision you will look back upon your former path and realize how much energy it took. Loving everyone takes no energy at all. It is what your soul longs for, but has been denied. The moment you give yourself to this practice it will rejoice, and effort will disappear, replaced forever by the peace that passes all understanding.

—Brother

Daily Spiritual Peacemaking Lesson – Day 339

The mind judges and discriminates between one thing and another because this is the job it does best. It does have a place in this world you have created, but it is a very small place. The larger role belongs to your heart, which is completely indiscriminate. Live there, and only visit the mind.

—Brother

Daily Spiritual Peacemaking Lesson – Day 340

Lay aside the need to do anything at all. Love will guide you in ways you cannot imagine now, and will perform every task you give it much better than you can imagine. A gentle smile is better than a keen mind. It will draw everything to your side without effort. A kind word will get you further than a well-rehearsed speech. Let your heart speak for you in everything. It is a better advocate than your mind in every situation.

—Brother

Daily Spiritual Peacemaking Lesson – Day 341

I hope you are integrating these lessons because you want them more than anything else. You may think that there could be another reason, but there isn't. It is fine to want what we want, as long as we understand the path to receiving it. Give to others and you will understand.

—Brother

Daily Spiritual Peacemaking Lesson – Day 342

The seeming distance between my mind and yours is disappearing. What was once perceived has now vanished, for you are no longer focused on shadows, but on the realities that never change. My mission is yours, though it may look different, and time seems to separate us. In the end, you will prove only one thing—that time cannot separate what is forever joined. If this is true, and I assure you that it is, then your enlightenment is occurring now, as are the results of that. What result do you need other than love? This is the only gift we bring the world, for it is the only gift it needs. The love of God flows through you now, as it always has. The only difference is that you will no longer deny that love, for it has never denied you. Give, then, to everyone the Light that has been offered to you, then you will stand upon new ground, and an Awakened World will be yours.

—Brother

Daily Spiritual Peacemaking Lesson – Day 343

You have chosen to stay awake with me to assist in the awakening of all other minds. Blessed be your holy name, for it is the name of all who walk this path. You cannot be alone in this, for you are now able to SEE the gifts given to you by God and, seeing them, you share them with ALL. No one is waiting for you, no matter how it seems to the mind still asleep. And this is your greatest power, knowing that the gift you offer is already received, for no one can be separated from everything that exists. Separation falls away from your mind like a shadow that disappears when the light comes. You are that light, Beloved, for I have seen it in myself. Do you understand what I am saying to you? I know you do understand, for we have walked together long enough to share One Mind, in holiness and in grace. We will walk together a little while longer, for the sun has yet to reach the horizon.

—Brother

Daily Spiritual Peacemaking Lesson – Day 344

You have chosen to stay awake with me to assist in the awakening of all other minds. Sleep now seems like such an unworthy state for one so holy, for you are no longer content with the sights and sounds that appear only in dreams. You have claimed your role as a Spiritual Peacemaker, an Emissary of Light, and so you are that. God will not keep you away from what has always been yours, and yet you have kept yourself away from it. Thank God for your transformation, for you will no longer allow these empty dreams to control you so. Why? The answer is so simple, an answer you have always known: What God has created as perfect, remains as it was created. You can change God's will in your dream, but not in reality, and dreams cannot hold the attention of the perfect creation of God forever. Share the gift you have received so well, for it is not beyond you to forget again. And yet, it will never be taken away from you.

—Brother

Daily Spiritual Peacemaking Lesson – Day 345

You have chosen to stay awake with me to assist in the awakening of all other minds. Thank you for your humility, your willingness to realize that God is working through you now. You would not have come this far if you thought that it was you doing the work. That is the thought that lulled you into the sleep of forgetfulness. Now you have been awakened from that sleep, not by me, but by the truth itself that flows through you. The truth stirs within, no matter how deeply you sleep, or how far you think you have wandered from your home. The stirring finally becomes so loud that you can no longer remain wrapped in bed. Your eyes are now open, and together we will help others awaken. This is all you need do to receive this gift over and over through each Beloved you encounter, simply by seeing the light in their eyes and knowing them as God knows them in perfection.

We are almost there. Stay awake with me.

—Brother

Daily Spiritual Peacemaking Lesson – Day 346

Peace comes to the world through you and as you. This is the essence of your function of being a Spiritual Peacemaker. Peace comes through you as you surrender and allow the Holy Spirit to use everything that makes you who you are, all your gifts and all your talents. Peace comes into the world "as" you because you cannot be separated from the Peace of God, except in your imagination. If such a thing were possible, then we would all be in a very different position, one whose ending could never be assured. If there is anything you have learned, let it be simply that the ending that is given to you by God is always assured, and that end is peace. You are that now! Let that be the beginning and the end of everything you offer today, to yourself and to everyone you encounter.

—Brother

Daily Spiritual Peacemaking Lesson – Day 347

Don't ever forget why you entered this path, or how you will achieve your goal. The goal is not to See as God Sees, or to Feel what God Feels. They are the means through which you will achieve a higher goal, one the world can never understand. You are here to Know what God Knows and, in doing so, redeem the whole world. Forgiveness is your path, and humility will guide you into everything you really desire. Lay aside all the things you thought you wanted, in favor of that which will satisfy all your longings. Then the Sight, the Heart, and the Knowledge of God will be yours.

—Brother

Daily Spiritual Peacemaking Lesson – Day 348

The world you see with your eyes is not the real world, and yet it can reflect reality if you choose for it to do so. Choose the world you can perceive with your soul, and it will flow naturally into every world. The physical world seems to be forever removed from peace, and so it will remain until you change your mind about this. Your inner experience alone will determine the outer. Use all the evidence you see outside to reveal the decisions made within, then you will know how to change both. This is why you chose to be a Spiritual Peacemaker in the world. Answer this call by answering your Self. The call and the answer come from the very same place within you.

—Brother

Daily Spiritual Peacemaking Lesson – Day 349

The world you perceive, or SEE, with your soul is eternal, and is therefore true. You have learned to seek this truth without regard to the evidence of the world, all the things that seem to prove peace unreal and, in doing so, a new possibility has entered. We are very near the end of this course, and yet it never truly ends, for the transformation of your mind has no real conclusion. We will draw deeper together into the world made for us by God, and the treasures we will discover have no end. How can you end if you, too, were created for Heaven? Peace is within you now, and it is being revealed to every mind. This is your choice as a Spiritual Peacemaker, and it is honored in Heaven as well as on earth. Take my hand and we will step together into the Light, and all creation will surely follow.

—Brother

Daily Spiritual Peacemaking Lesson – Day 350

When you seek this Truth above all things, then you discover who you are, for you cannot be separated from the Truth except in your dreams. Seek to Know by Giving what you Know. Let this be the only thing you think about, the all-pervading desire of your whole mind. Wholeness has returned to you now, for it never left. You are discovering this NOW, since NOW is the only moment such a discovery is possible. Step forward into the Light that cannot be dispelled. Only a shadow has blocked your sight of reality, but now even that has passed. I am telling you that you are ready to take the next step alone, without my help. You have been prepared well, and nothing stands in your way. Peace has come to your mind, Beloved, and nothing can interrupt the Divine Flow of Grace that comes to and through you now.

—Brother

Daily Spiritual Peacemaking Lesson – Day 351

Feel the greatness of the Beloved moving through you now. This is what you have come to know, only this, and knowing this, you share it that it may continue to be yours. Sharing the truth, the truth is seen where it has always been, where it sat still and motionless waiting for your Sacred recognition. And now, after so many centuries, you realize that no time has passed at all. You are still as God created you, perfect and whole. You tried to change the unchangeable, and you failed. Praise God that you failed, for this alone has assured your ultimate success. You step through the door of Light, now fully recognized. I SEE you, for you have SEEN your Self.

—Brother

Daily Spiritual Peacemaking Lesson – Day 352

Feel the holiness of the Beloved moving through you now. You are but a reflection of this Grace, though in a way you are not accustomed to in this world. You believe that the reflection and the source are two different things, separated by space. This is not true in Heaven, and therefore it is not true for you. You have not left your source, and that is why you are able to SEE now. Keep your eyes open with me for a little while longer, and I will show you an even deeper vision of your truest Self. Then you will understand this journey we have been taking together in a way you were not able to till now.

—Brother

Daily Spiritual Peacemaking Lesson – Day 353

You and I are able to SEE for the same reason, and this is what you will share as a Spiritual Peacemaker: God SEES, and that is enough. Are you able to grasp the simplicity of this? You have not left God except in your imagination, and therefore you are still within the Vision of God. You have always seen the truth, but your denial of what it shows you has kept you blind in spite of it. Have you ever seen something without really SEEING it? This has happened to everyone, even in the most mundane ways. God SEES what is really there, while you SEE and deny. But your denial is now seen for what it really is—a futile attempt to change reality into what it isn't. But all dreams must end, and so does this one fade into the dark shadows that do not really exist. You are here, and God is with you. Amen a thousand times, for that is all you need to know.

—Brother

Daily Spiritual Peacemaking Lesson – Day 354

Perfect joy has been the only goal of this course, as well as the experience (as opposed to the intellectual understanding) that your ability to keep this gift is in direct proportion to your willingness to share it. We will soon begin a time of celebration as we end our first year together. But first we must allow a time for evaluation, then integration. Are you willing to be honest with your Self as to the openness you have allowed in this process? Have you taken these lessons to heart as completely as you initially chose, rising above the world of form into the formless embrace of the Beloved? Do not judge yourself as right or wrong no matter how you answer, but do be honest. Then ask yourself the question—where do I go from here? Can I go deeper into these mysteries, releasing my hold on this meaningless world a little more? The rewards, as you have seen, are so great for those who choose to SEE with the Eyes of God. Choose it now, and all the lessons we have covered will fall into perfect place.

—Brother

Daily Spiritual Peacemaking Lesson – Day 355

This is a day for pure experience. Do not seek to give anything to anyone today. Simply be the source. Do not seek to perceive anything anywhere. Simply SEE what is real wherever you go. Do not seek to change the world. Simply change your own perceptions, and watch as the world changes on its own. You have come far enough to know that you are not here to "do" anything. As you allow God's will to be "done" through you, all things find their perfect rhythm.

Give thanks for the gift of being a Spiritual Peacemaker NOW.

—Brother

Daily Spiritual Peacemaking Lesson – Day 356

As often as you can, pray these words for the next several days, feeling that they are true:

"My life is now used as a radiating beacon, bringing peace into the life of all beings, wherever they may be. It does not matter what I say, for the words that stream from my mouth are not my own. It does not matter what I do, for it is not me who is acting, but the Beloved who is acting through me. I offer an ocean of gratitude for this gift, flowing through and as me now. I am an instrument of peace, and the universe is healed."

This is your path, the path of a Spiritual Peacemaker. This is who you are. Give thanks, Beloved.

—Brother

Daily Spiritual Peacemaking Lesson – Day 357

You are nearing the end of a journey you never really began. Does this surprise you? It may have surprised you a year ago, but it shouldn't now. That is because you are now able to realize within your mind what you have always known in your heart—that only the Love of God is real, as well as anything that extends from that love. You are that! Do you understand what I am saying to you? You are the extension of the love of God, perfectly revealed NO MATTER HOW IT APPEARS IN THIS WORLD. This is what you came to learn, and you have learned it well. Now give this gift to everyone you meet so that it may remain in your mind. Your heart is secure, but we must be gentle with your mind for a little longer, that it may remain strong. I am always with you to assure this.

—Brother

Daily Spiritual Peacemaking Lesson – Day 358

If there were any distance at all to this journey we have taken together, it would not be measured in miles, or even feet. Our journey, if it truly does exist, has been a journey of only a few inches. Perhaps you can measure it for yourself, the distance between your head—and your heart. The illusion of time has also fallen away, replaced by the timeless embrace that has awaited your return to the Home you never left, except in your imagination. How simple this journey has been, and how easy it has been to release its tiresome grip upon your sleeping mind. A single word was all that was required, perfectly felt for a single instant. YES! There is no magic in this word, for that would imply that it has power over the truest part of You that the Beloved has yet to forget. You have not been forgotten, for the Eyes of God have never left you. Now you are home, and time has no more hold upon you. Blessed be the One whose eyes are now open to the New Sun.

—Brother

Daily Spiritual Peacemaking Lesson – Day 359

We are Brothers and Sisters together in Light, fully revealed and suddenly felt. Until now you have listened to my voice and have received what I have to give. But now I turn to you, for we take this next step together. There is only one YES that can be spoken before the Holy Altar where all our dreams are forever forgotten. As we speak this word together, and all that it reveals, the clouds part and the sun is seen at last. Look also to the others who follow you, just as you have followed me. Now it is up to you to offer this gift, just as I have offered it. There is no final end to this great path, for it winds forever as an eternal labyrinth of Light. They are waiting for you to open your eyes and SEE them as I have seen you. Turn back to the world you created, Beloved and be their savior. Then will you be saved.

—Brother

Daily Spiritual Peacemaking Lesson – Day 360

As we approach the final stage of our one-year study, I feel it is time to offer some simple definitions of what it means to be a Spiritual Peacemaker in the world. Remember first that these concepts, like everything in this world, are open to interpretation, and so in the end, even they are not real. Therefore, breathe them into your heart and ask to be shown the truth that lies behind these concepts, revealing a deeper truth your mind cannot comprehend.

• A Spiritual Peacemaker blesses everything exactly as it is, and does not expect anything to change.

If you learn this one lesson, then you have everything you need to save the world. We are not here to change anything, but to KNOW that everything is perfect. Then, and only then, will the world change on its own to reflect your holy decision.

• A Spiritual Peacemaker chooses to SEE what cannot be seen and release what has never been bound.

If you look to the world hoping to see what is real, you will be condemned to illusion. The world was made to hide reality from you. Who made it that way? You already know the answer to that question.

• A Spiritual Peacemaker seeks his or her own release from the imagined universe, and realizes that that release only comes through offering the same gift to others.

There is no difference between what you give and what you receive, simply because both actions are to the Beloved. Therefore, decide what you most want to have, and give only that. Then every desire will be satisfied, for the only desire of your heart is to know who you are.

—Brother

Daily Spiritual Peacemaking Lesson – Day 361

• A Spiritual Peacemaker is patient with everything, because they know that the end is assured.

The one who knows that salvation is assured does not lose themselves to small details. You cannot be kept from the Beloved forever, and so, at the end of time, when all things of time fall away, you will remember who you are. Live in the world with this confidence, and everything will be yours.

• A Spiritual Peacemaker asks everything of Everything.

What more can I add to this? Your problem has not been that you have asked for too much, but that you have asked for too little. Everything that is real is already yours, and what isn't real is not worthy of you. Live in this knowledge.

• A Spiritual Peacemaker sees everyone as the same, and offers love without discretion.

If you decide that one person is more deserving of love than another, then you are lost. That is why the world you have created is lost, because it lives by this supposed law. You have learned the higher law of the VISION OF GOD. Accept this Vision and you will SEE that everything and everyone is deserving of love, simply because you are.

—Brother

Daily Spiritual Peacemaking Lesson – Day 362

These next three statements are the foundation of your experience as a Spiritual Peacemaker:

Peace prevails in my heart now, because the Beloved has never left me.

Love fills me now, because the Beloved has never stopped loving me.

Salvation is secured now, because the Beloved has never abandoned me.

All of our lessons have led us here, to the realization that only the Beloved's version of reality is real. You have learned to surrender what seemed to be true in favor of Truth itself. Now you must live this new vision in a world that responds only to your will. It has no will of its own, but was made to reflect the decisions you make about yourself and everyone around you. When those decisions align with the Decision of God, then you are free, and freedom flows from you to all beings. Open your heart and drink this cup of peace. You are indeed a Spiritual Peacemaker now.

—Brother

Daily Spiritual Peacemaking Lesson – Day 363

There are only three lessons left in our year's course. What have you learned? Hopefully nothing at all. Choose instead to remember the truth that lives within you and within all beings. Choose to SEE what is real, and reality is yours.

My words have been simple because the Truth itself is simple. There is nothing complex about the fact that your holiness cannot be threatened by anything that was created "for" you. And yet, the way that that holiness manifests may seem very complex. This is one of the great wonders of "time," but even it must pass away in the end. Our goal is and will always be PEACE, and it is assured. These lessons never really end, simply because your experience of peace never ends. Peace moves and shapes itself to the lessons you are choosing to learn every moment, and even within "no moment." You are an eternal being, Beloved, and the dream of separation is nearly over.

—Brother

Daily Spiritual Peacemaking Lesson – Day 364

You started this course asking yourself the question: "How may I best be used to heal the world?" Your intent was pure, asking to be an Instrument of the Peace of God, a channel of healing Light and joy. There is no space between the moment we began and the moment we find ourselves in now. And yet, the question we ask may have shifted, refined into a statement so simple that it may easily escape us. Now we resolutely claim: "I am an Instrument of Peace now, and the world is healed." Will you wait for the evidence to be discovered? If you do, then you will be waiting for a very long time. The world you see was made to block your vision of the world that can be SEEN. This is our only goal, and we proclaim it as accomplished. Who but you can claim this and know that it is so? Who will claim otherwise when your heart and soul have been quickened by this new song we sing together? Yes, our goal has been accomplished, and the world we made cannot escape this wave that sweeps across us now. It is yours but to KNOW that this is true, and to continue on as a Spiritual Peacemaker. Peace begins and ends within your heart. You are now ready to see that your heart and the heart of God are the same, and when you decide for peace along with God, which you have done, then there is nothing in the universe that dissuades this river of Light.

—Brother

Daily Spiritual Peacemaking Lesson – Day 365

Stepping Forward in Power.

What is power? Has your idea of being powerful changed at all since we began this journey? To the world you created in your imagination, power is the ability to assert your will over another person or the environment itself. By now you have realized that everything this world claims to be true is actually the opposite of what is really true. The world's idea of power is in reality the definition of powerlessness, simply because it is based upon a false foundation: that you can decrease another person's power and, in doing so, increase your own. In reality, decreasing another person's power is the same as decreasing your own. Therefore, the opposite must also be true: increasing another person's power increases yours.

You are now a powerful Spiritual Peacemaker because you have aligned your life with the Power of God, which only increases as it is shared. As you share your Light, Light increases all through the world. As you share your power, then the world and everything in it is empowered. What other reason but this leads to your decision to give everything to Everything? You are here to be truly happy, and that will only happen as you make others happy. Now you SEE with the eyes that were given to you by God, rather than the eyes fashioned by the world that were made not to see at all. Now that you can clearly see what is around you, you rejoice, for you See everything exactly as God Sees it. Praise the Beloved for this small gift that changes everything, letting time itself return to where it came from. At last you are home, Beloved. At last you are able to See who you are, and to share that vision with everyone you meet. Let it increase, then, by allowing it to increase in others. You are here to serve, just as I served. Then you will never lose this gift of sight, the gift that was given you by God before time began. This is the moment you have been waiting for. Claim it with the authority that has been given to you as a Peacemaker.

We have only just begun.

—Brother

Study Groups and Retreats

There are currently Art of Spiritual Peacemaking study groups and retreats forming around the world. If you would like to get more information or join a group, please visit James' website: www.jamestwyman.com, or call the office in the US at (541) 482-5941.

You may also consider joining "The Seminary of Spiritual Peacemaking," a ministerial program offered by The Beloved Community. Hundreds of people have been ordained by the seminary and are now serving in a variety of different ministries worldwide. Visit the website for more information.

Also available at the site are the many books, cd's and movies produced by James Twyman.

Other works by James Twyman
available from Findhorn Press

Praying Peace

James F. Twyman in conversation with Gregg Braden and Doreen Virtue

144 pages paperback

ISBN 1-899171-48-7

This book is a practical guide to peacemaking. And yet it comes at the subject from a perspective that is perhaps different than most people expect. Through the 'Seven Pathways to Peace,' the book demonstrates that love is the only real force in the universe. Therefore, peace is always present, even when conflict seems to prevail. When we 'Pray Peace,' we actually increase the peace that is hidden beneath layers of hatred, pulling it into conscious experience. This is the basis of the entire book.

The Seven Pathways to Peace

1. You are always praying; thought itself is prayer.

2. Whatever you focus your mind on increases.

3. To change the world, change your thoughts about the world.

4. If you want to experience peace--become peace.

5. Peace is always present, though it is sometimes hidden.

6. Love is the only force in the universe.

7. The world is already healed.

The Praying Peace Cards

Set of 52 cards + instruction sheet in tuckbox

ISBN 1-899171-09-6

The text on the first 47 cards comes from the peace prayers collected from the twelve major religions of the world by Peace Troubadour James Twyman. They can be used as a way to begin your day in prayer, or to focus throughout the day on peace. The instruction sheet in the pack suggests other possibilities, and you may well invent your own method. The cards can be used when on your own or within the context of a group, workshop or classroom discussion. The pack also includes three 'tone cards,' as well as two blank cards for adding your own prayers.

Messages from Thomas: Raising Psychic Children

224 pages paperback

ISBN 1-84409-014-0

In 2001, James Twyman, the internationally renowned author and musician who travels the world performing "The Peace Concert" in some of the greatest areas of violence and discord, traveled to Bulgaria to meet a group of psychic children living at a very special monastery. His bestselling book *Emissary of Love: The Psychic Children Speak to the World* recounts that amazing adventure.

In this new book, Thomas, one of the children he met, shares his insights on how to raise a child that exhibits psychic abilities. Over 40,000 people receive regular messages from Thomas through a special web newsletter, but this is the first time he has provided such detailed information. Other well-known authors and teachers (of which Doreen Virtue, Michael J Tamura, Drunvalo Melchizedek, etc.) have contributed to this special book, adding their insights on how to help our children change the world. The book also features in appendix letters from parents of psychic children.

The Secret of the Beloved Disciple

with a preface by Nick Bunick (*The Messengers, In God's Truth*)

160 pages paperback

ISBN 1-899171-08-8

Much of what you will read in this book may not make sense if you read it with your mind. But open your heart and it will speak directly to your soul, and you will understand some of the eternal secrets and mysteries of our purpose and destiny on this planet.

In 1995 James Twyman began an adventure that has touched the lives of millions of people around the world. While traveling through war torn Bosnia and Croatia he received a message from the Emissaries of Light (title of his previous book), an ancient community of spiritual masters said to have existed for thousands of years. Now, after three years, the story that was called "... the next Celestine Prophecy" by Variety Magazine continues. In *The Secret of the Beloved Disciple*, James Twyman finally learns the mysterious identity of the Emissaries of Light, and meets an amazing woman named Maria during a peace demonstration on the streets of Belgrade . He later learns that Maria is a physical manifestation of Mary, the Blessed Mother, and she leads him on a journey that changes his life forever. This is an unforgettable book, a story relevant to our times, exciting, inspiring and completely un-put-downable. If you open your heart to its message, you will never be the same again. You will become part of the solution to the challenges and problems facing the world today. You will find peace and hope inside you, and will want to radiate this out to your fellow travelers on the path. For peace and love is what you truly are.

The message of the Emissaries of Light.

"There are two simple truths you need to accept if you are to move effortlessly into the New World, the world which is based on the laws of love.

"The first message is **You're Ready.** *You are ready to release the fearful beliefs that have kept you bound to the concept of separation. You are ready to accept the reality of love that is the foundation of your existence. And you are ready to give love to everyone in every way, for that is the only way you will fully experience it for yourself.*

"The second message is **You Are Holy.** *Who you really are is beyond the scope of your imagination. If you are one with the Divine Pulse of creation, then you are also one with the holiness of God. When you realize this, when you begin to perceive this truth within everyone you meet, including yourself, then the world will change by itself. You are holy, and that cannot change. When you accept that you are ready, and that the truth in you is the very essence of holiness, then you will recognize the next teacher - the Messenger of Love. It is this teacher who will take you through the Door of Eternity, to the very seat of the soul."*

Portrait of the Master

160 pages hardback ISBN 1-899171-43-6, *or*

The Prayer of St. Francis

160 pages paperback ISBN 1-899171-54-1

St. Francis of Assisi is one of the most endearing and human characters of the Middle Ages. His influence today is just as strong as 800 years ago when he was founding his Order, talking to Popes and carrying the message of peace to the infidel. St. Francis traveled with the crusaders not to fight the Muslims, or even to preach to them, but to persuade them, and the Christians, to make peace and live together in harmony. This book focuses around his prayer, Lord, make me an instrument of thy peace, and in a series of charming vignettes, it shows how the prayer develops in the course of his pilgrimage through Italy towards the East and an uncertain fate.

This book reads like an adventure mystery story, yet also brings a message of peace, love and hope. We travel with Francis and Brother Leo from Assisi to Syria, meeting fascinating characters and learning life lessons along the way. While a certain element of fiction has been added, the basic story is true. The message of St. Francis is timeless, and this book brings him to life as few others have.

James F. Twyman has been drawn to the life of St. Francis since early childhood, and his own ministry as the Peace Troubadour has been based on the example of Francis's life, the simple way he expressed his love of God and his dedication to peace. It is the author's deep connection with the spirit of St. Francis that draws us deeply into this story up to the inspiring and surprising ending.

"James Twyman has written a timeless account of our own journey into the unchartered territory of life's fears, doubts and uncertainties."
—from the foreword by Gregg Braden, author of *The Isaiah Effect* and *Awakening to Zero Point*

"This story, based on the life of St. Francis, will stir your soul, and could become an instant classic."
— Neale Donald Walsch, author of *Conversations with God*

"Jimmy Twyman brings the vision of St. Francis to life. Seeking to change your world? Use these principles."
—James Redfield, author of *The Celestine Prophecy* and *The Secret of Shambala*

"Put 'The Prophet' and 'The Alchemist' together and you have James Twyman's classic, 'Portrait of the Master.' One hundred years from now people will still be raving about this book."
—Doreen Virtue, PhD, author of *The Care and Feeding of Indigo Children*

Ten Spiritual Lessons
I Learned at the Mall

128 pages paperback
ISBN 1-899171-83-5

- If you were told that you are already enlightened, would you believe it?

- If you were told that enlightenment is as easy as doing your weekly shopping, what would you say?

- If you were told that the person serving your cappuccino is your spiritual teacher, would you just laugh?

Most of us have been taught that we must enter a spiritual path in order to become enlightened. The idea is that if we work at it hard enough, attend dozens of seminars on spiritual topics, read enough books, etc., then someday, in this lifetime or the next, we will be struck by a cosmic lightning bolt, and in a sudden flash of insight will achieve full enlightenment. Consider the possibility that we have been sold a myth, the myth of enlightenment... In fact, we can find enlightenment anywhere, at any time, even in that most commercial and stressful place, the Shopping Mall. What if enlightenment is something you can pick up with your groceries, or doing your Christmas shopping? What if the person serving you behind the jewelry counter is as much your teacher as the leader of your latest workshop? What if it's all as simple as keeping your eyes and ears open while you live your daily life, doing all those mundane chores you dislike so much? This could change your attitude in every moment, making all that you do much more fun and interesting. In *Ten Spiritual Lessons I Learned at the Mall,* James Twyman takes a humorous and insightful journey through a place where few would ever go to attain enlightenment. He discovers that we can find ourselves anywhere, even in a place where we would rather not be... especially in such a place. You will be with him as he spends five days at a mall in Toronto, acting as if he was on a retreat in a monastery or an ashram, asking the big questions and finding some amazingly simple answers. This book will change the way you experience your ordinary environment.

FINDHORN
Press

For a complete Findhorn Press catalogue, please contact

Findhorn Press
305a The Park
Findhorn, Forres IV36 3TE
Scotland, Great Britain
tel +44 (0)1309-690582
fax + 44 (0)1309-690036
email info@findhornpress.com

or consult our website **www.findhornpress.com**